Lecture Notes in Computer Science 9249

Commenced Publication in 1973
Founding and Former Series Editors:
Gerhard Goos, Juris Hartmanis, and Jan van Leeuwen

More information about this series at http://www.springer.com/series/7409

Efthimios Tambouris · Panos Panagiotopoulos
Øystein Sæbø · Konstantinos Tarabanis
Maria A. Wimmer · Michela Milano
Theresa A. Pardo (Eds.)

Electronic Participation

7th IFIP 8.5 International Conference, ePart 2015
Thessaloniki, Greece, August 30 – September 2, 2015
Proceedings

 Springer

Editors
Efthimios Tambouris
University of Macedonia
Thessaloniki
Greece

Maria A. Wimmer
Universität Koblenz-Landau
Koblenz
Germany

Panos Panagiotopoulos
Queen Mary University of London
London
UK

Michela Milano
University of Bologna
Bologna
Italy

Øystein Sæbø
University of Agder
Kristiansand
Norway

Theresa A. Pardo
University at Albany
Albany, NY
USA

Konstantinos Tarabanis
University of Macedonia
Thessaloniki
Greece

ISSN 0302-9743   ISSN 1611-3349   (electronic)
Lecture Notes in Computer Science
ISBN 978-3-319-22499-2   ISBN 978-3-319-22500-5   (eBook)
DOI 10.1007/978-3-319-22500-5

Library of Congress Control Number: 2015945147

LNCS Sublibrary: SL3 – Information Systems and Applications, incl. Internet/Web, and HCI

Springer Cham Heidelberg New York Dordrecht London

Printed on acid-free paper

Springer International Publishing AG Switzerland is part of Springer Science+Business Media
(www.springer.com)

Preface

The annual International IFIP Conference on Electronic Participation (ePart) aims to bring together researchers of distinct disciplines in order to present and discuss advances in eParticipation research. As the field of eParticipation is multidisciplinary in nature, ePart provides an excellent opportunity for researchers with backgrounds in different academic disciplines to share and discuss current research on foundations, theories, methods, tools, and innovative applications of eParticipation. In addition, ePart provides a fruitful ground for nurturing and planning future cooperation.

The 7th ePart conference was organized by members of IFIP Working Group 8.5 and was supported by a multidisciplinary Program Committee from around the globe. As always, the conference was organized along with the International Conference on Electronic Government (IFIP EGOV).

IFIP EGOV and ePart have established a reputation of successful high-quality conference organizations. At the same time, they continue innovating in an attempt to increase the value they provide to their attendees. In this respect, this year, for the first time, the conferences were organized around five tracks:

- The General E-Government Track
- The General eParticipation Track
- The Open Government and Open and Big Data Track
- The Policy Modelling and Policy Informatics Track
- The Smart Governance, Smart Government, and Smart Cities Track

The five tracks of the dual IFIP EGOV and ePart conference highlight core areas of importance for the domains of study. The overall objective of the dual conference remains to attract scholars coming from different academic disciplines to present and discuss their latest research and to shed light on advancements in the field from different, sometimes even diverse, perspectives. With the introduction of a new organizational model of the dual conference, we were also happy to have as co-chairs a number of distinguished scholars who provide fresh insights into the conferences and who attract new relevant communities.

These proceedings cover completed research accepted in the General eParticipation Track and in the Policy Modelling and Policy Informatics Track. The completed research papers accepted in the other three tracks are published in the LNCS proceeding of IFIP EGOV. Like last year, accepted contributions of ongoing research, innovative projects, and PhD papers as well as abstracts of posters and workshops of the dual IFIP EGOV and ePart conference are published in joint complimentary proceedings by IOS Press.

The call for papers of the eParticipation and Policy Modelling Tracks attracted a wide range of topics with 32 submissions, which included 12 accepted completed research papers (published in these proceedings) and 10 accepted ongoing research papers (published in the joint IFIP EGOV and ePart proceedings of ongoing research).

This volume includes completed research organized in four topical threads as follows:

- eParticipation and Social media
- Deliberation and Consultation
- Evaluation
- Policy Formulation and Modelling

All ePart submissions were blind peer reviewed by at least three reviewers (and in most cases by four reviewers) from the Program Committee. The quality of the conference is directly related to the quality of peer reviews and we would like to once again acknowledge the work that has been done.

The Paper Awards Committee of IFIP EGOV and IFIP ePart was again led by committee chair Olivier Glassey of IDHEAP, Lausanne/Switzerland. The Organizing Committee carefully reviewed the accepted papers and granted outstanding paper awards to the winning authors. The winners were awarded in the ceremony during the conference dinner, which has become a highlight of each year's conference. The names of the award winners can be found on the conference website: http://www.egov-conference.org/egov-conf-history/egov-2015/.

This year, EGOV and ePart were organized in Thessaloniki, Greece, under the aegis of the University of Macedonia. The University of Macedonia has long been active in research in the areas of eGovernment and eParticipation. However, the success of a conference takes much more. We would therefore like to thank the team of the University of Macedonia and particularly Eleni Panopoulou but also Maria Zotou, Elina Nanopoulou, and Eleni Kamateri for their efforts in the excellent organization of the dual conference.

The University of Macedonia is a relatively new and small university. Its departments of Applied Informatics and Business Administration have worked together for these conferences. The University of Macedonia is located in Thessaloniki, Greece; a city with 2,500 years of history and at the same time a lively, artistic city and one of the largest student centers in South-Eastern Europe. The conference dinner was held at the Byzantine Museum and was preceded by an exclusive museum tour especially organized for conference participants. It could not have been more appropriate!

It was a real pleasure to have the conferences in such a suitable location and we are looking forward to IFIP EGOV 2016.

August/September 2015

Efthimios Tambouris
Panos Panagiotopoulos
Øystein Sæbø
Konstantinos Tarabanis
Maria A. Wimmer
Michela Milano
Theresa A. Pardo

Organization

Conference Chairs

Efthimios Tambouris   University of Macedonia, Greece
Hans Jochen Scholl   University of Washington, USA
Marijn Janssen   Delft University of Technology, The Netherlands
Maria A. Wimmer   University of Koblenz-Landau, Germany
Konstantinos Tarabanis   University of Macedonia, Greece

General eParticipation Track Chairs

Efthimios Tambouris   University of Macedonia, Greece (Lead Chair)
Øystein Sæbø   Agder University, Norway
Panos Panagiotopoulos   Queen Mary University of London, UK

Policy Modelling and Policy Informatics Track Chairs

Maria A. Wimmer   University of Koblenz-Landau, Germany, (Lead Chair)
Michela Milano   Bologna University, Italy
Theresa A. Pardo   Center for Technology in Government, University
      at Albany, SUNY, USA

Program Committee and Reviewers

Lasse Berntzen   Vestfold University College, Norway
Laurence Brooks   Brunel University, UK
Yannis Charalabidis   National Technical University Athens, Greece
Soon Ae Chun   CUNY, USA
Peter Cruickshank   Edinburgh Napier University, UK
Todd R. Davies   Stanford University, USA
Sharon Dawes   Center for Technology in Government, University at
      Albany/SUNY, USA
Fiorella De Cindio   Università di Milano, Italy
Paulo Depaoli   LUISS Guido Carli, Italy
Annelie Ekelin   Linneaus University/BTH, Sweden
Elsa Estevez   United Nations University, Macao, SAR China
Olivier Glassey   Lausanne University, Switzerland
Dimitris Gouscos   University of Athens, Greece
Johann Höchtl   Danube University Krems, Austria
M. Sirajul Islam   Örebro University, Sweden
Nikos Karacapilidis   University of Patras, Greece

Contents

Policy Formulation and Modelling

eParticipation and Social Media

Affordances and Effects of Promoting eParticipation Through Social Media

Fathul Wahid[1,2] and Øystein Sæbø[1(✉)]

[1] Department of Information Systems, University of Agder,
Kristiansand, Norway
{fathul.wahid,oystein.sabo}@uia.no
[2] Department of Informatics, Universitas Islam Indonesia, Yogyakara, Indonesia

Abstract. A growing body of literature highlights the adoption of social media for eParticipation, focusing on the identification of processes and structures through which ICT supports the relationship between citizens, governments and public bodies. There is a need to better understand the role of technology in such initiatives. This paper addresses this issue by introducing the concept of affordance. We used a case study approach to investigate an Indonesian eParticipation projects from Bandung, identifying affordance perceptions, enabling and inhibiting factors, actualized affordances and affordances effects. From the use of social media we identify nine actualized affordances and their effects, and we discuss the relationship between them. The case introduces findings from a developing country, a context that has largely been ignored within eParticipation research. Our findings provide lessons learned for practitioners on how to organize their eParticipation projects, as well as for researchers identifying future research avenues to strengthen our understanding of the role of ICT by introducing the concept of affordances.

Keywords: eParticipation · Affordances · Indonesia · Social media

1 Introduction

Information and communication technologies (ICTs) are increasingly being adopted to involve citizens in decision-making processes [1], intending to recapture citizens' declining interest in politics. eParticipation, research focuses on the identification of the processes and structures through which ICT supports the relationship between citizens, governments and public bodies [2, 3]. The introduction of social media may change the political landscape [4] and enable new opportunities for communication, consultation and dialogue between public bodies and citizens [1]. ICTs may also be used in political debates and decision-making processes to complement or contrast traditional means of communication and to coordinate participation in political processes [5].

The majority of eParticipation research focus on projects from the traditional context of ICT-related studies in the developed world, focusing on how traditional e-government stakeholders, such as political parties, citizens and public administrations [4], incorporate ICT-based services in an interplay with traditional communication channels [6]. The implementation of ICT is often done through the incremental development of existing services, based on the idea of continuously developing better

© IFIP International Federation for Information Processing 2015
E. Tambouris et al. (Eds.): ePart 2015, LNCS 9249, pp. 3–14, 2015.
DOI: 10.1007/978-3-319-22500-5_1

and more mature eParticipation services. There is a need for further investigation into the "black box" of eParticipation initiatives—that is, an exploration of the internal processes and concurrent consequences of the use of ICT [7] and of the challenges and opportunities for both institutional and non-institutional stakeholders.

In this landscape, the use of ICT to encourage direct participation in political processes in the city Bandung in Indonesia represents an exceptional case through which to generate new knowledge within this area. First, this case represents novel initiatives from the research context of developing countries. Cultural, political, economic and social contextual issues differentiate our case from the majority of reported research within the area. Second, the strategy in Bandung represents a disruptive approach [8], where the use of social media is introduced both to communicate with citizens and other external stakeholders and to coordinate internal processes, despite the lack of widespread inclusion of ICT in most governmental services. Hence, their strategy is differentiated from the traditional incremental and stepwise approach otherwise reported in the field. Third, by introducing the concept of affordances in the analysis of our cases, our study contribute to an increased understanding of the role that technology plays in relation to goal-oriented actors.

In this paper, we analyse this the Bandung case with the aim of investigating and reflecting on the use ICT (particularly emphasising social media) to promote eParticipation within developing countries. Topics of interest include how and why social media are used (or not), the impact of so doing and the enabling and inhibiting factors influencing this use. We introduce the concept of affordances to explore these issues. The concept has become popular within the area of IS to explore the adoption of technology within organizational arrangements resulting from the combination of work practices and features offered by the innovative use of IT [9].

2   Affordances: Theoretical Premises

Originating from the work of ecological physiologists [10], the concept of affordances focuses on interactions between actors (those being involved) with the environment (the surroundings of the actors), including the properties of actors and the environment [10]. The concept of affordance has become popular within the area of IS to explore adoption within organizational arrangements resulting from the combination of work practices and features offered by innovative use of IT [9].

The concept originates from the argument that people pick up rich information relevant to their needs from objects within their environment, representing the affordances of the object, not the properties [11]. Affordances are neither properties of the environment nor the characteristics of the individual but are relative to the interaction between the actor and the artefact [12]. Affordance exists as a relationship between an actor and an artefact, being relative to the action capabilities of the actor and reflecting the possible actions on the artefact itself [13]. This relativity implies that affordances are specific to one actor; hence, an affordance for one actor may be completely useless for another [11], who may not perceive or actualize the affordance. Affordances may be latent to begin with, needing to be perceived and actualized by a goal-oriented actor to achieve an outcome [11, 14].

The term was brought into IS to describe the action possibilities allowed by material properties within information systems [11], proposing a bridging concept to explain the intersection between IT systems and organizational systems [9]. This concept of affordances allows for the examination of how goal-oriented individuals interpret (and actualize) material properties within information systems to create changes in organizational practices [15]. As such, the concept of technological affordances relates not only to the individual level, but also to the action potential of what an organization can do with information systems with the intention to support organizational goals [13]. Organizational affordances relate to "the potential actions enabled associated with achieving organizational-level immediate concrete outcomes in support of organizational level goals" [16], resulting from the collective actions of the individuals.

Our motivation for introducing the concept of affordances here is to address our questions regarding how social media is being used (IT artefact), by whom (goal oriented actors), the consequences of the contextual factors (within a setting) and the consequences of this use (the resulting adoption). Our analyses are influenced by the work of Pozzi et al. [13], who proposes a theoretical framework (Fig. 1) for affordances, which is introduced as a basis the empirical analyses here. In this study, we focus on affordances perception to some extent but mainly on affordance actualization and the effect of affordances in the context of ICT use, particularly social media, in promoting eParticipation. Pozzi et al. [13] found that there is a lack of research focused on those aspects of affordances.

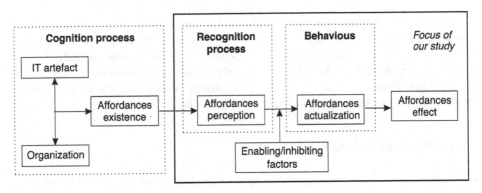

Fig. 1. Affordances theoretical framework inspired by Pozzi et al. [13]

3 Research Context and Method

Indonesia is among the top users of social media in the world. There are more than 70 million (out of around 250 million population) Facebook users and around 30 million Twitter users. The most active users of social media come from several big cities including Jakarta, which has the most active Twitter and Facebook users in the world, and Bandung. At the end of 2012, Bandung, the study site, had already the sixth most active Twitter users in the world[1]. Nowadays, WhatsApp – a cross-platform social media[2] – is also very popular[3] as 57 % of smart phone users in Indonesia are WhatsApp users[4].

In this paper, we empirically analyse the Bandung case by adopting an interpretive approach with the aim of investigating and reflecting on the use social media to promote eParticipation within developing countries. Topics of interest include how and why social media is used, the impact of so doing and the enabling and inhibiting factors influencing such use, based on the concept of affordances.

We interviewed key actors and included online archival data in order to gain an understanding of the contextual conditions. Archival data included statistical material, reports from the projects and analyses of social media activities in Bandung, including more than 6,000 tweets posted by the mayor. Table 1 summarizes the distribution of the interviews in terms of roles.

Table 1. Distribution of interviews

Role	Code of informant
- Secretary of the Department for Communication and Informatics	B1
- Secretary of the Department for Education	B2
- Head of the Section for Public Services in a sub-district	B3
- Vice- head of a village	B4
- Head of Ombudsman	B5
- Head of the Section for Village Empowerment	B6
- Head of the Section for Sub-district Empowerment	B7

The analysis began with the evidence emerging from the data, moving to a description of the structures and contexts. First, we used open coding to individually identify concepts. Second, the affordance perspective was introduced. Affordances produce immediate outcomes and events that were empirically observable; we looked for them in our empirical material by investigating our data sources to identify actual events, allowing us to identify the existence of affordances.

4 Findings and Analysis

eParticipation services in Bandung have been highly influenced by the inauguration of a new mayor in September 2013. Unlike his predecessors, who came from bureaucratic circles, the new mayor has a professional background as an architect, a lecturer at a

---

[1] http://www.forbes.com/sites/victorlipman/2012/12/30/the-worlds-most-active-twitter-city-you-wont-guess-it/.

[2] http://www.forbes.com/sites/benedictevans/2012/10/19/whatsapp-the-biggest-social-network-youve-never-heard-of/.

[3] http://www.thejakartapost.com/news/2013/06/24/whatsapp-ri-strong-market-usage-growth.html.

[4] http://www.thejakartapost.com/news/2014/10/28/telkom-s-q3-earnings-lifted-internet-data-services.html.

reputable national university, and a social activist. Soon after his inauguration, he asked all regional governmental agencies and their top management to establish e-mail, Twitter, Facebook, and WhatsApp accounts. Some of them also established BlackBerry Messenger (BBM) access. The mayor himself is an active Twitter user, posting more than 6,000 tweets in his first 11 months of service.

Such use of ICT is part of a larger scheme to enhance the overall functioning of the city. According to one informant, "To provide public services, the government of Bandung attempts to utilise IT optimally" (B1). And indeed, under the new mayor's direction, these agencies have used e-mail, Twitter, and Facebook as channels to encourage public participation. Furthermore, their use of the WhatsApp application enables information sharing, visual reporting, and discussion and internal coordination —effectively allowing for the dynamic inclusion of relevant external actors such as representatives from the police department, the military, and youth organisations.

The function of Bandung's ICT-based eParticipation initiatives is, specifically, "to capture inputs and complaints from citizens directly. The mayor should be well informed about this, and the department should respond to these inputs and complaints directly" (B1). In October 2013, Bandung officially adopted LAPOR, a national complaint-handling system developed by the President's Delivery Unit for Development Monitoring and Oversight. The mechanism for processing the incoming messages is depicted in Fig. 2. The system can be accessed through various channels, namely a website (i.e., www.lapor.ukp.go.id), social media sites and mobile applications (for Android, Blackberry, and IOS gadgets).

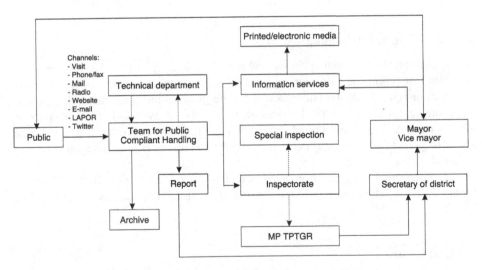

Fig. 2. Flow of incoming messages and responses in Bandung

Statistics from the first quarter of 2014 indicate that 2,723 incoming messages were recorded in LAPOR: 29 % using the website and 71 % using SMS. Of these 2,723 messages, 78 % were appropriately responded to; the rest were archived for several reasons, such as they contained overly general suggestions, they were unclear in their meaning, or they were inappropriate (e.g., mocking). When the incoming messages deal with corruption practices the follow-up will involve inspectorate, special inspection, and Advisory Council for Compensatory Claim (Majelis Pertimbangan Tuntutan Perbendaharaan dan Ganti Rugi [MP TPTGR]). Figure 2 depicts the overview of the system used to encourage public participation, both with and without the help of ICT.

4.1 Actualised Affordances

We identified nine actualised affordances emerged from the relation between Bandung's local government (Table 1). Some of these actualised affordances are directly related to the use of social media, such as facilitating direct communication and eliminating power distance; others are generated by other types of ICT use, such as supporting the internal business process and working ubiquitously.

4.2 Affordances Effects

Our data indicates that the actualised affordances identified above have resulted in six affordances effects (Table 2). Some of these effects, such as better public services and improved transparency, can be observed or experienced by citizens immediately. Other effects, such as improved institutional capacity and better working morale, are primarily experienced by the local government officers directly, though eventually they trickle down to impact citizens (Table 3).

4.3 Enabling and Inhibiting Factors

Seven enabling and inhibiting factors where identified, in terms of converting the possibility of action (i.e., affordances perception) into actual action (i.e., affordances actualisation) (see Table 4). These factors can be grouped into four categories: (i) top management (political goodwill, focus shifting, reward systems); (ii) government officers (technical skill and knowledge readiness, transparency culture); (iii) external actors (supports from the local parliament); and (iv) citizens (social media use among citizens).

The connection between affordances perception, affordances actualisation, and affordances effect, along with the associated enabling/inhibiting factors, is depicted in Fig. 3.

5   Discussion

When studying affordances, it is necessary to understand the motivation in which the actor's goals are embedded. Motivation is particularly important to the current case study as it influences affordances perception [13]. Affordances perception yields awareness of the possibilities of action [19]. It is about recognising the possibilities brought about by the technology in question—in this case, ICT. Indeed, in our case

Table 2. Identified actualised affordances

Actualised affordances	Excerpts
Facilitating direct communication	"All departments should have e-mail, Twitter, WhatsApp, and Facebook accounts. Their function is to capture inputs and complaints from citizens directly." (B1)
Inviting citizen participation	"I invited citizens [through Twitter] to participate in [the] trash picking movement every Monday, Wednesday, and Friday. Now, Bandung is clean." (The mayor of Bandung, quoted in [17])
Maintaining integrity	"So, there is no chance left to deceive, when we are using WhatsApp." (B1)
Eliminating power distance	I was aware, when I was elected as mayor, that social media would be an integral part of staying close to the citizens." (The mayor of Bandung, quoted in [17])
Supporting the internal business process	"Each department should have at least five IS applications, to support the internal business process and to provide services to citizens." (B1)
Reporting activities visually	"When offices at all levels, until village, are performing an activity, they should take a picture of it and post it through WhatsApp. All people [in the WhatsApp group] will know about it, as well as the mayor." (B1)
Assessing officer performance	"[Social media activity] is used as one of the indicators in assessing the officers' performance. When a head of a sub-district is working in the field, but she/he does not report it, the mayor will not know it." (B1)
Facilitating internal coordination	"When we are going to hold a meeting, we inform [staff] about it through WhatsApp.... We still ... make a regular invitation letter [on] paper. We take a photo of it and share it through WhatsApp." (B6)
Speeding up processes	"We send an activities report by e-mail to make sure it is quickly received, especially by the current mayor. It was not so with the previous one." (B3) "With eKelurahan[a] we can work more quickly." (B4)
Working ubiquitously	"As the data is stored in a server, we are not dependent on a specific computer." (B4) "The head of a sub-district may see the incoming letters through the system, and make his disposition. ... I will get notification of that through SMS." (B3)

[a]eKelurahan is a web-based system developed to facilitate administration processes at the village level. It has been used in Bandung since December 2013

study, we found that the mayor of Bandung was very aware of the potential for social media to promote citizen participation:

I see it from a different perspective. Social media is not my personal domain. I consider it as part of work. When I respond to a tweet, I am working. A lot of benefits can be harvested from using social media. Bandung has become clean because of social media. (The mayor of Bandung, quoted in [17]).

Table 3. Identified affordances effects

Affordances effects	Description/excerpts
Improved citizen participation	This has been indicated by the significant number of incoming messages sent by citizens in the form of complaints, questions, requests for information, suggestions, etc
Improved transparency	The use of Twitter made what the local government was doing transparent to the public eye. In many cases, citizens demand information or clarification on certain issues; thus, the local government should respond to it accordingly
More responsive government	The mayor often mentions the Twitter account of relevant technical department to follow up the reported issues/problems by citizens. In some cases, the mayor himself make a field visit All technical departments should respond to incoming messages immediately, within an agreed-upon timeframe
Better public services	Feedback provided by citizens through the eParticipation systems (i.e., LAPOR) force the local government to assure and improve the quality of public services "SIP[a] is the mayor's idea to provide zero-complaint services." (B6) "[The] ombudsman changed the status of 18 technical departments from yellow to green[b]." (B1)
Improved institutional capacity	"[Information systems are developed] to improve institutional capacity, both at the sub-district and the village level, which essentially [offers] better public services." (B6)
Better working morale	"In some cases, the officers are not ready yet when they are 'attacked' on Twitter or Facebook. They have no choice. The have to have resilience […] to work properly." (B1)

[a]SIP (i.e., www.sip.bandung.go.id) is a web-based system that enables citizens to assess the quality of the public services they experience from a specific government office
[b]Green status is the highest status level, indicating that the technical department meets the minimum standard of public service. Yellow status is the intermediate status level, indicating that the technical department does not yet meet the minimum standard of public service

Affordances perception can be viewed as inductive thinking [20]. In contrast to deductive thinking, inductive thinking can lead to more disruptive and innovative uses of technology, as asserted by [20] (pp. 84–85):

> Most executives and managers know how to think deductively. That is, they are good at defining [a] problem or problems, then seeking and evaluating different solutions to it. But, applying information technology to business reengineering demands inductive thinking—the ability to first recognize a powerful solution and then seek the problems it might solve, problems the company probably doesn't even know that it has.

Affordances perception influences affordances actualisation [13]. For example, all of the affordances presented in Fig. 3 have been actualised in the case of Bandung, exemplified by the official use of social media such as Twitter, and WhatsApp. As one informant asserted of Bandung's local government, "[To obtain feedback] our Twitter is the most active [channel used by citizens]" (B2).

The connection between affordances perception and affordances actualisation has emerged from the empirical evidence on whether the enabling/inhibiting factors impact

Table 4. Identified enabling and inhibiting factors

Affordances effects	Excerpts
Political goodwill	"This initiative can be copied by other local governments. All is dependent on the goodwill of the top management." (B1) "In coping with tweets containing criticism, mockery, and intimidation, my patience already reaches to the God level." (The mayor of Bandung, quoted in [18]
Technical skill and knowledge readiness	"Fortunately, our operator has … good skill in computer and Internet, and she graduated from communication studies, so we have no significant burden. … But, [at the beginning,] the dubiety of the operators in answering the incoming messages could be a challenge. We classified the messages, which ones … can be answered by her directly, which ones … need to be filtered, and which ones need to be consulted about with the top management." (B2) "The basic IT skill of the officers [at] the village level is inadequate. … We gave them technical assistance in collaboration with the developer of the system. We also recruited skilled officers." (B7)
Focus shifting	"Our department's focus was on managing public relations, as a government representative to balance the media reporting. … Nowadays, we are responsible [for developing] IT-based service. Each department should have at least five IS applications, to support the internal business process and to provide services to citizens." (B1)
Reward systems	"[Social media activity] is used as one of the indicators in assessing the officers' performance. … We rank the performance of the heads of the sub-districts. The best ten have been sent to South Korea for a comparative study." (B1)
Social media use among citizens	"A study conducted in Bandung, inhabited by 2.5 million people, found that most citizens have a social media account, including students of junior and senior high schools. Another study told us, in accessing information, that television is the first source [for information], and the second one is social media." (B1)
Supports from the local parliament	"At the beginning, the benefits of using such a system were unclear. … The nature of budget allocation for developing IS applications is abstract. It can be either cheap or expensive. They [the local parliament] were in doubt. … But, finally our proposal was] granted." (B3)
Transparency culture	"[In the beginning], their acceptance varied, since they were not used to being transparent, but now they have to. Citizens can give corrections and input." (B1)

whether or not officials are able to act in relation to their goals. Our analyses explored both the positive and the negative influences on affordances actualisation. Though the concept of affordances is usually discussed from the positive perspective [9, 15, 21],

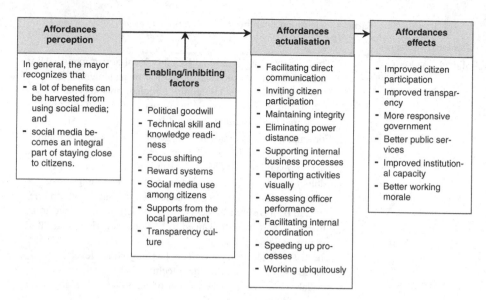

Fig. 3. The connection between affordances perception, affordances actualisation, and affordances effect, and its relation to associated enabling/inhibiting factors

affordances are defined in the literature as a dual concept [22, 23], emphasising that technology can both enable and constrain.

Our data indicates that affordances perception may play a very general role in identifying the action possibilities provided by certain technologies (such as social media) when they interact with specific contexts (e.g., eParticipation). However, in practice, this may lead to the emergence of unanticipated affordances actualisation. For example, at the beginning of a eParticipation initiative, it might be difficult to imagine how the use of social media could eliminate power distance; however, it does—and it is realised only after the affordances have been actualised. We could relate this to the concept of 'bounded rationality,' which holds that decision making is often conducted based on limited information [24]. Even more, some affordances actualisation may emerge to respond to new possibilities, as noted by [13]; indeed, the actualisation of an affordance may result in enabling conditions for additional affordances. For example, affordances facilitating internal coordination and enabling working ubiquitously may lead to another affordance (e.g., speeding up processes). This finding leads to a discussion regarding how useful it actually is to make a plan (e.g., a plan to use social media to increase citizen participation), especially in the context of developing countries. Likely, in such cases, a general plan would still be needed—but not necessarily an exhaustive one.

6   Conclusion

In this paper, we have employed a case study approach to identify instances of affordance perception, affordance actualisation, and affordance effects, as well as a number of influential enabling and inhibiting factors. By so doing, we have contributed to the area of eParticipation by demonstrating how the concept of affordances helps to make sense of the consequences of introducing ICT for the sole purpose of citizen participation. We have shown this by analysing the interactions between a goal-oriented actor (i.e., the new mayor of Bandung), the ICT artefacts, and the surrounding environment. Our contribution includes identifying nine actualised affordances, isolating the link between these nine affordances and certain affordances effects, and exploring the relationship between affordances perception and affordances actualisation (as enabled or inhibited by various identified contextual factors).

The case findings introduced here is based on empirical evidence collected at a single point in time, without access to longitudinal data. The concept of affordances (with a particular focus on action possibilities and the relationship between perception, actualisation, and effects) allows for further investigation into cause and effect by exploring how actions lead to the actualisation of affordances. Future research is needed to further our understanding of causal effects, particularly in terms of exploring longitudinal data from Bandung.

Practical implications of our work include disseminating the lessons learned from the success story of Bandung, where the introduction of LAPOR has boosted civic participation from citizens and other public stakeholders. Practitioners could learn from these experiences by, for instance, exploring how the various factors influence affordance effects. Such an inquiry would lead to increased understanding of how perceptions and enabling/inhibiting factors influence affordances actualisation and effects —the main objectives for any eParticipation initiative. Another important lesson that can be taken from the Bandung case is related to disruption and the disruptive perspective [8], which helps us to understand how ICT innovations can exhibit fundamental discontinuity. More research is needed before we can fully understand how disruptive moments can influence the success of eParticipation initiatives.

Our findings provide ample avenues for future research. First, the nature of our identified affordances and the relationship between them should be further investigated to enhance our understanding of collective actions within eParticipation projects. Questions to be answered include what motivates people to join and how knowledge-sharing processes take place within eParticipation projects [25]. Secondly, affordances have a relative nature [13], which implies that affordances actualised by some individuals might be of no use to other individuals. Hence, our contributions provide a starting point for research within different empirical settings. For instance, researchers could extend our theoretical approach by identifying different affordances, different relationships between the concepts, and different interaction patterns. Our findings could also be introduced to confront different eParticipation projects through comparative studies.

References

1. Medaglia, R.: eParticipation research: moving characterization forward (2006–2011). Gov. Inf. Q. **29**, 346–360 (2012). doi:10.1016/j.giq.2012.02.010

2. Rahman, M.M., Ahsan Rajoin, S.A.: An effective framework for implementing electronic governance in dveloping countries: bangladesh perspective. Int. J. Comput. Inf. Technol. **3**, 360–365 (2012)
3. Veit, D., Huntgerburth, J.: Foundations of Digital Government. Leading and Managing in the Digital Era. 158 (2014). doi:10.1007/978-3-642-38511-7_9
4. Criado, J.I., Sandoval-Almazan, R., Gil-Garcia, J.R.: Government innovation through social media. Gov. Inf. Q. **30**, 319–326 (2013). doi:10.1016/j.giq.2013.10.003
5. Van Dijk, J.: Models of democracy and concepts of communication. Digital Democracy Issues Theory Practice. Sage Publications, New York (2000)
6. Kavanaugh, A.L., Fox, E.A., Sheetz, S.D., et al.: Social media use by government: from the routine to the critical. Gov. Inf. Q. **29**, 480–491 (2012). doi:10.1016/j.giq.2012.06.002
7. Borins, S.: A holistic view of public sector information technology. JE Gov. **1**, 3–29 (2005). doi:10.1300/J399v01n02_02
8. Lyytinen, K., Rose, G.M.: Disruptive information system innovation: the case of internet computing. Inf. Syst. J. **13**, 301–330 (2003). doi:10.1046/j.1365-2575.2003.00155.x
9. Zammuto, R.F., Griffith, T.L., Majchrzak, A., et al.: Information technology and the changing fabric of organization. Organ. Sci. **18**, 749–762 (2007). doi:10.1287/orsc.1070.0307
10. Gibson, J.J.: A theory of affordances. In: Shaw, R. (ed.) Perceiving, Acting, Knowing Toward an Ecology Psychology, pp. 67–82. Lawrence Erlbaum Associates, Hillsdale (1977)
11. Markus, M.L., Silver, M.S.: A foundation for the study of it effects: a new look at DeSanctis and Poole's concepts of structural features and spirit *. J. Assoc. Inf. Syst. **9**, 609–632 (2008)
12. Chemero, A.: An outline of a theory of affordances. Ecol. Psychol. **15**, 181–195 (2003). doi:10.1207/S15326969ECO1502_5
13. Pozzi, G., Pigni, F., Vitari, C.: Affordance theory in the IS discipline: a review and synthesis of the literature (2014)
14. Bernhard, E., Recker, J., Burton-Jones, A.: Understanding the actualization of affordances: a study in the process modeling context. In: Proceedings of ICIS 2013 (2013)
15. Seidel, S., Recker, J., Vom Brocke, J.: Sensemaking and sustainable practicing: functional affordances of information systems in green transformation. MIS Q. **37**, 1275–1299 (2013)
16. Strong, D.M., Johnson, S.A., Tulu, B., et al.: A theory of organization-EHR affordance actualization. J. Assoc. Inf. Syst. **15**, 53–85 (2014)
17. Derby, D.: Ini trik Walikota Bandung agar dekat dengan rakyat. Tangerangnews.com (2014)
18. Yudiman, M., Sufyan, M.: Twitter Power @Ridwankamil. Publika Edu Media (2014)
19. Michaels, C.F.: Affordances: four points of debate. Ecol. Psychol. **15**, 135–148 (2003)
20. Hammer, M., Champy, J.: Reengineering the Corporation: A Manifesto for Business Reengineering. Nicholas Brealey Publ, London (1993)
21. North-Samardzich, A., Braccini, A.M., Spagnoletti, P., Za, S.: Applying media synchronicity theory to distance learning in virtual worlds: a design science approach. Int. J. Innov. Learn. **15**, 328–346 (2014)
22. Hutchby, I.: Technologies, texts and affordances. Sociology **35**, 441–456 (2001)
23. Volkoff, O., Strong, D.M.: Critical realism and affordances: theorizing IT-associated organizational change processes. MIS Q. **37**, 819–834 (2013)
24. Simon, H.A.: Bounded rationality and organizational learning. Organ. Sci. **2**, 125–134 (1991). doi:10.1287/orsc.2.1.125
25. Federici, T., Braccini, A.M., Sæbø, Ø.: "Gentlemen, all aboard!" using ICT to directly involve citizens in party politics. Lessons learned from the Italian Five Stars Movement. Gov. Inf. Q. (2015)

Please Like and Share! A Frame Analysis of Opinion Articles in Online News

Marius Rohde Johannessen[✉]

Department of Business and Management,
Buskerud and Vestfold University College, 235, 3603 Kongsberg, Norway
marius.johannessen@hbv.no

Abstract. In this paper, I apply framing theory to the online newspaper opinion articles that were most shared and most liked in social media in 2014. The articles were published in two of Norway's largest and most influential online newspapers; Dagbladet.no and Aftenposten.no. Frame analysis makes visible how people define and construct a given issue, and as such can provide valuable input on how to write when you want a topic put on the political agenda. The findings show that the most popular opinion articles have one common theme: They are written in a personal tone, and aimed at our private sphere. The paper concludes by discussing what this means for agenda setting and for the public sphere.

Keywords: eParticipation · Frame analysis · Framing theory · Social media · Online newspapers · Norway

1 Introduction

Agenda setting is a very important element in the political decision making process, and some scholars argue that there is a direct link between agenda setting and new legislation [1]. Agenda setting can be defined as the ability to influence our perceptions of the importance of a topic [2], where the objective is to achieve consensus among the members of a public [3]. The news media is traditionally viewed as a very important actor in agenda setting [3], and issues that are high on the agenda of the news media are often prioritised by politicians [4]. Opinion articles, in the form of letters to the editor, are debate-focused genres in the newspaper, written by readers. These articles often address political issues, and can to some extent be seen as insight into the topics that are of interest to the general public, or at least to the more politically interested parts of the general public [5].

In recent years, social media, defined as "a group of Internet-based applications that build on the ideological and technological foundations of Web 2.0, and that allow the creation and exchange of User Generated Content" (p. 61) [6] has become increasingly important as a communications channel, also for political issues. The Internet and networks of engaged citizens have created a new space for engagement [7]. In a social context which fosters participation and action, the Internet and social media can attract more citizens to participate in political processes [8, 9].

A recent study [10] found social media to be increasingly important for agenda setting. And while Facebook is the most important social medium, the strength of

© IFIP International Federation for Information Processing 2015
E. Tambouris et al. (Eds.): ePart 2015, LNCS 9249, pp. 15–26, 2015.
DOI: 10.1007/978-3-319-22500-5_2

social media is its diverse user base and the sum of many social media applications [10]. Perhaps even more important is the finding that social media and news media have a symbiotic relationship where stories from the news media are shared to, and discussed by, a larger audience in social media [10]. Drawing on the power of weak networks to form communities of individuals with similar interests can facilitate the formation of social movements, political campaigns and various protest groups [11, 12]. The objective of such groups will often be related to agenda-setting and to gaining the attention of the media [13].

According to framing theory, the way in which a story is framed is an important part of the agenda setting process [14], as the framing process is essential for 'level 2 agenda setting', the process where a set of attributes, or themes, are defined for the issues being discussed [15]. It is this very process of shaping the message which is known as framing: "Framing is the process by which a communication source, such as a news organization, defines and constructs a political issue or public controversy" (p. 567) [16].

This short introduction leads us to the objectives and research questions of this paper: To analyse the framing of content in successful online newspaper opinion articles, and to examine the potential implications this has for agenda setting and the public sphere. These objectives translate into the following research questions:

RQ1: How are the most liked and shared newspaper opinion articles framed?
RQ2: What are the implications of framing for agenda setting?

The rest of the paper is structured as follows: Sect. 2 provides an overview of related research, specifically on the topics of framing theory and the role of the media in shaping public opinion. Section 3 presents the research approach of the study, and Sects. 4 and 5 present the findings and conclusions with some possible directions for future research.

2   Related Research

2.1   Framing Theory

Framing is concerned with how we construct the stories we tell about the world [17]. Framing theory has its roots in several disciplines, especially psychology and sociology [18]. One of the first to introduce the concept was sociologist Erving Goffman in his 1974 book "Frame analysis. An essay of the organization of experience" [19], where he used the concept of frames to show people organize their perceptions of society as a whole and of specific aspects of society. Framing relates to attitudes, and can be measured as the sum of positive and negative associations with a given issue [17]. These attitudes then influence how we choose to talk about the issue. For example, if a company wants to build office buildings in your city, which will generate jobs and income but have a negative effect on the local environment, your attitude towards the project can be determined by the value you put on the economy vs environmental and "green" issues. These attitudes then frame how you talk about the issue. A newspaper reporter in favour of the environment will write more about the negative environmental impacts of the build, while another reporter focused on the economy will write about how the project is great for the local economy.

Several studies have examined the effects of framing on the public's perceptions of an issue. These studies show that framing has a clear impact on our perceptions, especially when we do not have a clear preference on the issue, or if the framing supports our own views. A survey asking people about their willingness to pay more for products in order to offset the products' carbon emissions, showed that especially republican voters were more likely to accept paying more only if asked about "carbon offset". When the extra amount of money was referred to as a "carbon tax", the number of republican voters willing to pay more dropped substantially [20]. Another survey asked about attitudes to free speech. When respondents were asked if they would support the right of a hate group to hold a rally, the survey questions tested framing by first asking "given the importance of free speech, would you support...", then "Given the risk of violence, would you support...". For the first question, 85 % of respondents were positive towards allowing the rally. For the second, only 45 % were positive [17]. In Norway, the protest group ATTAC was successful in gaining media attention and managed to become an important voice in the late 90's and early 2000's debate on globalisation. This success was due to the successful framing of their message, which were embedded in the popular discourses surrounding globalisation at the time, using the protests in Seattle and other cities as part of their framing process [21].

Studies of framing effects are useful in showing that framing works. Other scholars have studied how and why framing works. One study found two factors that helped explain how framing affects us. The first factor was that framing changes the weight assigned to our beliefs. Read about global warming long enough, and we start being re concerned about it. The second factor was the introduction of new ideas and new information, showing us content we had no previous awareness of, i.e. reading about global warming for the first time [22]. A literature review found that successful framing had effects related to the dissemination of information, persuasion of readers and for agenda-setting [18].

2.2   Conducting Frame Analysis

Analysing the framing process can be done using a number of different approaches. This section provides an overview of the most common approaches to frame analysis. Table 1 summarises the different approaches identified in literature.

Reese points out that empirical analysis of frames can be both quantitative/positivist and qualitative/interpretive [23]. Bishop [24] applied frame analysis to media coverage of play. He collected texts from US newspapers and transcripts from national TV news and performed a qualitative content analysis because "a quantitative content analysis would not have enabled the author to unpack the layers of meaning found in the texts" (p. 513). His unit of analysis was the entire article, and he coded the articles looking for keywords, stock phrases, stereotypes and judgments connected with the themes he identified. This allowed him to create labels for the frames he found in the texts. This approach allowed him to identify eight distinct frames for talking about children's play, ranging from play as a form of learning to the need for physical exercise.

Table 1. Summary of research methods, frame analysis

Approach	Purpose	Insights gained
Qualitative content analysis Coding of qualitative data: keywords, key phrases, judgment statements	Identify themes and topics Interpret meanings of texts to identify frames for the different themes and topics	Rich description of the frames used to talk about a specific issue
Quantitative content analysis Follows pre-defined coding scheme based on hypotheses	Using frames to examine issues of statistical significance. Impact over time	Time series data, tendencies/consequences of frames
Mixed methods Approach varies according to research question	In-depth analysis and identification of frames, and of the impact of frames	Impacts and tendencies mixed with a deep understanding of context and the individual frames

Kang [25], in his study of autism, follows a similar approach of identifying themes and following a coding scheme for the identification of frames, but applies quantitative content analysis and statistical methods to identify frames and to examine how these frames have changed over time. Liu and Pennington-Gray [26] also argues for quantitative content analysis in their study of the media's coverage of bed bugs. Again, the unit of analysis is the news article. They develop a coding scheme and perform various statistical analyses. These two studies both had a somewhat different objective in that they were interested in following the news framing over time.

Silberberg [27] argues for a mixed-methods approach, where the research methods applied varies according to the research question being asked. Her study on newspaper framing of the US Food and Drug administration (FDA) applies quantitative methods to examine the number of positive, negative and neutral articles from three selected newspapers about the FDA, as well as identifying bias and any ideological differences in the newspapers. He applies qualitative analysis for identifying specific framing techniques, general discussion of results, textual patterns in the reporting, and to present example content from the different frames. Yarnell [28] similarly argues for a mixed-method approach, pointing out that a pure quantitative framing analysis lacks context and depth, while qualitative framing analysis can lose out on important statistical facts.

2.3 Online Newspapers' Role in Shaping Public Opinion

The news media is traditionally viewed as a very important actor in agenda setting [3], and issues that are high on the agenda of the news media are often prioritised by politicians [4], as successful framing of newspaper stories have proven successful in persuading the public about the merits (or negative sides of) an issue [18]. For example, a study of news coverage of the funding of children's programs showed significant changes in the city budget before and after an editorial campaign calling for increased spending on children's related policies [4].

In Norway, both the Internet and newspapers have a strong position. According to the Bureau of Statistics[1], 75 % of Norwegians read a printed newspaper at least once a week, and 85 % use the Internet every day. 61 % of Internet users visit at least one online newspaper. While print readerships have dropped significantly in recent years, online readerships and subscriptions are on the rise, and newspapers remain one of the most important sources of information for Norwegians. However, social media is on the rise, and according to the TNS media survey[2], 56 % of Norwegians use social media to meet their needs for information, and 71 % respond that the newspaper (on- or offline) meets their needs for information. As there is some overlap between the media channels, these numbers support the findings of Grzywinska and Borden, which claims that social media and traditional media are in a symbiotic relationship where traditional media extends its user base through sharing in social media [10].

The importance of this symbiotic relationship becomes even more visible when we take into account the notion of the network society. Western society is increasingly organized through networks, and networks influence culture, business and politics alike [29]. A network consists of nodes (the individual parts of the network) and the connections between these nodes. Nodes can be individuals, organizations, societal institutions, business and government [30]. Studies in marketing have shown powerful network effects from the sharing of content, especially when the one sharing is seen as an influencer in the network [31]. This combination of the media's agenda setting power and the network effects that brings content to an even larger audience is part of what makes understanding framing so important. An increased awareness of the fact that content is framed can aid us in being more critical citizens, as being part of a social network where you are exposed to alternative arguments and different sources of information leads to a more informed public, which is less likely to be persuaded by how others frame an issue:

"Deliberation, discussion, and exposure to information and alternative arguments can raise the quality of public opinion by reducing ambivalence and uncertainty. People who are better informed about the issues are more likely to have established a frame of reference for their opinions and are less likely to be swayed by how other people frame the issues for them" (p. 121) [17].

3   Research Approach

The objectives of this paper is to analyse the framing of content in successful online newspaper opinion articles, and to examine the potential implications this has for the public sphere. In order to address these objectives, I chose to follow a qualitative research approach with an interpretivist epistemology. This approach is appropriate because framing concerns the creation of meanings, and meanings are in their very

---

[1] http://www.ssb.no/medie.

[2] http://www.tns-gallup.no/medier/avis.

nature interpretive [23]. The empirical basis for the paper is the lists of the most shared and most liked opinion articles from two of Norway's leading online newspapers. This provided me with 40 articles for analysis, covering different topics and published throughout 2014. The data was imported to the Nvivo software package for qualitative research, and analysed using a frame analysis approach, as outlined by Reese [23] and Bishop [24]. Because the number of articles is limited and the selection is so hetero-geneous in terms of the topics addressed, I have chosen to identify frames from a macro-perspective. For example, the frame "deliberation" could easily be broken down into smaller frames based on the actual argument. Given the limited number of articles within the frame, this would however not allow me to identify patterns of interest in the data.

Reese [23] points out that the frame analyses should always start with answering a set of questions: Where does the frame reside? In text, culture or in the mind of the receiver? How do we know that a frame actually exists, or is it simply a construction by the researcher or the reader? What is the unit of analysis? What is the relationship between frames and agenda setting, and how do we separate topics and themes from the frames used to present them? For this paper, the answers are as follows: The frame resides in text, in the arguments structuring the opinion article. Being an interpretive study, the frame exists as a construction based on the researcher's interpretations of text. We can code the story about the drunk driving of famous cross-country skier in several ways, such as justice, celebrity blunders or drunk driving. I have attempted to code using relatively broad categories, so in this case I would code the article as "justice". The unit of analysis is the individual article. Topics and themes are separated from frames through the coding process, as these are the first items to be identified for each article. As for the relationship between frames and agenda setting, the literature section addresses this issue. The actual coding process is influenced by Bishop [24]: The individual article is coded by first identifying the theme of the article, then searching for key words and phrases, as well as judgment claims.

The coding process followed a grounded, iterative approach. Specific sections of the texts were coded as different themes and frames, in order to create a coding scheme. In the second round of coding, the texts were coded with the identified themes and frames. I performed the first two rounds of coding, and verified my findings through having a colleague examine and comment on the data set and findings.

In addition to the frame analysis, I performed a set of descriptive statistical anal-yses. Word-frequency analysis, and cross coding of nodes to identify issues such as how many women and men used specific frames for their articles, and how many of these were unknown writers (people who are not hired as comment writers, run a popular blog or are frequent writers in the letters to the editor section). This allows for a more mixed-method approach, as argued for by [28].

4   Findings

The two newspapers selected for analysis are two of the largest online newspapers in Norway, based on number of readers. Dagbladet.no had 1,906,000 readers in 2014, and Aftenposten.no had 1,162,000. Looking at the list of most visited web sites in Norway, published by the **Norwegian Media Businesses' Association**[3] **(NMBA), we find newspapers at five of the top ten most read web sites. The other sites are weather forecasting service yr.no, classifieds site finn.no and the national broadcaster NRK, as well as "other services", where we find social media and other web sites. Both Dagbladet.no and aftenposten.no ranks in the top ten most read web sites in Norway. This is a clear indicator of the importance of newspapers in Norway.** Table 2 **shows a summary of statistics for the two newspapers, including their Facebook and Twitter readership (both newspapers have "share on Facebook/Twitter buttons attached to each story). On Facebook, both newspapers have a separate page for opinions and letters to the editor. This page is also included.**

Table 2. Statistics for the two newspapers in the study.

Title	Web	Twitter	Tw., opinion	Facebook	FB, opinion
Aftenposten	1,162,000	65600	13200	194248	21680
Dagbladet	1,906,000	5677	4035	95010	64781

Facebook is by far the most popular channel for sharing. 42,000 people on Facebook, and only 452 times on Twitter shared the article that was on top of the most shared list. We see this trend across all the examined articles, where 100+ people share in Twitter, while Facebook sharing is in the tens of thousands. The articles were published throughout the year, at different times of day.

4.1   General Findings – Closeness, Personal Issues and New Voices

The word frequency shows that the issues close to home get more attention. Norway/Norwegian is mentioned 136 times, while Europe/European is only mentioned 15 times, and only in four of the 40 articles. Frequently used nouns give us a hint of the themes that are important. These include "children", "school", "work", and "women", reflecting the most common themes found in the articles. Unknown writers (writers who are not regular columnists, well-known bloggers or frequent contributors to the opinion section of newspapers) write more than half of the articles, and around half of the writers are women. Only six writers have an academic background. This indicates that social media sharing does help new to include new voices in the public sphere. Personal issues are the most popular themes: Health, gender/body, parenting and education make up 75 % of the articles. This supports Graham's [34] view that the personal sphere has become an important part of public debate.

---

[3] http://www.mediebedriftene.no/Tall–Fakta1/Lesertall/lesertall-avis-host-2014/.

4.2   Frames

Six frames were identified. The first frame, *metaphor,* was found in one article that used a fairy tale figure to discuss current social issues. "Askeladden" is a stereotype of the idealized Norwegian, the underdog who succeeds by being creative and thinking outside the box, and who thinks more about others than about himself. The article uses the metaphor to show everything that is wrong with Norwegian society today:

> "Askeladden helped those in need. When others needed him, he forgot about his own issues and
> needs. Personal kindness translated to politics is solidarity... However, now the welfare state is
> threatened. Social inequality is on the rise. The number of poor children increases. The wealthy
> do not have to pay taxes"

The second frame is *satire/irony.* Three articles use this to frame their message. They do this to ridicule the position they are arguing against, in order to convince the reader that there is only one way of interpreting said issue. A columnist comments on the teacher's strike in the autumn of 2014, ridiculing the arguments made by those who oppose the strike:

> "After all, the strike affects an innocent third party. I am not thinking about the students. No
> one cares about students. I am of course thinking about myself. And people like myself."

Another article discusses gender stereotypes used in advertising, and uses male stereotypes to argue against this form of advertising:

> "How many of us see these images and think 'yes, we can relate to this. Party and drinking trips
> to European brothels, where we party all night with heavy-chested women who has no
> personality?"

The third frame identified is *Justice,* The frame uses arguments related to justice, fairness and equal treatment to frame the message. Two articles use this frame, one discussing terrorism and the treatment of Anders Behring Breivik, the other discussing the drunk driving of a famous cross-country skier:

> "You can't call yourself a victim of the media in this case. No one in VG [Norwegian news-
> paper] gave you a bottle of vodka and Audi the last time I checked. You are a huge role model
> for young kids, who now might think that drinking and driving is ok. Therefore we should all be
> happy that this episode is so massively criticized in the media."

Another frame, used in four articles, is *pressure.* This frame focus on the psychological pressure that faces us in modern society, and argues that we need to find ways of lessening pressure. Peer pressure, parenting and the pressure to be the best at everything are topics within this frame, which has a clear "them and us" perspective. A liberal Muslim woman is tired of the peer pressure she claims comes from conservative Muslims in her surroundings:

> "I am sick and tired of Muslims who think they are better than the rest of us. Why do they insist
> on being so different? Do they believe God loves them more than us? The Niqab does not just
> represent oppression, but also arrogance."

Pressure related to parenting and testing in schools are other issues. The following quote is an example from an article incorporating both of these topics:

"At supper, 6.30 PM a Tuesday in May, we receive a call from a concerned teacher. Our six year old boy is having trouble separating the letters 'b' and 'd'...and there is a test tomorrow... It is thought provoking that a teacher has to call parents late at night about this. Who is it really that is being tested tomorrow? The pupil or the teacher?"

Deliberation is the frame of the classical debate article. This frame presents arguments backed up by reasoning and references to literature. The objective is to convince the reader through presenting facts and rational arguments. It is not surprising that the six academic authors and the established commentators are the most frequent users of this frame. The topics found in this frame relates to politics and society, discussing the dangers of drugs, financial policies, international politics and women's rights. Ten of the examined articles falls within this frame. While the topics vary, their content is such that they are relevant to large numbers of people. For example, the article discussing NATO does so in a context of Russian expansion in the Ukraine, and the dangers a strong Russia poses for Norway:

"The Russian insurances comes after Russia several times the past few months have entered Swedish airspace with their fighters, and after several military provocations of all their European neighbours, including Norway"

The last frame is perhaps the most interesting one. More than half of the articles are framed as a *personal account* of events, where the author describes his or her experiences in relation to a theme, and discusses the theme based on these experiences. The articles framed as personal accounts are the most shared articles by far, showing that content we as readers can relate directly to, which addresses issues we are concerned with, is perhaps the best way of gaining attention and reaching a broad audience. The topics in this category varies greatly, ranging from terrorism to education and parenting. What the articles do have in common is how they address something they perceive as a societal issue through personal experience, and how they relate these personal experiences to a broader context. An anonymous mother discusses the failure of kindergartens to avoid bullying through an account of her three-year-old daughter's daily life:

"Now I suddenly understand the more than 50 necklaces she has brought home from kindergarten the past few months. Each piece is made out of loneliness, exclusion and small children's hands, alone at a table"

In another example, a woman discusses the pressures of modern work life through the story of her own illness:

"I'm burnt out. Exhausted and depressed. On sick leave because I could not handle it all anymore. They call it hitting the wall. I would rather compare it to walking off a cliff. I did not see a wall, I did not feel a crash, and it never stopped. Suddenly I just lost my footing and fell."

This frame most clearly reflects the general findings in Sect. 4.1. The issues that seem closest are the most engaging ones. The writers are new voices in the public sphere, and while their message is personal, the readers seem to find something universal in the stories they read.

5 Discussion and Conclusion

In this paper, I have examined popular opinion articles from two online newspapers, using frame analysis to identify how writers frame a popular article. The analysis revealed six frames. One of these, the *personal account*, accounts for more than half of the examined articles. Except for an article by Steven Hawking the articles using this frame are at the very top of the list of shared content.

We can interpret the meaning of this for the wider public sphere and for agenda setting in politics in several ways. A sceptic would perhaps say that this fascination for the private and personal is a sign that we should stop worrying about including citizens in the public debate. Aftenposten commentator Thorgeir Kolshus points us in another direction, claiming that the "idea of our private stories having public value is an expression of societal trust. My issues are relevant for others, and other people's issues are relevant to me. This helps build community"[4]. Kolshus' interpretation is also found in research claiming that the private realm is becoming more and more relevant for the public sphere [32]. While the stories are private, they contain arguments related to important societal issues. This framing brings new issues to the attention of thousands of new people through sharing in social media. If we assume that every user sharing an article has 100 unique friends, an article that is shared 42,000 times potentially reaches out to 4 200 000 people. That is 85 % of the Norwegian population. The sum of this sharing certainly has implications for agenda setting both in the media and in parliament. Political parties spend many resources following the stories that trend in the media, looking for issues to comment on. Thus, it is likely that over time, the personal framing of opinions will have implications for which cases are put on the agenda of political parties.

This paper has a few limitations that are worth noticing. First of all, existing studies of framing (see for example [22, 25, 26]) tend to focus on one topic or issue, and examine the framing surrounding this issue. As my approach was to examine what makes us share content, the analysis process was slightly different in that I had several topics and a limited number of articles to analyse. Thus, the frames "deliberation" and personal account" should be seen as meta-frames, overarching frames that contain more specific framing about the topic. The data set is somewhat limited, covering only 40 articles. I did attempt contacting the other leading newspapers in order to have a larger data set to work with, but I was not successful in getting answers from them. Even so, the findings in this paper shows some interesting trends that are worth reporting. In addition, the paper identifies several possibilities for future research.

The framing analysis includes only a small subsection of opinion articles, and it would be useful to examine a larger sample, which also included an examination of the comment fields in newspapers, as well as comments on Facebook and Twitter conversations. The role of technology in this process also needs a more thorough investigation, and a study of the affordances of social media in relation to agenda setting and framing could be an interesting approach for this purpose. Another interesting approach

---

[4] http://www.aftenposten.no/meninger/kronikker/Var-private-offentlighet-7833509.html.   Quote   is   translated from Norwegian.

would be a Social network analysis examining the sharing of content, as well as examining the discussion that follows a shared article in social media.

Acknowledgement. I would like to thank my brother, sociologist Lars Emil Johannessen, for fruitful discussions on frame analysis and framing theory.

References

1. Zucchini, F.: Government alternation and legislative agenda setting: government alternation and legislative agenda setting. Eur. J. Polit. Res. **50**, 749–774 (2011)
2. Mccombs, M., Reynolds, A.: News influence on our pictures of the world. Media Effects: Advances in Theory and Research. Routledge, New York (2002)
3. McCombs, M.: Building consensus: the news media's agenda-setting roles. Polit. Commun. **14**, 433–443 (1997)
4. Brewer, M., McCombs, M.: Setting the community agenda. J. Mass Commun. Q. **73**, 7–16 (1996)
5. Dalton, R.J., Beck, P.A., Huckfeldt, R., Koetzle, W.: A test of media-centered agenda setting: newspaper content and public interests in a Presidential Election. Polit. Commun. **15**, 463–481 (1998)
6. Kaplan, A.M., Haenlein, M.: Users of the world, unite! the challenges and opportunities of Social Media. Bus. Horiz. **53**, 59–68 (2010)
7. Castells, M.: The new public sphere: global civil society, communication networks, and global governance. Ann. Am. Acad. Pol. Soc. Sci. **616**, 78–93 (2008)
8. Roberts, B.: Beyond the "networked public sphere": politics, participation and technics in web 2.0. Fibreculture (2009)
9. Rose, J., Sæbø, Ø., Nyvang, T., Sanford, C., Svendsen, S.B.: The role of social networking software in eParticipation. DEMO-net: Democracy Netw. (2007)
10. Grzywinska, I., Borden, J.: The impact of social media on traditional media agenda setting theory. the case study of occupy wall street movement in USA. Agenda setting: old and new problems in old and new media, Wroclaw (2012)
11. Svendsen, G.T., Svendsen, G.L.H.: Social Kapital - en introduktion. Hans Reitzels Forlag, København (2006)
12. Benkler, Y.: The Wealth of Networks: How Social Production Transforms Markets and Freedom. Yale University Press, New Haven (2006)
13. Carroll, W.K., Hackett, R.A.: Democratic media activism through the lens of social movement theory. Media Cult. Soc. **28**, 83–104 (2006)
14. McCombs, M., Ghanem, S.I.: The Convergence of Agenda Setting and Framing. Framing Public Life Perspectives on Media and our Understanding of the Social World. Taylor & Francis e-library, London (2001)
15. Weaver, D.H.: Thoughts on agenda setting, framing, and priming. J. Commun. **57**, 142–147 (2007)
16. Nelson, T., Clawson, R., Oxley, Z.M.: Media framing of a civil liberties conflict and its effect on tolerance. Am. Polit. Sci. Rev. **91**, 567–583 (1997)
17. Chong, D., Druckman, J.N.: Framing theory. Annu. Rev. Polit. Sci. **10**, 103–126 (2007)
18. Tewksbury, D., Scheufele, D.A.: News Framing Theory and Research. Media effects: Advances in Theory and Research, pp. 17–33. Erlbaum, Hillsdale (2009)
19. Goffman, E.: Frame Analysis. An Essay on the Organization of Experience. Northeastern University Press, Boston (1974)

20. Hardisty, D.J., Johnson, E.J., Weber, E.U.: A dirty word or a dirty world?: attribute framing, political affiliation, and query theory. Psychol. Sci. **21**, 86–92 (2010)
21. Sandberg, S.: The success of ATTAC in Norway: an approach synthesising discourse analysis and framing theory (2003)
22. Lecheler, S., de Vreese, C.H.: News framing and public opinion a mediation analysis of framing effects on political attitudes. J. Mass Commun. Q. **89**, 185–204 (2012)
23. Reese, S.D.: Finding frames in a web of culture. 2010 Doing News Fram. Anal. Empir. Theor. Perspect., 17–42 (2010)
24. Bishop, R.: Go out and play, but mean it: using frame analysis to explore recent news media coverage of the rediscovery of unstructured play. Soc. Sci. J. **50**, 510–520 (2013)
25. Kang, S.: Coverage of autism spectrum disorder in the US television news: an analysis of framing. Disabil. Soc. **28**, 245–259 (2013)
26. Liu, B., Pennington-Gray, L.: Bed bugs bite the hospitality industry? A framing analysis of bed bug news coverage. Tour. Manag. **48**, 33–42 (2015)
27. Silberberg, R.: Journalistic framing of the food and drug administration: how do our nation's most respected newspapers report about the FDA? (2008)
28. Yarnell, S.M.: Frame analysis. Psychol. Mark. **2**, 31–40 (1985)
29. Castells, M.: Materials for an exploratory theory of the network society1. Br. J. Sociol. **51**, 5–24 (2000)
30. Barney, D.: The Network Society. Polity Press, Cambridge (2004)
31. Katona, Z., Zubcsek, P.P., Sarvary, M.: Network effects and personal influences: the diffusion of an online social network. J. Mark. Res. **48**, 425–443 (2011)
32. Graham, T.: Beyond "political" communicative spaces: talking politics on the wife swap discussion forum. J. Inf. Technol. Polit. **9**, 31–45 (2011)

The Influence of Social Media on Social Movements: An Exploratory Conceptual Model

Carla Danielle Monteiro Soares[✉] and Luiz Antonio Joia

Getulio Vargas Foundation,
Praia de Botafogo, 190 – 5th Floor, 22253-900 Rio de Janeiro, Brazil
carla.soares@fgvmail.br, luiz.joia@fgv.br

Abstract. Information and communication technology affects all issues in the modern world, including social movements. The impact of these technologies on such movements has been felt worldwide in recent years, affecting both developed countries, such as Spain and the United States, as well as developing countries, such as Brazil, Egypt, and Tunisia. Interestingly, the intensive use of the Internet and especially social media has been a common denominator in the popular demonstrations that have occurred in the past few years in the most diverse scenarios. Social movements appear to have been influenced by social media, particularly with respect to their organization and communication. Therefore, based on a review of the extant literature on the topic, this paper seeks to propose an exploratory conceptual model about the influence of the use of social media on social movements, whereby possible scenarios in which these social demonstrations tend to occur can be identified.

Keywords: Social movements · Internet · E-Participation · Social media

1 Introduction

Contemporary social movements[1] like so many other aspects of the modern world begin to suffer gradual transformation, starting to have similar characteristics, even when sparked off in completely different scenarios. Information and communication technology (ICT) has a dual role in this context, since the Internet is now used at times for the mere diffusion of information, and at other times as the very means by which the demonstrations are organized, in a process that feeds back on itself [1].

In the case of social movements, Internet and social media in particular facilitate the events and also brings them to international attention at an unprecedented pace, enabling the uprisings to be literally monitored in real time [2, 3].

Among these movements, the highlights were those that took place in Istanbul, the Arab Spring, Occupy Wall Street, the *Indignadas* in Spain, the 20 Cents movement in

---

A definition of Social Media can be found at http://webtrends.about.com/od/web20/a/social-media.htm, accessed on March 10, 2015.

[1] A definition of Social Movement can be found at https://www.ebscohost.com/uploads/imported/thisTopic-dbTopic-1248.pdf, accessed on May 25, 2015.

© IFIP International Federation for Information Processing 2015
E. Tambouris et al. (Eds.): ePart 2015, LNCS 9249, pp. 27–38, 2015.
DOI: 10.1007/978-3-319-22500-5_3

Brazil, among others. These movements were mostly composed of young people called to action through social media, without the presence of parties, trades unions, and traditional mass organizations [4, 5].

In order to contribute to the understanding of the relationship between the use of the Internet and especially social media with the social movements, this theoretical paper proposes the development of a conceptual model, rendering possible to discuss the potential and limitations of social media on social movements, thereby providing insights for the understanding and ongoing enhancement of academic research in this knowledge area.

2   The Context of Internet, Social Media, and Social Movements

The networks represent the new social morphology of our societies, since the diffusion of network logic substantially modifies the operation and the results of processes of production, experience, power and culture [6]. This society, named as the "network society" [7], uses information and communication technologies to establish its social structure. However, the Internet is a tool that develops but does not change behavior; on the contrary, behavior takes advantage of the Internet to broaden and organize itself into what it represents [8].

In spite of this, the Internet has proved to be an essential medium of expression and organization for the social demonstrations. It is a means of communication to which much of the world population has access, reconfiguring the map of relationships, in which ideas and information flow and some boundaries become fluid. In this respect, one argues that the importance of social networking sites (SNS) has grown so swiftly that they have become one of the tools of the social and political movements [9].

The popularity of the SNS, making them the most well-known websites in the world from October 2011 onwards, has contributed to a considerable extent to the spread of social demonstrations [10]. To give an idea of scale, in different regions such as the Middle East, Latin America, Europe, and Africa, SNS represented about 24 % of all time spent on the Internet in 2011, an increase of 35% compared to 2010 [11]. Moreover, YouTube has become the most popular online video platform worldwide, offering two out of five videos viewed worldwide [10].

With respect to the social movements, one stresses the fact that major mass demonstrations of the population were organized by mobilization via social media and thereafter showed their strength with the massive presence of people on the street [12]. They were united around calls for change, such as the Arab Spring, which began in late 2010, the *Indignadas* movement in Spain in 2011, and the protests in Brazil in 2013. In these cases, there was no mediation of the mobilization along classic lines, namely political parties, trade unions and conventional communication channels [13].

One deals with a standard feature of the social movements, namely that they spill over from social media onto the streets [12]. Anger and indignation with the current reality is the trigger for this feature, though fear is a suppressor for the outbreaks. Fear, however, is overcome by sharing the indignation via the network, which generates the awareness that one is not alone. Based on that, enthusiasm arises, which fosters the hope that things can be different, after which mass mobilization occurs. Furthermore, the interactive dynamics of the highly interconnected modern world has established a favorable environment for the reinvention of democracy [14]. Social media enables social movements to spread extremely swiftly and comprehensively, with technology rendering the physical distance between participants irrelevant.

As one states, occupation of the public space is essential at a given point for the visibility of the social movement, even though the origin and support structure of the social movement is in the open territory of the Internet and its social media [12].

Moreover, social movements mediated by the Internet intentionally have no leaders or hierarchy, mimicking the horizontal playing field of the Internet and reflecting distrust both of established leaders as well as of crises of representation [12]. Therefore, one points out that social movements enabled by social media are popular P2P (peer-to-peer) movements, in other words they have the same features as a point-to-point protocol computer network [15]. Thus, they arise when the decentralized and horizontal communication capacity of society makes it possible to build communities, share ideas and – in the case of demonstrations – express indignation. It is also stated that networks composed of many connection points and actors can be established anywhere and that all its points need to use compatible programs to connect to each other as, for example, Facebook [15]. This means that different actors can be in different places, though using the same social networking platform to link up. It is also stressed the importance of P2P processes arising from the high degree of connectivity of social media in real time (mobile phone, Internet, Twitter, and Facebook) for synchronization of a collective intelligence in what one calls the third reinvention of democracy and politics [14].

In the next section, it will be set forth the methodological procedures undertaken in this article to propose an exploratory conceptual model aiming at addressing the relationship between social movements and social media.

3 Methodological Procedures

After having defined the topic of this theoretical essay, the search for literature started. The first phase of this process was trying to find papers published in the leading journals of Information and Communication Technology. This search was not fruitful. Only a literature review on *Information, Communication, and Society* written by Garrett [16] about the subject of this research was found. One broadened the scope of search and included the principal journals in the field of sociology, anthropology, communication, marketing, politics, etc. The *Journal of Communication* and *The Communication Review* both dedicated a special issue on social media and political change. *The Journal of Communication* titled its issue: *Social Media and Political Change: Capacity, Constraint, and Consequence* and covered a wide range of protests.

After the review of the results accrued from the first search phase, a more general search among journals from different disciplines was undertaken, including backward and forward search as suggested by Webster and Watson [17]. This search resulted in 64 articles, all containing the following key words, independently or combined, namely: social media, manifestations, social protest, uprising, rebellion, Arab Spring, Tunisia, Egypt, Iran, Brazil, Occupy movement, and Occupy Wall Street.

The papers were classified based on their contents. That is, some articles address the structural factors related to the use of social media on social movements, i.e. the contextual conditions of each country wherein the popular movements took place. On the other hand, others articles tackle the contextual factors related to the use of social media on social movements, namely the factors considered closest to the movements per se, being them specific moderating factors that can help revealing the evolution and dynamics of social movements mediated by social media.

In order to comply with the suggestions accrued from Webster and Watson [17] and Okoli and Schabram [18] on literature review development, one analyzed the papers trying to triangulate them [19–21], as well as find commonalities and differences both in theory and methodology used. Attention was also paid to their recommendations for future research, as recommended by Webster and Watson [17].

After that, the aforementioned structural and contextual factors accrued from the papers analyzed were consolidated into an exploratory conceptual model to be tested in further studies.

4   Social Media and Social Movements: A Proposal for an Exploratory Conceptual Model

As already said, this article aims to develop an exploratory conceptual model to analyzing the influence of social media use in the organization of local social movements. This conceptual model consists of structural and instrumental factors discussed below and identified by means of the main contributions of the extant literature on social movements mediated by ICT that occurred in several countries since 2011.

4.1   Structural Factors

Based on the analysis of the extant literature about the subject addressed in this paper, one can realize the importance of structural factors on the using of social media on popular movements. These structural factors in the conceptual model are the contextual conditions of each country, namely the macro elements that demonstrate the overall living conditions and political activity in the nation. They can foster the emergence of agendas and ideas (e.g. improved living conditions, better transport, and the fight against corruption), as well as their dissemination to society in general. They include the technological, political, and socioeconomic context, as listed below according to the extant literature analyzed.

4.1.1   Technological Context

From the literature review conducted, one have noticed that several authors point to the importance of access to ICT by society as a way of having independent sources of information, sharing such information, and acquiring greater knowledge about leaders and governments [6, 12, 22–24]. In addition, access to ICT provides opportunities to express opinions, support social movements and even coordinate initiatives [16]. These authors support the existence of a strong linear relationship between the degree of Internet penetration in a given country and the current social movements.

In this manner, the technological context is used in the conceptual model for definition of the degree of Internet penetration in a given country. In preparing this construct, an international index can be used covering aspects such as: degree of territorial Internet signal coverage via the telecommunications infrastructure; degree of openness of the regulatory framework by means of universal access policies, especially for economically prejudiced people; degree of digital education of society such that individuals can exercise their civic rights independently and autonomously via the Internet.

The International Telecommunication Union Development Index [25], more commonly known as the ICT Development Index of the International Telecommunication Union (ITU) - the UN specialized agency for information and communication technologies - is an international index that takes into account the above aspects. Therefore, it might be used (among others) as a *próxis* for measuring this construct.

4.1.2 Political Context

Based on the studies of several authors [26–30], the political context of a country, namely its degree of democracy, influences the social movements that take place there. Therefore, it is relevant to analyze the political context associated with the degree of democratic freedom in a given country. Thus, when preparing this construct, an international index can also be used covering aspects such as: breadth of the electoral process; degree of independence and representativeness of Powers; degree of freedom of speech and press; degree of protection of human rights; degree of social participation.

Thus, the index of democracy compiled by The Economist (Democracy Index) [31] might be used (among others) as a *próxis* for measuring this construct, as it assesses democracy (or lack thereof) in 167 countries on a regular basis.

4.1.3 Socio-Economic Context

For several academics [12, 32–35], the socio-economic conditions of a country interfere directly in the collective actions of its citizens, who express their complaints and/or conceptualize their participation in social movements, inviting others to join them. Thus, the socioeconomic context – that defines the economic conditions that influence the quality of life of society in a given country – is also used in the proposed conceptual model. In the creation of this construct, an international index might be used to assess aspects such as: degree of economic activity relating to the production of goods and services and degree of distribution of income throughout society. Thus, the Human Development Index (HDI) – a statistical tool used to measure the overall development of a country in its social and economic dimensions –might be used (among others) as a *próxis* for measuring this construct [36].

That index sets out to measure the development of a country in accordance with the United Nations Development Programme (UNDP). The calculation of same combines four main indicators: life expectancy for health; expected years of schooling; average years of schooling for education; and gross national income per capita for the standard of living.

4.2   Instrumental Factors

Based on the analysis of the extant literature about the subject addressed in this paper, one can also realize the importance of instrumental factors on the using of social media on popular movements. These instrumental factors in the conceptual model are those considered closest to the movements per se. They are specific moderating factors, which may help to reveal the evolution and dynamics of social movements mediated by social media.

By using the literature review, the following factors can are considered to be instrumental: the agenda of claims; the traditional media; the repression of the demonstration; and the international repercussion, as explained below.

4.2.1   Agenda of Claims

Social movements occur for various reasons, such as political, social, and economic claims, which reveal the hope for new eras of self-determination after the struggle, demonstrations, and riots [35]. In addition to the increasing dissatisfaction with the dictatorial regimes, youth unemployment, corruption, poverty, inflation, social exclusion, and violent repression are among the main reasons for the revolts [35].

The beginning of movements on the Internet occurs as a result of existing economic, political, and social conditions [12]. In other words, the agenda arises from the moment citizens, who are either dissatisfied with the economic and social conditions and/or with repression, express their indignation via social networks, or when indignation is provoked by some image showing repression that spreads rapidly via social media and, in the current Internet jargon, 'goes viral.' [12].

In turn, one points out that the concerns of the people are shared by means of tools (platforms like Facebook and Twitter) that increase the intensity of social connection, thereby fomenting social movements [37]. Furthermore, an increase in the intensity of information flow (the number of times that people listen to the issues) and in the emotional intensity (how individuals experience the perception of events) lead to an increase in the likelihood of radicalization [38]. Thus, there is a strong connection between social media and the agenda of claims of the movements.

4.2.2   Traditional Media

Traditional media which performs the mediation of reality by means of formal journalism – collecting and disseminating information on events, within and beyond national borders – suffered from the inversion in the flow of news [39]. Social media with input from the public began to influence the content of the traditional media, which transmitted information on the manifestos, scheduling of gatherings, and images and videos taken during the protests [40].

One highlights the fact that during the social movements, as participation and trust of the population increased in relation to the news posted on social media, public trust in the traditional media vehicles diminished [37]. A search then began for information on social media (videos, photos, and declarations) that did not appear to be edited and that had been obtained by ordinary people. This established an inversion in the flow of news, where content and/or the agenda of claims produced by the public, which were posted on social media, were reproduced in the traditional media. Thus, the traditional communication media began to use information available in the social media to establish the agendas of their news [37].

Interestingly, those who do not yet have access to social media take advantage of the traditional media, such as newspapers, magazines and television, to get information on the social movements. Moreover, public acts gain visibility through media coverage and give the participants added incentive to stage further demonstrations [41].

4.2.3   Repression of Demonstrations

When there is suppression of protests, either by the government or by the media, social media is increasingly used for sharing text, video, audio, and photos of the events. A quest for the legitimation of the movements with the support of the population has been detected. The evidence of truculent oppression leads to heavier traffic on social media, with numerous shared photos and videos, accompanied by indignant texts posted by the population [42]. Besides, when repression is related to social media, as was the case in Egypt, ironically this action can exacerbate the revolt and make the citizens angrier, thus promoting greater interaction between them and leading them to seek new hybrid communication tactics to overcome the barriers imposed by the repressive government [43].

4.2.4   International Repercussion

In their studies, several authors stress the strong ties between new technologies and the international political world, highlighting the dissemination and monitoring of news through social media to promote the spread of ideas and tactics for protest swiftly and efficiently across national borders [44–46]. Thanks to network technology, the mobilizations can achieve transnational scale in record time [47]. Moreover, digital tools, including networks and mobile technology, are evidence of a snowball effect, which is only possible because of the structure and design of modern digital communications that transcend the traditional geopolitical boundaries [48].

As a result of the aforementioned analysis, the reference sources that have supported the choice of both the structural and instrumental factors, as well as their components, are presented in a consolidated way in Figs. 1 and 2 below.

Structural Factors	Reference Sources
Technological Context	[6,7,26,27,28]
Political Context	[26,27,28,29,30]
Socio-Economic Context	[12,32,33,34,35]

Fig. 1. Reference sources for the structural factors

Instrumental Factors	Reference Sources
List of Claims	[12,14,35,38]
Traditional Media	[39,41]
Repression of Demonstrations	[42,43]
International Repercussion	[44,45,46,47,48]

Fig. 2. Reference sources for the structural factors

4.3 Exploratory Conceptual Model of Influence of the Use of Social Media in Social Movements

From the structural and instrumental factors explained above, an exploratory conceptual model of influence of the use of social media in social movements can therefore be proposed, as shown in Fig. 3.

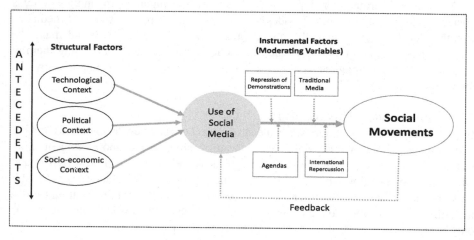

Fig. 3. Exploratory conceptual model of the influence of social media use in social movements

According to the proposed exploratory model, the analysis of social movements in each country must consider the dynamics of the sundry structural factors, namely the technological, political, and socio-economic scenarios, as well as their modification over the course of time. For example, in the case of the technological context, an increasing trend in the degree of Internet penetration in a country signifies greater access to information. Thus, with access to ICT, citizens acquire information, self-organization and self-mobilization spontaneously that they did not previously have [12]. In the case of the political context, by using, for instance, the democracy index of The Economist, it is possible to evaluate a country according to the following indicators: "full democracy," "imperfect democracy," "hybrid regime", and "authoritarian regime" [36]. Moreover, one can analyze the regression, progression or stalemate of the country's democracy index, in addition to considering the causes for this. These include: poor economic performance; decreased public trust in political institutions; increased violence and drug trafficking; democratically-elected leaders replaced by technocrats; among others [36].

In the case of the socio-economic context, the classification of the country in relation to its Human Development Index, for instance, makes it possible to analyze its evolution or involution, and compare it with that of other countries where there were also social movements mediated by ICT. The decrease of this index may signify increased unemployment among young people, increased levels of poverty and violence, which can lead to the indignation of citizens and demonstrations on the Internet in response to the prevailing economic, political, and social conditions in the country [12].

With respect to the instrumental factors, it is necessary to analyze to what extent these specific items – namely the agenda of claims, traditional media, repression of demonstrations, and international repercussion – contribute to the increased dissemination of social movements via the social network.

These instrumental factors are relevant, since it has been realized from the literature review that the evolution of social demonstrations occurs in an interactive manner. That is, they begin with specific agendas aired in minor protests, which increase in size as they suffer repression and/or suffer repercussions in the media [45–47], until they become widespread protests with international repercussions. This process of evolution of social movements occurs as an escalating force driven by social media. In other words, the interactions increase in line with the way that these factors interact with the main players in the demonstrations, and so on [14].

In this context, the occurrence of a feedback process is detected in which the social movements increasingly foster the use of social media. This, in turn, is configured and reconfigured by the information disseminated among the players, namely the demonstrators, thereby providing feedback for the next social protests, such as, for example, the sharing of actions in the protests and dissemination of agendas.

5 Final Remarks

This theoretical paper proposed an exploratory conceptual model in order to evaluate how the use of social media influences the social movements of a country, by considering its degree of Internet penetration, the maturity of its democracy, and the socio-economic conditions of its citizens. Thus, the influence of the use of social media can be evaluated by assessing the technological, political, and socio-economic scenarios. These contexts, identified in the literature review on social movements and social media, are the macro elements that are proof of the living conditions in general and socio-political activity in the country and are therefore considered to be the structural factors.

In addition to the structural factors, one was identified from the literature review the need to use elements inherent to the movement per se, acting as specific moderators that can assist in understanding the evolution and dimension of social movements via social media. These elements are considered to be instrumental factors, namely agenda of claims, traditional media, repression of demonstrations, and international repercussion.

Thus, the proposed exploratory conceptual model might enable analysis of the influence of the use of social media in social movements in order to identify possible scenarios where demonstrations tend to evolve, scrutinizing their antecedents and possible causes, and establishing if there is a pattern in the emergence of these social movements mediated by social media.

Lastly, as this is an exploratory and theoretical paper, further research must test the proposed conceptual model by means of analysis of social movements mediated by ICT that have occurred in different political, socio-economic, and technological scenarios.

References

1. Nicoletti, A.S.: Participação política e as nuances das manifestações populares de junho de 2013 no Brasil (2014). http://www.encontroabcp2014.cienciapolitica.org.br/resources/anais/14/1403288098. 10 March 2015
2. Pereira, M.A.: Internet e mobilização política: os movimentos sociais na era digital. Encontro da compolítica (2011). http://tede.ucsal.br/tde_arquivos/3/TDE-2010-11-04T102328Z164/Publico/20Maria%20Carvalhal%20Britto%20Pimentel.pdf. 10 March 2015
3. Lévy, P.: A inteligência coletiva: por uma antropologia do ciberespaço. Tradução de Luiz Paulo Rouanet. Loyola, São Paulo (2011)
4. Harvey, D., Maricato, E., Zizek, S., Davis, M., Maior, J.S., Iasi, M., e de Oliveira, P.R.: Cidades rebeldes: Passe livre e as manifestações que tomaram as ruas do Brasil. Boitempo Editorial (2013)
5. Ramos, A., Oliveira, R. Indivíduos, sociedade, tecnologia: as manifestações nas ruas das cidades brasileiras e as redes sociais. Revista Tecnologia e Sociedade **10**(20) (2014)
6. Castells, M.: The Internet Galaxy. Oxford University Press, Oxford (2001)
7. Castells, M.: Communication, power and counter-power in the network society. Int. J. Commun. **1**(1), 29 (2007)
8. de Moraes, D.: Por uma outra comunicação: Mídia, mundialização cultural e poder, 2nd edn., pp. 255–287. Editora Record, Rio de Janeiro (2004)
9. Segerberg, A., Bennet, W.: Social media and the organization of collective action: using Twitter to explore the ecologies of two climate change protests. Commun. Rev. **14**(3), 197–215 (2011)
10. Mansour, E.: The role of social networking sites (SNSs) in the January 25th revolution in Egypt. Libr. Rev. **61**(2), 128–159 (2012)
11. ComScore: ComScore video metrix (2011). http://www.comscore.com/por/. 10 March 2015
12. Castells, M.: Redes de indignação e esperança: movimentos sociais na era da Internet. Jorge Zahar Editor Ltda (2013)
13. Peruzzo, C.: Movimentos sociais, redes virtuais e mídia alternativa no junho em que "o gigante acordou". MATRIZes **7**(2), 73–93 (2013)
14. Franco, A.A: Terceira Invenção da Democracia. Curitiba: Escola de Redes (2013). http://escoladeredes.net/group/a-terceira-invencao-da-democracia/page/a-terceira-invencao-da-democracia-texto-base. 10 March 2015
15. Zarur, F.: PQP este é um movimento popular P2P! Comunicação, Internet e Web (2013). http://www.comunicacao-Internet.com.br/. 10 March 2015

16. Garrett, R.K.: Protest in an information society. Inf. Commun. Soc. **9**, 202–224 (2006)
17. Webster, J., Watson, R.T.: Analyzing the past to prepare for the future: writing a literature review. MIS Q. **26**(2), xiii–xxiii (2002)
18. Okoli, C., Schabram, K.: A guide to conducting a systematic literature review of information systems research. Sprouts Working Papers Inf. Syst. **10**(26) (2010). http://sprouts.aisnet.org/10-26
19. Patton, M.Q.: Qualitative Evaluation and Research Methods, 2nd edn. Sage, Newbury Park (1990)
20. Yin, R.: Case Study Research: Design and Methods, 2nd edn. Sage Publications, Thousand Oaks (1994)
21. Scandura, T., Williams, E.: Research methodology in management: current practices, trends, and implications for future research. Acad. Manage. J. **43**(6), 1248–1264 (2000)
22. Livingston, S.: A evolução dos sistemas de informação em África: um caminho para a segurança e a estabilidade. Centro de Estudos Estratégicos de África (2011)
23. Stepanova, E.: The role of information communication technologies in the "arab spring". PONARS Eurasia Policy Memo **159**, 1–6 (2011)
24. Bokor, M.J.: New media and democratization in Ghana: an impetus for political activism. http://www.netjournals.org/pdf/NJSS/2014/1/13-039.pdf. 10 March 2015
25. ITU: Yearbook of statistics 2014 (2014). http://www.itu.int/en/ITU-D/Statistics/Pages/publications/yb2014.aspx (2015)
26. Kedzie, C.: Communication and democracy: coincident revolutions and the emergent dictators. Santa Monica, RAND Corporation, CA. http://www.rand.org/pubs/rgs_dissertations/RGSD127 Accessed on 05 March 2015.
27. Fishkin, J.S.: Virtual democratic possibilities: prospects for Internet democracy. In: Conference Internet, Democracy and Public Goods, B.H., Brazil (2000)
28. Benkler, Y.: The Wealth of Networks: How Social Production Transforms Markets and Freedom. Yale University Press, New Haven (2006)
29. Kavanaugh, A., Kim, B.J., Perez-Quinones, M.A., Schmitz, J., Isenhour, P.: Net gains in political participation: secondary effects of Internet on community. Inf. Commun. Soc. **11**(7), 933–963 (2008)
30. Best, M.L., Wade, K.W.: The internet and democracy global catalyst or democratic dud? Bull. Sci. Technol. Soc. **29**(4), 255–271 (2009)
31. The Economist Intelligence Unit: Democracy index (2013). http://www.eiu.com/public/topical_report.aspx?campaignid=Democracy0814
32. Wiktorowicz, Q.: Islamic Activism: A Social Movement Theory Approach. Indiana University Press, Bloomington e Indianápolis (2004)
33. Aguiar, S.: Formas de organização e enredamento para ações sociopolíticas. Informação & Informação, Universidade Estadual de Londrina, vol. 12 (2007)
34. Joffé, G.A.: Primavera Árabe no Norte de África: origens e perspectivas de futuro. Relações Internacionais (R:I) **30**, 85–116 (2011)
35. Farah, P.D.E.: A Primavera Árabe no Machriq, Maghreb e Khaly: motivações e perspectivas. Política Externa (USP) **20**, 10–25 (2011)
36. UNDP: Human development report (2014). http://hdr.undp.org/en/data. 10 Mar 2015
37. Boyd, S.: Revolution=Messiness at Scale, Again (2011). http://www.stoweboyd.com/post/3105227293/revolution-messiness-at-scale-again. March 10 2015
38. Vieira, V.P.P.: O papel da comunicação digital na Primavera Árabe: Apropriação e mobilização social. In: V Congresso da Compolítica, realizado em Curitiba/PR (2013)
39. Figueiredo, R.: Junho de 2013: A sociedade enfrenta o Estado, Edição 1. Summus Editorial, São Paulo (2014)

40. Fattori, M.: Protestos e Manifestações: Redes Sociais X Mídias Tradicionais. In Marketing Digital, Social Intelligence (2013). http://www.dp6.com.br/protestos-e-manifestacoes-redes-sociais-x-midias-tradicionais/. 10 March 2015
41. Pujol, A.F.T., Rocha, F.G., Sampaio, F.S.: Manifestações Populares no Brasil Atual: Sociedade Civil em Rede e Reivindicações Sobre o Poder Político. In: XIII Coloquio Internacional de Geocrítica. El control del espacio y los espacios de control, Barcelona (2014)
42. Pavlik, J.V.: A tecnologia digital e o jornalismo: As implicações para a Democracia. Braz. Journalism Res. 7(2), 94 (2011)
43. Hassanpour, N.: Media disruption exacerbates revolutionary unrest. In: American Political Science Association (APSA) Annual Meeting Paper (2011)
44. Kluver, A.R.: The logic of new media in international affairs. New Media Soc. 4(4), 499–517 (2002)
45. Wenger, A.: The internet and the changing face of international relations and security. Inf. Secur. 7, 5–11 (2001)
46. Westcott, N.: Digital Diplomacy: The Impact of the Internet on International Relations. Oxford Internet Institute, Research Report 16, July 2008
47. Norris, P.: Digital Divide: Civic Engagement, Information Poverty, and the Internet Worldwide. Cambridge University Press, Nova York (2001)
48. Hands, J.: Is for Activism: Dissent, Resistance and Rebellion in a Digital Culture. Pluto Press, London (2010)

Deliberation and Consultation

e-Consultation Platforms:
Generating or Just Recycling Ideas?

Efthimios Tambouris[(✉)], Anastasia Migotzidou,
and Konstantinos Tarabanis

University of Macedonia, Thessaloniki, Greece
tambouris@uom.gr

Abstract. A number of governments worldwide employ web-based
e-consultation platforms to enable stakeholders commenting on draft legislation. Stakeholders' input includes arguing in favour or against the proposed
legislation as well as proposing alternative ideas. In this paper, we empirically
investigate the relationship between the volume of contributions in these platforms and the amount of new ideas that are generated. This enables us to
determine whether participants in such platforms keep generating new ideas or
just recycle a finite number of ideas. We capitalised on argumentation models to
code and analyse a large number of draft law consultations published in
opengov.gr, the official e-consultation platform for draft legislation in Greece.
Our results suggest that as the number of posts grows, the number of new ideas
continues to increase. The results of this study improve our understanding of the
dynamics of these consultations and enable us to design better platforms.

Keywords: Online consultation · e-Forum · e-Rulemaking

1 Introduction

During the last years, the Internet has been extensively used for engaging large
numbers of citizens in policy making. Relevant research and practice is heavily
influenced by deliberative democracy theory, which is based on the assumption that
"public, plural discussions offer a superior form of collective decision making" [1].
Consequently, preferences should not just be aggregated (as in voting) but should be
rather "revised in the light of a preceding debate" [2]. Despite its promises however,
scholars soon concluded that putting the theory in practice is a challenging task [1, 3].

A prominent area of relevant research and practice involves the use of Web-based
platforms to support online deliberation on policy material such as draft laws and
regulations, which is provided by relevant agencies. These platforms enable users to
argue in favour or against the proposed draft legislation as well as to propose new ideas
for the relevant policy topics. This area is sometimes termed *open consultation,* while
in the USA it is closely associated with *e-rulemaking*, which refers to the use of digital
technologies in the development and implementation of regulations [4]. For the purposes of this study, we will restrict the use of the terms *open consultation platform* to
refer to *an e-consultation platform dedicated to commenting on draft legislation.*

© IFIP International Federation for Information Processing 2015
E. Tambouris et al. (Eds.): ePart 2015, LNCS 9249, pp. 41–52, 2015.
DOI: 10.1007/978-3-319-22500-5_4

Research in this area has followed various areas and has provided some interesting findings. Early research revealed that various non-technological barriers, including deep motivational, cognitive, and knowledge-based chasms stand in the way of citizen participation in the regulatory process [5]. Other research suggests that the possibility of deliberation is affected by political choices made both about the format and operation of the online discussion [2]. More recent research revealed that online participation mechanisms require careful design considerations as well as a cultural change on behalf of public administrators [6]. The differences between those using online forums with those of online discussions in a forum designed according to deliberative principles have been also investigated [3]. A comprehensive meta-analysis of working with the pioneering "Regulation Room" provided significant insight in a number of areas ranging from identifying the different types of potential participants to presenting relevant barriers and how they can be overcome [7]. From a technological point of view, various platforms have been investigated. Regulations.gov, the official USA website for e-rulemaking, has been heavily investigated (e.g. [4]) however other platforms have been also studied (e.g. [5, 8]).

In our work, we are interested in examining the characteristics of discussions that take place in such platforms. More specifically, we aim to investigate the relationship between the number of contributors and the new ideas that are contributed to the discussion. This can provide a better understanding of the social capital that is accumulated in such platforms as the level of participation increases. It can also facilitate designing better platforms to support the process.

Therefore, the study objective is to experimentally investigate the *relationship between the volume of contributions and the new ideas that are contributed in e-consultations on draft legislation*. For this purpose, data from the Hellenic official online consultation platform for draft legislation, namely *opengov.gr*, were obtained, coded and analysed.

The rest of this paper is organised as follows. In Sect. 2 we outline the motivation of this study along with background material. In Sects. 3 and 4 we present the method of work and scope of our study respectively. In Sect. 5 we provide the employed data selection method. In Sect. 6 the main results of our study are presented while in Sect. 7 the main conclusions as well as study limitations and future work are discussed.

2   Background Material and Motivation

Online deliberation is associated with an emerging body of practices, research and software that purposely foster open, fair, and rational discussions over the Internet [9]. It has been argued that "the online environment erodes physical, psychological, and social barriers" [6]. On the other hand, online debates are often characterised by repetitive contributions, digressions, argumentative fallacies, rhetorical flourishes, manipulative framing and personal attacks that result in a high noise-to-signal ratio and confusion rather than clarity [10]. Furthermore, the levels of engagements do not seem to increase while online deliberation results can be superficial and polarised particularly when using inappropriate tools [6]. A recent literature review has accumulated relevant challenges [11].

ICT tools used to support online deliberation range from general-purpose e-forums to Argument Visualisation (AV) tools and to tools developed exclusively for supporting online deliberations. We now briefly outline e-forums and AV tools.

An e-forum is structured around discussion topics (termed *threads*). Topics are pre-defined or can be created by users. In each topic, users can hold online conversations in the form of posted messages (aka *posts*). Replies to posts are often also possible. These tools however run the risk to drown under their own success. Indeed, as the number of posts increases, discussions within forums tend to be extremely large and complex resulting in poor deliberation quality (e.g. from repetitive contributions and argumentative fallacies).

AV tools represent discussions in terms of ideas, positions and arguments. Discussions are usually depicted as graphs (often called *argumentation maps*) containing nodes that can be joined by lines (or arrows) to display inferences [12]. Efforts to include argumentation concepts in e-forums have also emerged (e.g. [13]). Proponents of AV tools suggest they provide an unprecedented opportunity to facilitate rational and, therefore, concise online discussions.

In a panel discussion of Politics Online Conference, Fig. 1 was presented to argue that using AV tools, online discussions will be much smaller since as the number of contributors in any discussion increases the number of new ideas contributed levels [14]. This actually seems to be a logical claim. After all, how many new ideas can potentially exist in any single discussion? Interestingly enough, however, our literature review failed to reveal any experimental evidence to support this claim.

Figure 1 provided the main inspiration behind the work presented in this paper. Figure 1 suggests there is a logarithmic relationship between contributors and new ideas contributed in any discussion. In other words, our study objective is equivalent to investigating the claim *"as the number of contributors in a discussion increases the number of new ideas levels"*.

However, we restrict our study to a specific category of online deliberations, i.e. open consultation. The difference is significant. In an online deliberation the participants are often asked to brainstorm, i.e. contribute new ideas to a specific topic or

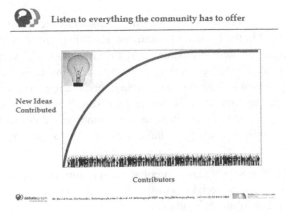

Fig. 1. Contributors vs. New Ideas Contributed in a deliberation (from [14])

problem. It is often the case that there are no pre-existing solutions, thus ideas generation is a major objective. On the other hand, in open consultations, the draft law or regulation already provides a concrete set of ideas and solutions. Here, the participants are primarily asked to argue in favour or against these solutions. The participants can still contribute new ideas but this is not the main objective. Thus, ideas generation is not the primary objective of open consultations. As a result, one can assume that there are less ideas generated in open consultations when compared on online deliberations aiming to facilitate brainstorming.

3   Method of Work

The method of work that we followed included four steps.

Step 1: Define study scope
In this step we present important context information. Relevant research has revealed that the context is particularly important when studying or operating open consultations [1]. We therefore start by presenting the main design decisions behind Opengov, the e-forum consultation platform that will be used for analysis purposes.

Step 2: Map posts to argumentation maps
In this step we present how posts from Opengov were mapped into new ideas. This is an important step as it outlines the method employed for coding the posts.

Step 3: Select data for analysis
In this step we examine the content of Opengov and select a number of laws and articles for coding and analysis.

Step 4: Conduct analysis and report results
In this step we present that analysis results. More specifically, we plot relevant scatter graphs and perform trend analysis using the standard functionality of MS Excel for a number of cases. Finally, we discuss the results.

4   Study Scope

In Greece, online public consultations on draft legislation are conducted before the relevant laws are voted in the Hellenic Parliament. For this purpose, a specific technical infrastructure is employed, which is managed by the Greek Open Government Initiative (Opengov) of the Hellenic Parliament [8]. The corresponding technical infrastructure, also termed Opengov (www.opengov.gr), employs open source applications and tools and contains various applications. However, for simplicity we will use the term Opengov to refer to the specific application for online public consultations on draft legislation. Online public consultations have a life cycle comprising four successive phases.

- Preparation: The Opengov's team, in collaboration with the relevant ministry, sets up the platform and the material of consultation and ensures the overall approval of content by the prime minister's office.

- Public comment: Once approved, the consultation is published and opens to commentary from anyone interested (posts from both registered and anonymous users are allowed). Partners of the relevant ministry are moderating the comments before these are published.
- Edit Conclusions: After the end of the consultation period, the relevant ministry posts in Opengov a message containing initial consultation results. In addition, the ministry takes into consideration the comments and prepares a full report on the consultation, as suggested by relevant legislation.
- Completion: When the law is voted by the Parliament and the report on the consultation results is posted, the consultation is considered as completed.

In this study, *discussion* refers to online consultations on draft legislation. Furthermore, the term *contributions* refers to *posts*, since contribution to Opengov is usually anonymous and hence there is no way to determine who the actual contributor is.

The last point we need to clarify in our study objective is the concept of *"new ideas"*. In order to define new ideas, we examined the literature on argumentation models. This is a common approach followed when analysing online political content. More specifically, we examined the Issue-Based Information System (IBIS) [15], gIBIS [16], the Representation and Maintenance of Process Knowledge (REMAP) approach [17], the Procedural Hierarchy of Issues (PHI) approach [18], Questions, Options, and Criteria (QOC) [19] and Potts and Bruns approach [20] amongst others. Our review revealed there is no *"idea"* argumentation concept. However, in most models the concept *position* is proposed to suggest solutions to *issues*, which represent problems or topics for discussion. Thus, we will use *position* to denote ideas. We note here that for the purpose of our study, it is sufficient that our argumentation maps include two only concepts, namely *issue* and *position*. We acknowledge this is not sufficient for constructing a complete argumentation map as at least *argument* should be also included according to the IBIS model. Actually, in our research we have included various other concepts in the mapping. However, *issue* and *position* are still sufficient for the purposes of this paper.

Concluding, our study objective is now operationalised as follows: *to investigate the relationship between the number of posts and the number of citizens' new positions in an official e-consultation on draft legislation.*

5 Mapping Framework

In this section, we develop a simple model and a process to enable us coding the content of Opengov platform using concepts from argumentation theory. We start by listing three important design characteristics of the Opengov platform:

- Citizens are allowed to provide posts only per article and not for the entire draft law.
- Citizens can only post on articles and not on other citizens' posts (i.e. replying to a post is not enabled).
- Both registered and anonymous posting is allowed.

In open consultations, *issues* (which are the actual topics of a debate) refer to the contents of draft laws and/or regulations. Draft laws are divided into articles with each article focusing on one or more topics. Thus, it seems reasonable to suggest that one article is represented by one *issue*. Our analysis however revealed that in certain cases, one article may contain more than one different *issues*. In addition, the main body of the draft law contains the proposed *Government Positions* (*Gov Positions*) on these issues. As a result, in our argumentation model we need to distinguish between *Government Positions* and *Citizen Positions*. Citizens' posts in Opengov platform contain, amongst others, *citizen new positions*, i.e. new ideas.

The main entities in Opengov platform and their relationships are depicted in Fig. 2 using UML notation. In UML, a diamond represents aggregation (e.g. *has* relationship) while an arrow represents generalization (e.g. *isA* relationship) between classes (i.e. concepts). A class in italics (e.g. position) denotes an abstract class, i.e. a class that cannot be instantiated. This actually means that in our coding we may have government positions or citizen positions; not just positions.

In order to investigate our study objective, we developed one simple argumentation map for each article consultation. We acknowledge existing research aiming to automatically derive arguments from text using natural language processing techniques (e.g. [21]). Nevertheless, we opted for a manual approach which is usually more accurate. Thus, the process that we followed in order to code Opengov contents (i.e. draft law text and posts) using our simple argumentation map is:

Step 1: Analysis of draft law text
We read each article to determine (a) the relevant problem statement, which was coded as *Issue*, and (b) the positions of the government in the proposed law to address that problem, which were coded as *Government Positions*.

Step 2: Analysis of posts
We read all posts related to each Article. The aim was to identify new ideas to address the Issue. These were coded as *Citizen (New) Positions*.

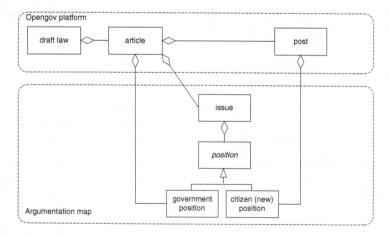

Fig. 2. Simple model for transferring Opengov content to an argumentation map

6 Data Selection

Since the start of its operation, a large number of consultations have been conducted in Opengov. Table 1 presents the consultations per ministry and the number of posts per consultation (as of June 2011 when data were collected).

Table 1. Draft laws published per ministry (from http://www.opengov.gr/, as in 2011)

Ministry of	Consultations	Posts
Interior, Decentralization & eGovernment	10	14.069
Finance	9	18.713
Foreign Affairs	0	0
National Defence	0	0
Regional Development and Competitiveness	24	4.138
Maritime Affairs and Fisheries Islands	0	0
Environment, Energy and Climate Change	29	7.760
Education, Lifelong Learning and Religion	19	9.577
Infrastructure, Transport and Networks	14	2.154
Labour and Social Insurance	7	1.790
Health and Social Solidarity	1	1.146
Rural Development and Food	8	3.053
Justice, Transparency and Human Rights	17	1.956
Citizen Protection	5	1.910
Culture and Tourism	2	580
OpenGov	5	366
Total	150	67.212

The first step was to calculate the number of posts per article per consultation. For this purpose, the following have been considered:

- Opengov platform accepted posts at the article only level. Thus, general posts on the whole draft law are not possible.
- The first article is not considered in the analysis. In most consultations, the first article contained a significantly larger number of posts than the rest of the articles. The reason is that citizens tend to post general comments referring to the whole draft law in the first article. Thus, in general, posts in the first article do not necessarily relate to the content of the first article only. For this reason, the analysis of these posts is excluded from our study.
- Consultations of very brief draft laws, i.e. having up to two articles, have not been considered.
- Obviously, articles with zero (0) number of posts have been excluded from the study. This includes "Locked for comment" articles. These are articles that the Opengov platform administrators have selected to exclude from commenting. Thus, no posts exist for these articles.

- Taking into consideration the above restrictions, the total number of articles presented in all ministries' consultations is 1,132 while the total number of posts is 42,263. The average number of posts published per article is 30. The maximum number of posts in one article was 2,546. Due to the extremely large number of posts that some articles had, we decided to restrict our research to articles having less than 70 posts. These represent 91,43 % of the total number of posts in all articles.

Based on the above, we decided to study consultations with number of posts in the following ranges: 0–10, 11–20, 21–30, 31–40, 41–50, 51–60, 61–69 posts per article. From each group below the average number of posts (i.e. 30 posts) we selected and analysed two articles that were close to the high-end of the area, while for groups above the average number we selected one article per group, except for the last group where we also sampled two articles. This gave us a total of 17 articles belonging to 5 different law consultations. These were: (a) Public Consultation on the implementation of the electricity social tariff (termed here Public Consultation 1, or PC1), (b) Pubic consultation on the implementation of the biodiversity strategy in Greece (PC2), (c) Pubic consultation on reengineering the supporting structures of the Ministry of Education (PC3), (d) Public consultation on the technological high education (PC4) and (e) Public consultation on gambling (PC5).

7 Results

Following the method of work presented in the previous section, we started by reading and coding each of the 5 draft laws and 17 articles under investigation. As a result, we were able to identify the relevant *issues* along with the *government positions*. A first result here is the fact that in most cases each article included one only issue. In other words, each article was concentrated around one topic. In some articles however, this was not the case. For analysis purposes, we decided to discard all articles containing more than one issue leaving us with 4 draft laws and 14 articles to examine. We thereafter read and coded one by one each and every post for each remaining article. As a result, we were able to identify the new ideas suggested by citizens. These were coded as *citizen positions* (or *new positions*). For each article, a table was created presenting new positions as the number of posts grows. Table 2 presents the overall results.

Based on the detailed tables for each article we created a graph depicting the number of citizen positions as the number of posts increases. As the graph accommodates all 14 data sets (one for each article), we have employed a line chart instead of the, more accurate, scatter plot (Fig. 3).

Table 2. Analysis overall results

PC id	PC1		PC2							PC3	PC4			
Article id	2	3	15	12	11	10	9	8	7	3	2	3	5	6
# Posts	3	7	6	6	9	18	12	10	12	25	69	38	61	58
# Citizen Positions	2	3	2	6	5	8	5	9	10	13	23	11	15	20

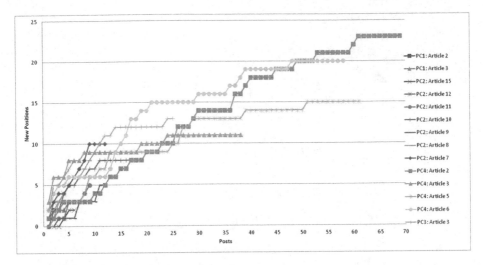

Fig. 3. Number of new positions per post (for all Articles)

The figures suggest that most consultations follow a similar pattern. We thereafter examined in detail two cases that we consider as having particular interest.

In the first case, we consider all 14 articles that we analysed. Here, we calculate the average of all citizen positions for each value of the number of posts. Clearly, as the number of posts increases, the average is based on a continuously smaller number of consultations (with the last 8 values calculated from only one consultation). The standard deviation is about 22 % different from the average value (without considering the last 8 values). In the second case, we consider only the consultation with the largest number of posts, i.e. Article 2 of PC4 having 69 posts. The resulting scatter plots are depicted in Fig. 4.

We thereafter use the standard "Trendline" functionality of MS Excel in order to examine which trend/regression type better fits the data. We present the analysis results for the largest article only in Fig. 5. By observing the different trendlines, we conclude that, within the limitations of our study, there is no evidence that the number of new positions tends to level. Instead, it seems there is an almost linear relationship between the number of posts and number of new positions.

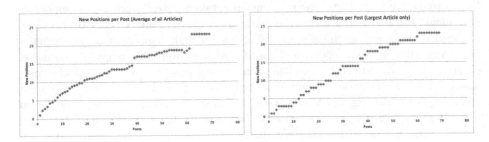

Fig. 4. Number of new positions per post

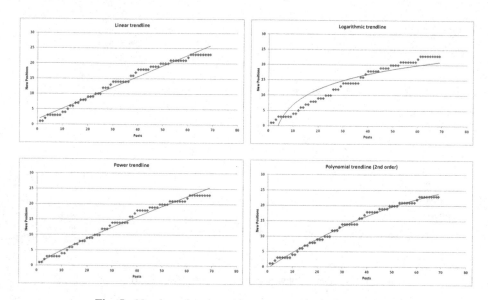

Fig. 5. Number of new positions per post including trendline

This result suggests that increased participation in open consultations has an impact in terms of new ideas generated. We should therefore expect that by mobilising more citizens we can anticipate more different ideas. Clearly, in this study we did not evaluate the quality of those ideas. However, we only kept legitimate positions, i.e. we excluded spam, personal attacks etc., following the principles of argumentation models. This finding might be also interesting to the developers of tools for massive partici-pation in e-rulemaking, online deliberation or idea generation in general. More spe-cifically, the evidence that the number of new positions seems to constantly increase poses a significant challenge to those designing user interfaces for such applications. It seems it cannot be assumed that the number of ideas will eventually level, hence there is a challenge on how to fit ideas in the screen when having massive participation. As a result, new ways of accommodating the volume of positions are needed.

8 Conclusion and Future Work

In this study, we investigated the relationship between citizens' posts and number of new ideas. For this purpose, we used data from the Hellenic Open Government's platform (Opengov). Specifically, consultations on draft legislation using Opengov were manually obtained, coded and transferred into argument maps. For analysis purposes, we concentrated on e-consultations having less than 70 posts, which repre-sented 91.43 % of the total number of consultations at the time when data were obtained. The remaining 8.57 % comprised of articles consultations having from 71 up to 2,546 posts. The analysis was performed at the article level, since posts in Opengov are allowed only at that level. We thereafter randomly selected and coded the consultations of 17 articles with varying numbers of posts. The maximum number of posts in one article was 69.

Our results suggest that, for the range of values that we examined (up to 69 posts), the relationship under investigation does not seem logarithmic, as suggested in Fig. 1.

We should note, however, that our approach has a number of limitations. First, we examined only one platform. Second, we measured the number of posts instead of contributors i.e. actual persons. Third, we equated new ideas with citizens *positions* (as defined in argumentation models). Forth, the extraction of new positions from posts was performed manually by one only author. Fifth, we only examined e-consultations having up to 69 posts. Although these represent 91.43 % of the total number of e-consultations, there were still consultations with significantly more posts (up to 2,546 posts). All these limitations indicate possible routes for future research.

Acknowledgments. The authors would like to acknowledge the high-quality comments received by the four peer reviewers. We have tried to address as many comments as possible within the existing time and space limitations. Many comments provided us with new ideas and perspectives for extending this work in the future.

References

1. Gonzalez-Bailon, S., Kaltenbrunner, A., Banchs, R.E.: The structure of political discussion networks: a model for the analysis of online deliberation. J. Inf. Technol. **25**, 230–243 (2010)
2. Wright, S., Street, J.: Democracy, deliberation and design: the case of online discussion forums. N. Media Soc. **9**(5), 849–869 (2007)
3. Strandberg, K.: Designing for democracy?: an experimental study comparing the outcomes of citizen discussions in online forums with those of online discussions in a forum designed according to deliberative principles. Eur. Polit. Sci. Rev. **7**(3), 451–474 (2015)
4. Coglianese, C.: E-rulemaking: information technology and the regulatory process. Adm. Law Rev. **56**, 353 (2004). (KSG Working Paper No. RWP04-002)
5. Coglianese, C.: Citizen participation in rulemaking: past, present, and future. Duke Law J. **55**, 943–968 (2006)
6. Schulz, D., Newig, J.: Assessing online consultation in participatory governance: conceptual framework and a case study of a national sustainability-related consultation platform in Germany. Environ. Policy Gov. **25**(1), 55–69 (2015)
7. Farina, C.R., Epstein, D., Heidt, J., Newhart, M.J.: Designing an online civic engagement platform: balancing "more" vs. "better" participation in complex public policymaking. Int. J. E-Polit. **5**(1), 16–40 (2014)
8. Deligiaouria, A.: Open governance and e-rulemaking: online deliberation and policy-making in contemporary greek politics. J. Inf. Technol. Polit. **10**(1), 104–124 (2013)
9. Zhang, W.: Simulating the ideal eDeliberation: the roles of inclusion, equalization and rationalization. In: De Cindio, F., Macintosh, A., Peraboni, C. (eds.) e-Participation to Online Deliberation, Proceedings of the Fourth International Conference on Online Deliberation, OD2010, pp. 117–125, Leeds, UK, 30 June - 2 July 2010

10. Van Eemeren, F.H., Garssen, B.: Pondering on problems of argumentation: twenty essays on theoretical issues. Argumentation Library, vol. 14, XXII, 306 p. 9 illus. Springer, The Netherlands (2009)
11. Jonsson, M.E., Åström, J.: The challenges for online deliberation research: a literature review. Int. J. E-Polit. 5(1), 1–15 (2014)
12. Braak, S.W., van den Oostendorp, H., van Prakken, H., Vreeswijk, G.A.W.: A critical review of argument visualization tools: do users become better reasoners? In: Workshop Notes of the ECAI-2006 Workshop on Computational Models of Natural Argument (CMNA VI), pp. 67–75, Riva del Garda, Italy (2006)
13. Xenakis, A., Loukis, E.: An investigation of the use of structured e-forum for enhancing e-participation in parliaments. Int. J. Electron. Gov. 3(2), 134–147 (2010)
14. Price, D.: 'Debategraph - Politics Online Conference 2009', Presentation at Politics Online 2009 by David Price, Obtained through the Internet (2009). http://www.slideshare.net/davidprice/debategraph-politics-online-conference-2009. Accessed 18 March 2015
15. Kunz, W., Rittel, H.: Issues as Elements of Information Systems. Working Paper No. 131, California, Berkley (1979)
16. Conklin, E.J. Begeman, M.L.: gIBIS: a hypertext tool for exploratory policy discussion. In: Proceedings of CSCW 1988, pp. 140–152. ACM, New York (1988)
17. Ramesh, B., Dhar, V.: Representation and maintenance of process knowledge for large scale systems development. In: Proceedings of 6th Annual KBSE Knowledge-Based Software Engineering Conference, pp. 223–231, Syracuse (1991)
18. McCall, R.J.: PHI: a conceptual foundation for design hypermedia. J. Des. Stud. 12(1), 30–41 (1991). (MEDINA-MORA)
19. MacLean, A., Young, R., Bellotti, V., Moran, T.: Questions, options, and criteria: elements of design space analysis. In: Moran, T., Carroll, J. (eds.) Design Rationale Concepts, Techniques, and Use, pp. 53–106. Lawrence Erlbaum Associates, Mahwah (1996)
20. Potts, C., Bruns, G.: Recording the reasons for design decisions. In: Nam, T.N. (ed.) Proceedings of the 10th International Conference on Software Engineering, Singapore, pp. 418–427. IEEE Computer Society Press, Los Alamitos, 11–15 April 1988
21. Winkels, R., Douw, J., Veldhoen, S.: Experiments in automated support for argument reconstruction. In: Proceedings of the Fourteenth International Conference on Artificial Intelligence and Law (ICAIL 2013), pp. 232–236. ACM, New York, USA (2013)

Equality of Participation Online Versus Face to Face: Condensed Analysis of the Community Forum Deliberative Methods Demonstration

Eric Showers, Nathan Tindall, and Todd Davies$^{(\boxtimes)}$

Center for the Study of Language and Information, and Symbolic Systems Program,
Stanford University Stanford, Stanford, CA, USA
{eshowers,ntindall,davies}@stanford.edu

Abstract. Online deliberation may provide a more cost-effective and/or less inhibiting environment for public participation than face to face (F2F). But do online methods bias participation toward certain individuals or groups? We compare F2F versus online participation in an experiment affording within-participants and cross-modal comparisons. For English speakers required to have Internet access as a condition of participation, we find no negative effects of online modes on *equality of participation* (EoP) related to gender, age, or educational level. Asynchronous online discussion appears to improve EoP for gender relative to F2F. Data suggest a dampening effect of online environments on black participants, as well as amplification for whites. Synchronous online voice communication EoP is on par with F2F across individuals. But individual-level EoP is much lower in the online forum, and greater online forum participation predicts greater F2F participation for individuals. Measured rates of participation are compared to self-reported experiences, and other findings are discussed.

Keywords: Public deliberation · Participation equality · Discursive equality · e-participation

1 Introduction

The efficacy of face to face deliberation has been the subject of much discussion in the academic literature. According to some authors, it leads to better decision

T. Davies—*An extended version of this paper, with additional data, tables, figures, and analysis, is available at the SSRN open access repository* (see reference [27]). This research was supported by the Agency for Healthcare Research and Quality (AHRQ) under contract #HHSA290201000005C, through the American Institutes for Research (AIR), subcontract #641.02916. Additional funding was provided by the Vice Provost for Undergraduate Education at Stanford University. We thank AIR Staff members Coretta Mallery, Rikki Mangrum, Maureen Maurer, Manshu Yang, and Mark Rosenberg for helpful discussions and aid in obtaining the data. The views expressed in this paper are those of the authors, and have not been approved by AHRQ or AIR.

© IFIP International Federation for Information Processing 2015
E. Tambouris et al. (Eds.): ePart 2015, LNCS 9249, pp. 53–67, 2015.
DOI: 10.1007/978-3-319-22500-5_5

making and allows for a greater degree of public agency [6]. Others, however, claim that it is at best a waste of time, and at worst that it leads to bad decision making [25]. Beyond discussions of effectiveness, many authors focus on specific elements of deliberation that might prove problematic or worth looking at — the most important for the purposes of this paper having to do with the marginalization of participants according to race or gender. Some of these hypothesized effects are quantitative and can be easily identified or tested for — that men speak more than women in deliberative sessions, for example [13,29], and [21]. Other phenomena, such as domination or the idea that some demographic groups might be less likely to deliberate or have less influence, are harder to examine quantitatively [1,25]. Echoes of these phenomena, however, might be found in the measurable quantity of an individual's contributions. Much of this literature deals with face to face deliberation. We apply such methods to online participation as well.

As Internet access becomes more widespread and allows more users to make their voices heard, its potential as a tool for public deliberation cannot be overlooked. There is already a substantial body of literature discussing the Internet's capacity for use in this regard, e.g. [8,12,24,33]. This literature is particularly concerned with the ability to eliminate some of the inequalities present in face to face deliberation [26], and cites elements of online deliberation such as anonymity and remoteness as potential benefits. There are detractors as well, however, who cite issues with online deliberation including a potential lack of respect among participants and lack of Internet access among certain groups [2]. Another dimension that must be considered is facilitation style, which can impact the proceedings [31]. But while the literature often discusses online and face to face (F2F) deliberation in isolation, there are few sources that provide a *direct* comparison between the two [23]. We aim to provide a quantitative look at examples of both kinds of deliberation in order to highlight potential differences between the deliberative *modes* [8], and to examine the effects of other variables within both modes.

In order to compare online and F2F deliberation effectively, we will examine the Agency for Healthcare Research and Quality's Community Forum Project [4,5], which gathered together a large number of deliberative groups using different methods (as described in the next section) — one online, two offline, and one mixed. The Community Forum is beyond the scale of any controlled deliberation experiment done previously, and it sought to bring together a representative sample of the U.S. population. It is also one of the few *multiple-method* experiments that provides quantitative data on populations recruited specifically for deliberation. Our analysis is drawn from transcripts of all F2F and synchronous online meetings during the Community Forum project, archives of all online forum discussions, and records of surveys filled out by the participants that measure their knowledge, attitudes, and experience both pre- and post-deliberation.

2   Community Forum Project

A five-arm randomized controlled trial was conducted between August and November 2012 by the American Institutes for Research. This Deliberative

Methods Demonstration was intended to inform the Agency for Healthcare Research and Quality's research programs on public views regarding the usage of research evidence in health care decision making, and to expand the evidence base on public deliberation. The demonstration gathered empirical evidence about the *effectiveness* of deliberation, which has received minimal attention to date [8]. In the literature, effectiveness has been defined by the following parameters: (1) the quality of deliberative experience or discourse, (2) changes in participants' knowledge or attitudes about the deliberative topic, (3) changes in participants' empathy and concern for issues affecting the community at large, and (4) the impact of deliberation on decisions by the sponsoring agency.

For this Deliberative Methods Demonstration, participants were randomly assigned to one of four deliberative discussion methods, or to a reading-materials only (RMO) group. Participants were sampled from Chicago, IL, Sacramento, CA, Silver Spring, MD, and Durham, NC, where they were assigned into groups representative of the population of those areas with respect to gender, age, and ethnicity, as estimated by the U.S. Census. A total of 1,774 participants were recruited for the study, of whom 961 took part in a deliberative discussion method, and 377 were assigned to the RMO group.

The following deliberative question was posed to all participants: *Should individual patients and/or their doctors be able to make any health decisions no matter what the evidence of medical effectiveness shows, or should society ever specify some boundaries for these decisions?*

The participants were all given educational background materials to read. Those assigned to a discussion group then discussed the deliberative question in one of four distinct methods that have been advocated and used previously in prior public deliberations [5]. Additionally, some participants were only assigned reading materials. This was done to examine whether deliberation has a positive or negative impact on attitude change, and other measures of effectiveness. The main results of the study are reported elsewhere [4,5]. The methods were: **Brief Citizens' Deliberation (BCD)** – one two-hour session per group, active facilitation; **Community Deliberation (CD)** – two in-person deliberative sessions with active facilitation (**CD-F2F**), each 2.5 hours long, separated by a week during which participants interacted through the online asynchronous Deme discussion board (**CD-Forum**) [9]; **Online Deliberative Polling®(ODP)** – four 75-minute online sessions with minimal student facilitation; **Citizens' Panel (CP)** – 2.5 days of deliberation with three active facilitators per group, moderated breakout groups, and unfacilitated open spaces; and the **Reading Materials Only (RMO)** Control Group – educational materials received via an email link, with no discussion (these data were not used in our investigation).

3   Research Questions and Previous Findings

The following research questions have been prioritized and answered in our analysis:

1. Do the medium (online versus F2F) and/or modality (e.g. speech versus text) have effects on *equality of participation* (EoP) across demographic groups (ethnicity, gender, education, age)?
2. Do online methods differ from F2F on individual-level EoP?
3. Do online methods differ from F2F in the effect of group size on EoP?
4. Do individuals who participate more online also participate more F2F?
5. What is the relationship between objective measures of EoP and self-reported experience?

While we were interested in broad differences between deliberative modes, of particular concern was the effect the deliberative environment had on the contributions of individuals based on their demographic. Some literature claims, for example, that women say less than men online, e.g. [10,16–18,30]. Does online deliberation bias contributions in favor of male participants? Other authors emphasize online divides related to race/ethnicity [20], educational level [20], and/or youth, e.g. [10,30]. In terms of ethnicity, whites and males have been reported to say more than any other group in F2F deliberative settings as well [22,25]. On the other hand, multiple studies of F2F deliberation have found that women speak as much as, or more than, men in these offline settings [11,28,32]. Are online settings different? Examining the quantitative data from the online sessions could help answer these questions.

Some literature shows that group size has an effect on F2F deliberation, and our aim was to use the vast quantity of data that the Community Forum Project collected to map that effect across its F2F and online modes. Because group size is less salient in online settings, these data provide a unique opportunity to test the hypothesis under different conditions. Finally, although the value of participation equality in group deliberation brings forth varying opinions in scholars, e.g. [14,25], and [26], more unequal systems seem less desirable in cases such as public deliberation where a diversity of voices is a commonly agreed goal [7,15].

4   Methods

The present study utilizes data generated in the AHRQ Community Forum Deliberative Methods Demonstration [4,5], but this study was not conceived prior to the design of the Community Forum experiment. An optimal design for the present study would have an online forum-only group, allowing a more pure comparison between online asynchronous text forums and the other methods. The lack of such a condition reflects limitations in the budget and aims of the Community Forum project, but we believe that much can be learned by creatively exploring the data that *were* produced.

Each deliberative session was transcribed from audio and/or video recordings. For each contribution, the number of words it comprised was tabulated. From these data, the *frequency, volume*, and *average contribution length (ACL)* were calculated for each individual in the deliberative sessions. The frequency of contribution was calculated by dividing an individual's number of spoken continuous contributions by the total number of contributions spoken in the session.

Table 1. Mean values: demographic data

Method	Groupts	Sessions	Individuals	Size Range	Avg. Size	Avg. Age	Fem-Prop	Education	Hispanic	Native	Asian	Black	White	Other
BCD	24	1	309	9-14	13.0	46.9	0.55	5.49	0.13	0.02	0.03	0.27	0.60	0.10
CD	48	2	292	7-13	11.8	47.5	0.55	5.65	0.11	0.01	0.02	0.33	0.56	0.09
CP	12	3	98	20-28	24.3	48.5	0.57	5.39	0.10	0.00	0.01	0.47	0.43	0.10
ODP	72	4	262	5-12	9.5	45.6	0.52	5.87	0.11	0.01	0.01	0.25	0.64	0.11

The volume of contributed words for an individual was calculated by dividing the total number of words that an individual spoke by the total number of words that were spoken in the session by all participants. The average contribution length was calculated by taking the total number of words that an individual spoke and dividing it by their number of contributions. Measuring frequency and volume as percentages was necessary to perform analysis across methods due to variation in deliberation duration and group size.

The following were considered independent variables, as self reported by each participant: *age*, *gender*, *education*, and *race/ethnicity* (Hispanic, Native American, Asian or Pacific Islander, Black or African American, White, Other). Education was self-reported as one of eight categories, increasing from "less than high school graduate" to "more than 4-year college graduate." Individuals could indicate more than one race/ethnicity.

Table 1 shows the number of transcript files that were scraped from each method, the range in attendance for sessions, and the demographic makeup of the people who participated.

Analysis was performed across methods, across media (online/offline), and by looking at isolated subpopulations in order to investigate the behavior of different ethnic and gender subgroups. Deliberative experience surveys were also administered. An equality factor, calculated to have a Cronbach's alpha value of 0.64 as a function of three of the questions, was found by exploratory factor analysis [5]. (See also [27].)

5   Results

We divide the results into three parts. The first part compares the ODP (synchronous voice) data with the three F2F methods. The second compares participants in the CD group who posted on the online forum (asynchronous text) with those who did not. And the third reports findings that speak to EoP across deliberative modes.

5.1   Synchronous Voice vs. Face to Face

Tables 2 through 4 show the frequency, volume, and average contribution length correlations with different independent variables across all five environments: ODP and CD-Forum (the online environments), the F2F component of CD (which we call CD-F2F), the BCD, and the CP environments. Significant negative effects for attendance (group size) were found with respect to frequency and

Table 2. Frequency correlations

Mode	Method	Size	Age	Gender	Education	Hispanic	Native	Asian	Black	White	Other
Online	ODP	-0.304***	0.294**	0.015	0.042	-0.073	0.009	-0.050	-0.020	0.106**	-0.129***
	CD-Forum	0.010	0.106	-0.016	0.115	0.030	-0.081	-0.080	-0.033	0.097	-0.061
F2F	CD	-0.222***	0.107*	-0.041	0.101*	-0.064	0.002	-0.018	0.017	0.010	-0.059
	BCD	-0.150*	0.211***	-0.081	0.119	0.038	0.062	-0.068	-0.186**	0.190***	0.000
	CP	-0.134*	0.134*	0.012	0.118	-0.128*	—	-0.062	-0.127*	0.166**	-0.070

Table 3. Volume correlations

Mode	Method	Size	Age	Gender	Education	Hispanic	Native	Asian	Black	White	Other
Online	ODP	-0.252***	0.203***	-0.0156	0.160***	-0.066	0.037	-0.018	-0.134***	0.191***	-0.127***
	CD-Forum	0.008	0.112	-0.029	0.145	0.006	-0.072	-0.074	-0.055	0.122*	-0.068
F2F	CD	-0.196***	0.047	-0.055	0.138*	-0.045	0.022	-0.032	0.030	0.0035	-0.035
	BCD	-0.140*	0.087*	-0.147*	0.136	0.041	0.038	-0.065	-0.127*	0.147*	-0.004
	CP	-0.121*	0.023	0.001	0.185**	-0.011	—	-0.065	0.031	0.006	0.014

Table 4. Average contribution length correlations

Mode	Method	Size	Age	Gender	Education	Hispanic	Native	Asian	Black	White	Other
Online	ODP	0.060	0.063	-0.056	0.167***	0.023	0.023	0.087*	-0.149***	0.116**	-0.032
	CD-Forum	0.048	0.091	-0.056	0.151*	0.002	-0.085	-0.075	-0.030	0.094	-0.055
F2F	CD	-0.054	-0.166***	0.032	0.092*	0.043	0.175***	-0.044	0.032	-0.063	0.121**
	BCD	0.032	-0.161**	-0.117	0.156**	0.032	-0.099	0.019	0.084	-0.047	-0.033
	CP	0.075	-0.112	-0.083	0.129**	0.179	—	-0.043	0.024	-0.132*	0.163**

volume across all four methods but no effects with respect to average contribution length were found to be significant. Significant positive effects for age were found across the various methods as well.

With respect to education, a positive relationship between contribution and self-reported education was found. For the ODP, CD-F2F, and CP conditions, no significant effect was found between gender and contribution frequency, volume, or average length. However, in the BCD condition, female identification had a significant negative correlation with volume ($\rho = -0.147$, $p < 0.02$).

In the ODP condition, a participant indicating that they were white had a positive, significant correlation with all contribution metrics (frequency, $\rho = 0.107$, $p < 0.001$; volume, $\rho = 0.191$, $p < 0.001$; average length, $\rho = 0.116$, $p < 0.01$), while black identification had a negative correlation with volume ($\rho = -0.134$, p < 0.001). A similar trend was found in the BCD condition, where white identification had a positive, significant correlation with frequency and volume (frequency, $\rho = 0.190$, $p < 0.001$, volume: $\rho = 0.147$, $p < 0.02$), while answering the ethnicity question with "Black or African American" had negative contribution correlations (frequency, $\rho = -0.186$, $p < 0.002$; volume, $\rho = -0.127$, $p < 0.05$). For the CP condition, answering ethnicity with "White" had a positive, significant correlation with frequency ($\rho = 0.166$, $p < 0.01$), while black identification had a negative, significant correlation with frequency ($\rho = -0.127$, $p < 0.05$). No significant effects with respect to ethnicity were found for the CD-F2F method. Identifying as "Hispanic", "Native American", or

Table 5. Mean values: Posters vs. Nonposters

Subset	Avg. Age	Fem-Prop	Education	Hispanic	Native	Asian	Black	White	Other	Frequency	Volume	Avg. Length
Posters	50.0	0.58	5.74	0.12	0	0.01	0.35	0.56	0.08	0.10	0.10	35.8
Nonposters	46.7	0.52	5.52	0.10	0.03	0.03	0.30	0.55	0.118	0.084	0.085	41.1
p-value	0.31	0.15	0.25	0.51	0.01*	0.07	0.24	0.83	0.12	0.01**	0.03*	0.01**

Table 6. Frequency correlations

Mode	Subset	Size	Age	Gender	Education	Hispanic	Native	Asian	Black	White	Other
Online	Posters	-0.165*	0.1134	-0.069	0.136	0.006	—	-0.063	-0.104	0.158*	-0.034
F2F	Posters	-0.234***	0.177**	-0.100	0.050	-0.011	—	-0.122*	-0.047	0.059	0.018
	Nonposters	-0.225***	0.003	0.016	0.165*	-0.166*	0.030	0.074	0.122	-0.082	-0.138

Table 7. Volume Correlations

Mode	Subset	Size	Age	Gender	Education	Hispanic	Native	Asian	Black	White	Other
Online	Posters	-0.138	0.124	-0.080	0.181*	-0.026	—	-0.061	-0.126	0.187*	-0.051
F2F	Posters	-0.170**	0.119*	-0.135*	0.094	0.000	—	-0.115	-0.030	0.046	0.034
	Nonposters	-0.249***	-0.054	0.038	0.197**	-0.131	0.055	0.038	0.119	-0.070	-0.106

Table 8. Average contribution length correlations

Mode	Subset	Size	Age	Gender	Education	Hispanic	Native	Asian	Black	White	Other
Online	Posters	-0.082	0.0885	-0.140	0.201**	-0.041	—	-0.044	-0.107	0.159*	-0.02
F2F	Posters	0.034	-0.142*	-0.005	0.126*	0.102	—	-0.091	0.017	-0.25	0.124*
	Nonposters	-0.149*	-0.185**	0.103	0.065	-0.024	0.229	-0.039	0.061	-0.104	0.104

"Asian or Pacific Islander" showed no systematic correlations with contribution measures across methods.

5.2   Findings Within the Citizens' Deliberation Hybrid Method

Posters vs. Nonposters. Table 5 compares those who posted with those who did not post in the online forum of the CD method. The frequency, volume, and average length figures given there are for each group's average-member contributions in the F2F sessions of CD. Tables 6 through 8 compare the poster and nonposter groups in CD both online and F2F in terms of the demographic variables and sizes of the groups in which they were participating,

Posters and nonposters showed similar, significant effects with respect to attendance (group size). Posters showed positive effects for frequency and volume with respect to age, but nonposters showed no effect, a discrepancy from the findings of the other groups. Nonposters and posters shared significant negative correlations for average contribution length with respect to age, however. Posters showed positive, significant correlations with respect to education only for average contribution length, while nonposters showed positive, significant correlations with respect to education for frequency and volume. No systematic, significant correlations were found for ethnicity or gender among the poster and nonposter groups, with the exception that female identification had a significant, negative correlation with contributed volume in the F2F session ($\rho = 0.197$, $p < 0.05$). In comparing the total F2F contributions of posters and nonposters (Table 5), posters' contributions were of significantly higher frequency ($p < 0.005$), significantly higher volume ($p < 0.03$), and (interestingly) their average contribution lengths were significantly less ($p < 0.01$).

Face to Face vs. Asynchronous Text (Deme Forum). In the F2F component of CD, group size had a statistically significant negative correlation with both frequency ($\rho = -0.222$, $p < 0.001$) and volume ($\rho = -0.196$, $p < 0.001$), but no significant impact on average length. These results were mirrored in the online component (frequency, $\rho = -0.165$, $p < 0.05$; volume, $\rho = -0.138$, $p < 0.08$) although the effect was weakened. (See Tables 6, 7, and 8 for this subsection.)

There were no significant age effects in the online case, but in the F2F sessions, frequency was positively correlated with age ($\rho = 0.107$, $p < 0.02$), while average length was negatively correlated ($\rho = -0.166$, $p < 0.001$). There were no significant effects for gender in either medium. Educational level was positively correlated with all contribution measures both online (frequency, $\rho = 0.136$, $p < 0.08$; volume, $\rho = 0.181$, $p < 0.02$; average length, $\rho = 0.201$, $p < 0.01$) and in the F2F sessions (frequency, $\rho = 0.100$, $p < 0.03$; volume, $\rho = 0.139$, $p < 0.01$; average length, $\rho = 0.092$, $p < 0.05$), with slightly stronger effects online. There were no significant race/ethnicity effects among the F2F participants, but white identification had a positive, significant correlation with all metrics in the online case (frequency, $\rho = 0.158$, $p < 0.05$; volume, $\rho = 0.187$, $p < 0.02$; average length, $\rho = 0.159$, $p < 0.05$).

Face to Face (Posters Only) vs. Online Forum in CD. As shown in Tables 6 through 8, we also examined differences between the behavior of those who posted online and spoke offline in CD, in order to examine if the change in medium would impact individuals' contribution rates. Group size effects were consistent with the other methods, though the effect observed in the F2F mode (frequency, $\rho = -0.234$, $p < 0.001$; volume, $\rho = -0.169$, $p < 0.002$) was much stronger than in the asynchronous forum setting (frequency, $\rho = -0.153$, $p < 0.04$; volume, $\rho = -0.125$, $p < 0.08$).

Although no significant age effects were found in the online forum, the effect was significant across all metrics in the F2F setting, (frequency, $\rho = 0.176$, $p < 0.002$; volume, $\rho = 0.119$, $p < 0.04$; average length, $\rho = -0.143$ $p < 0.02$). In the F2F condition, education had a positive and significant effect on average contribution length ($\rho = 0.126$ $p < 0.02$), and was similar online (frequency, $\rho = 0.136$, $p < 0.08$; volume, $\rho = 0.181$, $p < 0.02$; average length, $\rho = 0.201$ $p < 0.01$). Among posters, women contributed less in the F2F setting (frequency, $\rho = -0.100$, $p < 0.08$; volume, $\rho = -0.135$, $p < 0.04$), though no significant gender effects were observed in the online setting. With respect to ethnicity, no systematic effects were observed in the F2F case. However, significant effects were observed for white identified posters on the online forum, who posted more than those who were nonwhite (frequency, $\rho = 0.158$, $p < 0.05$; volume, $\rho = 0.187$, $p < 0.02$; average length, $\rho = 0.159$ $p < 0.05$).

5.3 Equality of Participation Across Individuals

Although the most common application of the *Gini index* is its use as a measure of income inequality in a given nation, it also can be used as a general measure of inequality in a data set. In this context the Gini index ranges from 0, representing complete equality, to 1, representing complete inequality. Gini indices were calculated for each session, and the values analyzed for each medium, in order to investigate EoP differences across methods. The Gini index was calculated by the following formula, which fulfills the Transfer Principle of Inequality [19], where X_i is the amount that person i contributed and P_i is the contribution rank of person i such that the person who contributed most receives a rank of 1 and the person who contributed least a rank of N:

$$G = \frac{N+1}{N-1} - \frac{2}{N(N-1)\bar{x}} \sum_{i=1}^{n} P_i X_i$$

In comparing the synchronous voice method (ODP) against the other methods (Table 9), statistically significant differences were found for frequency between ODP and BCD ($p < 0.05$), and between ODP and the (Deme) Forum ($p < 0.05$). Significant differences for volume were found between ODP and both BCD and CD-F2F ($p < 0.001$). Additionally, significant differences for average contribution length were found between ODP and both BCD and CD-F2F ($p < 0.001$). For volume, ODP ($G = 0.439$) and CP ($G = 0.448$) reported the highest Gini indices, with the other F2F methods showing more modest, yet still fairly high, coefficients (BCD: $G = 0.351$; CD-F2F: $G = 0.368$). The Gini indices for the online forum when including all participants (both posters and nonposters) in the CD method were dramatically greater than for all the other methods, indicating, perhaps not surprisingly, that an optional online forum draws a more limited set of participants.

Gini indices for each metric were also calculated based on the F2F contributions of the people who posted (Table 10). Among those who posted, a statistically significant difference between online ($G = 0.467$) and F2F ($G = 0.345$)

Table 9. Gini indices across methods

Method	Frequency	Volume	Average length
BCD	0.329	0.351	0.204
CD-F2F	0.335	0.368	0.214
CP	0.400	0.448	0.283
ODP	0.362	0.439	0.279
CD-Forum	0.754	0.702	0.556

Table 10. Gini indices among posters across mediums

Method	Frequency	Volume	Average length
Forum	0.316	0.467	0.302
Face to face	0.322	0.345	0.203

media is prominent for volume ($p < 0.001$). Even among those who choose to participate in an online forum, there appears to be less EoP for volume and average length (thought not frequency).

Self Reported Experiences Regarding Equality of Participation. (See [27] for data.) In the post-deliberative experience survey, participants rated CD (F2F) and BCD the most equal of the methods, with CP being the least perceived equal, and ODP falling in between. An interesting comparison is with the measured Gini indices for each method (Table 9). The subjective equality factors roughly mirrored the pattern of Gini indices across the four rated methods, with BCD and CD(-F2F) scoring as the most equal on all three Gini measures and also on the subjective equality factor, CP scoring the least equal on all, and ODP scoring in the middle on all. Posters in the CD-Deme forum rated overall equality significantly lower in the CD-F2F environment than did nonposters, though posters were more satisfied that they personally said what they wanted to. We saw in Table 5 that posters exceeded the contributions of nonposters in the F2F sessions of CD by all three objective metrics, and their reported satisfactions can be reconciled with this fact. Posters appeared aware that they got more than their share of speaking in during the CD-F2F sessions, perhaps leading them to feel satisfied with their own participation but less satisfied that the process produced equal participation. In all but one of the methods (BCD), white identified participants rated the equality of the method significantly lower than did black identified participants, despite the fact that black identification predicted lower volume of participation in all but one of the method groups (see Table 14 in [27]).

Individual-Level Equality of Participation and Group Size Online Versus Face to Face. (See [27] for data.) The Gini index is a measure of how concentrated participation is across individuals (the higher the Gini, the more participation is dominated by a subgroup of participants). A natural question to ask is what effect the size of the group has on this measure. The Gini index rose substantially as group size increased in both the BCD and CP methods, but was unaffected by group size in the CD method. For the online environments, the relationship between Gini indices and group size was either flat or slightly negative for both ODP (synchronous voice) and CD-Deme (the asynchronous text forum). This provides some evidence that the two online methods each scale well, at least within the observed ranges (7–12 and 8–17 participants, respectively, for the ODP and CD groups). Adding more participants within these ranges does not seem to make participation more unequal across individuals in the two online methods, nor in the CD-F2F method. But adding participants does seem to reduce EoP in two of the F2F methods: BCD and CP.

6 Discussion

Some literature argues that women are less likely to participate online than are men, e.g. [2,3], though women may be more likely to participate equally with men online than offline [23]. We found no significant negative effects on EoP for women across methods, with the exception of the BCD method, which favors men in volume. This conclusion deviates from the sizeable body of literature arguing that women speak less F2F [7,21,23], and from the claim that women are less active in online contributing [2,23], in agreement with the idea that online environments do not adversely impact gender EoP (see [34]). One explanation for the F2F equality of contribution is that all of the F2F methods were facilitated, and there is evidence to support that facilitation eliminates the worst of the gender gap in deliberation [31]. The discrepancy in our findings lies with the BCD method, in which female identification negatively correlated with all contribution measures. One difference between BCD and the other F2F methods was that BCD used a male facilitator for half of the groups (rather than a female for all), although within the BCD method women were not significantly more inhibited under the male facilitator than under the female one. Despite this discrepancy, the results overall imply that the difference of mode (online vs. offline) is not causing the difference in and of itself. Indeed, in the CD condition we saw that female online forum posters participated equally with men, but the same women did not do so F2F. These findings agree with some other studies involving online deliberation, most notably another study in which participants deliberated on healthcare issues [24], but they are unique in being drawn from a within-group study. Previous examinations of online deliberation even when compared directly with F2F deliberation, have not used the same group that participated F2F when tracking online contributions.

In most of the methods, and most visibly online, there was a significant positive correlation between white identification and volume/frequency, and a significant negative correlation between black identification and the same measures. This was most prevalent in the online methods — ODP and the forum — where facilitation was the least present. The online and F2F environments showed relatively even participation levels across ethnicities in the three F2F environments, but noticeable differences in both ODP and the CD-Deme (Forum) setting (see Fig. 3 in [27]). ODP is unique in that there did not seem to be a tradeoff for white participants between volume/frequency and ACL, and the correlation with all three measures was positive. These results are consistent with other findings for gender, in which the gender gap is eliminated via facilitation [31].

Noticing that age and education had consistent positive relationships with contribution measures for all metrics, a multiple regression model was generated in order to investigate to what extent these factors could compensate for other discrepancies, especially between ethnicities. As shown in Table 14 in [27], the racial difference in participation is reduced when we control for age and education. A gap persists for the two online environments: ODP and CD-Deme (Deme is the Forum component of CD), though not for the F2F environments, including CD-F2F*, which represents just Deme forum posters in the F2F component of CD. This merits further study to determine whether the media difference is robust.

For further analysis and discussion, see [27].

7   Conclusions

While there have been a variety of studies of online and offline deliberation, none have as large a pool of information to work with as the Community Forum project, and as such it provides a unique opportunity to provide quantitative analysis of the difference between the two modes on a scale that has not been seen before. While this paper does not represent an exhaustive report of all the conclusions that can be gleaned from the data about the effect of deliberative mode on EoP, some conclusions appear well-supported based on our analysis so far:

1. *Online effects on demographic groups' participation equality.* Overall, we see no consistent effects of online versus F2F participation for gender equality of participation in these data. There is evidence that some deliberation methods (e.g. the F2F BCD method) may adversely impact female participation, independently of the offline-online dimension, and that an asynchronous forum produces higher EoP across genders than F2F discussion. For ethnicity, the online versus F2F picture is less clear, but the online settings in this study do seem to have depressed black participation relative to whites' (see Fig. 3 in [27]). Online deliberation appears to reduce black and increase white participation somewhat, relative to F2F, even when controlling for age and educational level (see Table 14 in [27]). This provisional finding requires further investigation, but may reflect the reduced level of facilitation in the online conditions of the Community Forum experiment. Older participants appear to contribute more in volume online (see Table 3), possibly because the negative effect of age on average contribution length that we see in F2F environments does not occur online. Online environments do not appear to amplify participation inequality related to educational level, which might be a bit of a surprise.
2. *Online effects on individual-level participation equality.* As measured by Gini indices, synchronous voice deliberation (ODP) is on par with F2F methods for individual-level EoP (Table 9). But the optional online Deme forum used in CD produced much greater concentration of participation volume than did F2F methods, including the CD-F2F environment that included the same participants (Table 10).

3. *Online environments and group size effects.* Although the methods tested here are too limited to say so definitively, in this study the online environments (ODP and CD-Forum) eliminated the amplification of inequality that we saw from group size in the BCD and CP (but not CD-F2F) methods.
4. *Online posting as a predictor of F2F participation.* In Table 5 we saw that Forum posters in the CD method out-participated nonposters on all three contribution metrics, indicating that the tendency for an individual to participate is correlated across online and F2F contexts.
5. *Relationship of self-reported experience to measures of participation equality.* The Gini coefficients for frequency, volume, and ACL, as measures of individual-level EoP, proved to be good predictors both of each other and of the subjective equality factor (Table 9, plus Table 11 in [27]). Interestingly, however, at the demographic level there was a more puzzling relationship. Black identified participants rated all but one of the methods more equal than did white participants, even when they participated less by volume than white identified participants did. The ODP method was the only pure test of subjective ratings for an online method, and, consistent with its Gini indices, participants rated it neither the most nor the least equal in comparison to the other (F2F) methods.

For further research, the results related to gender could be taken in a more focused direction. Though ODP was an exercise in synchronous voice deliberation, the purpose of the online forum was question-answering rather than deliberation proper. Using a method similar to CD in which the asynchronous text component were used to deliberate, rather than to share personal anecdotes and ask questions about the topic, would provide a better test of gender equality between online and offline methods. Future research might place more emphasis on individual group composition and its effects on individual contributions, to isolate the cause of demographic trends. Additionally, though outside the scope of this paper, looking at facilitator effects might prove especially useful.

References

1. Abdel-Monem, T., Bingham, S., Marincic, J., Tomkins, A.: Deliberation and diversity: perceptions of small group discussions by race and ethnicity. Small Group Res. **41**(6), 746–776 (2010)
2. Albrecht, S.: Whose voice is heard in online deliberation?: a study of participation and representation in political debates on the internet. Inf. Commun. Soc. **9**(1), 62–82 (2006)
3. Baek, Y.M., Wojcieszak, M., Carpini, M.X.D.: Online versus face-to-face deliberation: Who? why? what? with what effects? New Media Soc. **14**(3), 363–383 (2012)
4. Carman, K.L., Mallery, C., Maurer, M., Wang, G., Garfinkel, S., Yang, M., Gilmore, D., Windham, A., Ginsburg, M., Sofaer, S., et al.: Effectiveness of public deliberation methods for gathering input on issues in healthcare: Results from a randomized trial. Soc. Sci. Med. **133**, 11–20 (2015)

5. Carman, K.L., Maurer, M., Mallery, C., Wang, G., Garfinkel, S., Richmond, J., Gilmore, D., Windham, A., Yang, M., Mangrum, R., et al.: Community Forum Deliberative Methods Demonstration: Evaluating Effectiveness and Eliciting Public Views on Use of Evidence. Agency for Healthcare Research and Quality (2014)

6. Christiano, T.: The significance of public deliberation. In: Bohman, J., Rehg, W. (eds.) Deliberative Democracy: Essays on Reason and Politics, pp. 243–278. MIT Press, Cambridge (1997)

7. Dahlberg, L.: Computer-mediated communication and the public sphere: a critical analysis. J. Comput. Mediated Commun. **7**(1) (2001)

8. Davies, T., Chandler, R.: Online deliberation design: Choices, criteria, and evidence. In: Nabatchi, T., Weiksner, M., Gastil, J., Leighninger, M. (eds.) Democracy in Motion: Evaluating the Practice and Impact of Deliberative Civic Engagement, pp. 103–131. Oxford University Press, Oxford (2012)

9. Davies, T., Mintz, M.D., Tobin, J., Ben-Avi, N.: Document-centered discussion and decision making in the deme platform. In: 2012 International Conference on Collaboration Technologies and Systems (CTS), pp. lxv-lxviii. IEEE (2012)

10. Davis, R.: Politics Online: Blogs, Chatrooms, and Discussion Groups in American Democracy. Routledge, New York (2005)

11. Dutwin, D.: The character of deliberation: equality, argument, and the formation of public opinion. Int. J. Public Opin. Res. **15**(3), 239–264 (2003)

12. Fishkin, J.S.: Virtual public consultation: Prospects for internet deliberative democracy. In: Davies, T., Gangadharan, S.P. (eds.) Online Deliberation: Design, Research, and Practice, pp. 23–35. CSLI Publications, Stanford (2009)

13. Fraser, N.: Rethinking the public sphere: a contribution to the critique of actually existing democracy. Social Text **25**, 56–80 (1990)

14. Gerber, M.: Equal partners in dialogue? participation equality in a transnational deliberative poll (europolis). Polit. Stud. **63**, 110–130 (2015)

15. Graham, T., Wright, S.: Discursive equality and everyday talk online: the impact of superparticipants. J. Comput. Mediated Commun. **19**(3), 625–642 (2014)

16. Hargittai, E., Walejko, G.: The participation divide: content creation and sharing in the digital age 1. Inf. Commun. Soc. **11**(2), 239–256 (2008)

17. Harp, D., Tremayne, M.: The gendered blogosphere: examining inequality using network and feminist theory. Journalism Mass Commun. Q. **83**(2), 247–264 (2006)

18. Herring, S.: Gender differences in computer-mediated communication: Bringing familiar baggage to the new frontier. American Library Association Annual Convention (1994)

19. Jasso, G.: On gini's mean difference and gini's index of concentration. Am. Sociol. Rev. **44**, 867–870 (1979)

20. Johnson, T.J., Kaye, B.K., Bichard, S.L., Wong, W.J.: Every blog has its day: politically-interested internet users perceptions of blog credibility. J. Comput. Mediated Commun. **13**(1), 100–122 (2007)

21. Karpowitz, C.F., Mendelberg, T., Shaker, L.: Gender inequality in deliberative participation. Am. Polit. Sci. Rev. **106**(03), 533–547 (2012)

22. Marder, N.S.: Gender dynamics and jury deliberations. Yale Law J. **96**, 593–612 (1987)

23. Monnoyer-Smith, L.: The technological dimension of deliberation: a comparison between on and offline participation. In: Coleman, S., Shane, P. (eds.) Connecting Democracy: Online Consultation and the Future of Democratic Discourse, pp. 191–207. MIT Press, Cambridge (2011)

24. Price, V.: Citizens deliberating online: theory and some evidence. In: Davies, T., Gangadharan, S. (eds.) Online Deliberation: Design, Research, and Practice, pp. 37–58. CSLI Publications, Stanford (2009)

25. Sanders, L.M.: Against deliberation. Polit. Theory **25**, 347–376 (1997)

26. Shane, P.: Turning gold into epg: Lessons from low-tech democratic experimentalism for electronic rulemaking and other ventures in cyberdemocracy. Online Deliberation: Design, Research, and Practice, pp. 149–162 (2009)

27. Showers, E., Tindall, N., Davies, T.: Equality of participation online versus face to face: An analysis of the community forum deliberative methods demonstration (2015). http://ssrn.com/abstract=2616233

28. Siu, A.: Look who's talking: Examining social influence, opinion change, and argument quality in deliberation. ProQuest (2009)

29. Squires, J.: Deliberation, domination and decision-making. Theoria J. Soc. Polit. Theory **55**, 104–133 (2008)

30. Stromer-Galley, J., Wichowski, A.: Political discussion online. In: Consalvo, M., Ess, C. (eds.) The Handbook of Internet Studies, pp. 168–187. Wiley, New York (2011)

31. Trénel, M.: Facilitation and inclusive deliberation. In: Davies, T., Gangadharan, S.P. (eds.) Online Deliberation: Design, Research and Practice, pp. 253–257. CSLI Publications/University of Chicago Press, San Francisco (2009)

32. Wilson, P.A.: Deliberative planning for disaster recovery: re-membering new orleans. J. Public Deliberation **5**(1) (2008)

33. Witschge, T.: Online deliberation: Possibilities of the internet for deliberative democracy. In: Shane, P. (ed.) Democracy Online: The Prospects for Political Renewal Through the Internet, pp. 109–122. Routledg, New York (2004)

34. Zhang, W.: Deliberation and the Disempowered: Attendance, Experience, and Influence. Ph.D. Dissertation, University of Pennsylvania (2008)

A Knowledge Extraction and Management Component to Support Spontaneous Participation

Lukasz Porwol[✉], Islam Hassan, Adegbojega Ojo, and John Breslin

Insight Centre for Data Analytics, National University of Ireland,
Galway, Ireland
{lukasz.porwol,islam.hassan,adegboyega.ojo,
john.breslin}@insight-centre.org

Abstract. Harnessing spontaneous contributions of citizens on Social Media and networking sites is a major feature of the next generation citizen-led e-Participation paradigm. However, extracting information of interest from Social Media streams is a challenging task and requires support from domain specific language resources such as lexica. This work describes our efforts at developing a Knowledge Extraction and Management component which employs a lexicon for extracting information related to public services in Social Media contents or streams as part of a holistic technology infrastructure for citizen-led e-Participation. Our approach consists of three basic steps – (1) acquisition and refinement of public service catalogues, (2) organization of the public service names into a lexicon based on different semantic similarity measures and (3) development of a dictionary-based Named Entity Recognizer (NER) or "spotter" based on the lexicon. We evaluate the performance of the NER solution supported by contextual information generated by two well-known general-purpose information NER tools (DBpedia Spotlight and Alchemy) on a dataset of tweets. Results show that our strategy to domain specific information extraction from Social Media is effective. We conclude with a scenario on how our approach could be scaled-up to extract other types of information from citizen discussions on Social Media.

Keywords: e-Participation · Citizen-led e-Participation · Information extraction (IE) · Natural Language Processing (NLP) · Public services · e-Government

1 Introduction

e-Participation involves technology-mediated interaction between citizens and the politics sphere [1]. By leveraging information and telecommunication technology (ICT), in particular contemporary social software technologies, e-Participation facilitates ubiquitous public participation and instant feedback capabilities [2]. Certain contemporary e-Participation solutions attempted to augment the discussion platforms with Social Media as additional communication channel though with very limited success. This is due to the fact that the traditional conceptualizations of e-Participation as a consultative, democratic process with involvement of citizens in policymaking do

© IFIP International Federation for Information Processing 2015
E. Tambouris et al. (Eds.): ePart 2015, LNCS 9249, pp. 68–80, 2015.
DOI: 10.1007/978-3-319-22500-5_6

not sufficiently address the common spontaneous citizen participation on informal channels such as Social Media [3]. Our experience so far is that state-of-the-art e-Participation solutions integrated with Social Media directly or in particular, leveraging generic, of-the-shelf analytical solutions to harness the vast information on Social Media mainly through general-purpose NER tools, largely fail to achieve the desired performance level. This we argue is due to lack of specific mechanisms to deal with information overload and lack of domain-specific natural language propocessing tools to complement the popular general-purpose ones which offer relatively narrow range of general concepts like name of a person, organization, location, brand, product, a numeric expression including time, date, money and percent [4]. In particular, state-of-the-art solutions fall short in addressing e-Participation specific concepts such as public service names or policies. Therefore, progress in this area is contingent on developing domain-specific tools for processing political discussion by citizens and e-participation contents in general. Building on our previous work [5], we show how the Knowledge Extraction & Management component of a holistic infrastructure for e-Participation could be implemented using domain-specific lexical resource. We demonstrate and discuss the use of the component through a use case scenario. Thus, by our solution we exemplify the creation of explicit technological bridge between the citizen-political-discussion-sphere (Social Media) and public services sphere. The paper is structured as follows: In Sect. 2 we elaborate on related work in the context of use of social software, in particular Social Media for e-Participation; Sect. 3 presents important concepts essential to understand the of Knowledge Extraction and Management Component development process; In Sect. 3 we discuss the approach; Sect. 4 elaborates on the Knowledge Extraction and Management component creation and presents an example use case scenario. In Sect. 5 we discuss our contribution to the advancement of e-Participation domain with final conclusions presented in Sect. 6.

2 Related Work

2.1 Web 2.0 and Social Media in e-Participation

The last decade witnessed many examples of the use of social software as an infrastructure for realizing certain aspects of e-Participation. Social software is usually referred to as: Web 2.0 Software (or platform) that enables social networking by offering capabilities for people to contact and interact with each other [6]. The main principle of Web 2.0 is collective intelligence, collaborative content creation and composition by the user (here citizen) who contributes towards common knowledge [7]. Many e-Participation projects including HUWY,[1] U@MARENOSTRUM[2], VID[3],

---

[1] http://www.huwy.eu/vi.

[2] http://www.uatmarenostrum.eu/.

[3] http://www.vidi-project.eu/.

WAVE[4], VOICES[5], WEGOV[6], Puzzled by Policy[7], PADGETS[8], SPACES[9] employed Web 2.0 tools such as digital forums, blogs, wiki's and live-chat to provide dedicated e-Participation environment where citizens can express and discuss their needs, concerns and ideas. Those highly structured platforms, though supposedly well tuned to specific e-Participation needs, in principle suffer from abysmally low participation of citizens. In contrast, very specific, incredibly popular sub-group of social software tools: Social Media are widely used by citizens for spontaneous political discussions though without direct link to the formal e-Participation. This phenomena is referred to in the literature as Duality of e-Participation [8]. Therefore, in response to challenges faced by the dedicated e-Participation platforms some of the solutions indeed, introduced explicit support for the popular Social Media platforms with particular feed integration (in rare cases both ways content exchange is available) [9, 10]. Some more advanced solutions such as presented by PADGETS [11] with injection of special widgets into Social Media enable direct back-loop feed to the dedicated platform. However the big challenge remains unsolved as the prominent e-Participation solutions integrating Social Media largely do not address the issue of volume nor quality (lack of relevant selectivity) of the content produced [12], therefore do not ensure sufficient innovation to enable the dual e-Participation observed by Macintosh [8]. We are aware of certain original attempts to leverage the potential of spontaneous discussions on Social Media, such as the innovative approach presented in WEGOV project [13]. Nevertheless the methodology applied in the project appears to relay on relatively generic Social Media analytics tools (for topic detection, topic popularity, sentiment analysis and seed user detection) without explicit, direct links to the government sphere including for instance: references to governmental services, policy documents or newsletters. Moreover the methodology does not seem to give much of explicit thought to the essential synergy between current government-led solutions and processes, and citizen-led participation. Therefore the solution offered by the project, though advanced, appears to repeat the principles of the already available of-the-shelf, popular Social Media analytics solutions for businesses.

Considering Social Media and politics it is important to recall past miscellaneous attempts to harness Social Media for e-Participation, beyond e-Participation research projects. In particular, as it has been shown that successful Social Media campaign can influence political popularity (hence can have a significant impact on results of elections), many decision makers and government offices employed Social Media as a direct campaign communication channel [14, 15]. Another important e-Participation Social-Media use context has been: improved, Social-Media-supported Disaster and Crisis Management and Policy Development derived from Social-Media-facilitated citizen reporting capabilities [16, 17]. In particular Social Media have been playing

---

[4] http://www.wave-project.eu/.

[5] http://www.give-your-voice.eu/.

[6] http://www.wegov-project.eu/.

[7] http://join.puzzledbypolicy.eu/.

[8] http://www.padgets.eu/.

[9] http://www.positivespaces.eu/.

increasing role as rapid crowdsourcing and rapid response tools, especially in the events of crisis (including political crisis) [18] and natural disaster [19]. However, the Social-Media-applications for e-Participation, in the cases mentioned, focus rather on the use of popular Social Media platforms directly or use common, of-the-shelf (not a domain specific) analytical methodologies and solutions to harness the spontaneous political discussions what results in moderate performance. Therefore, a solution that would try to comprehensively address specific analytical needs of the e-Participation context, such as: effective methods for identifying political content on Social Media or contextual information clustering and linking is yet to be developed.

2.2 Semantic Web

The Semantic Web (Web 3.0) provides a framework that allows data to be shared and reused across applications, enterprises, and community boundaries [20] advancing the website-based Web 2.0 to the Web of Data. Semantic Web leverages ontologies for information modelling and knowledge representation. Ontologies provide a controlled vocabulary of terms that can collectively provide an abstract view of the domain [21]. Semantic Web technologies and ontologies are being used to address data discovery, data interoperability, knowledge sharing and collaboration problems. Ontologies can be described in RDF (Resource Description Framework) [22] which provides a flexible graph based model, used to describe and relate resources. The application of Semantic Web technologies to e-Government gained significant momentum with applications to several major areas including the use of ontologies to formally model different aspects of e-government; Structuring e-Participation research [23], Enabling personalized service delivery [24]; Enabling interoperability and integration of government resources and services [25].

In our work we leverage Semantic Web for constructing artefacts essential for Natural Language Processing and for storing all the data in a graph, in order to explicitly support better data discovery and interoperability for next generation e-Participation.

2.3 Natural Language Processing

2.3.1 Information Extraction

The goal of Information Extraction (IE) is to derive information structures directly from text with emphasis on the following aspects: identifying relations from textual content [26], automatic instantiation of ontologies and building knowledge bases tools [27]. Common methods on IE have focused on the use of supervised learning – SL techniques [28], self-supervised methods [29] and rule learning [30]. These techniques learn a language model or a set of rules from a set of manually tagged training documents and then apply the model or rules to new texts. The challenge for the SL approaches is the high cost of creating the labelled resources. In contrast, the unsupervised learning (UL) methods (also referred to as Open Information Extraction) attempt to fetch information automatically from the texts themselves [31].

2.3.2 Named Entity Recognition

A named entity can be defined as an entity classified accordingly to predefined set of categories for instance: person, organization, location, brand, product, time, date etc. [4]. The Named Entity Recognition applies multiple "classic" information extraction techniques listed before: SL, SSL and UL. However certain contemporary NER solutions apply lexical resources (e.g. WordNet[10]), lexical patterns and statistics computed on large annotated corpus [32]. The common processing pipeline for NER includes detecting named entities, assigning a type weighted by a numeric confidence score and by providing a list of URIs for disambiguation. The lexical resources and terminological databases are essential part of modern NLP systems consisting of large amount of highly detailed and curated entries [33]. A Lexicon can be developed to be domain independent or to support a specific domain. Thus, in our work we focus on the lexicon-based domain-specific approach to NER.

3 Approach

Design science creates and evaluates artefacts that define ideas, practices, technical capabilities and products through which the analysis, design, implementation and use of information systems can be effectively accomplished. Given that the goal of this work is to construct a technical artefact, our research follows the Design Science Research guidelines and process elaborated in [34, 35]. In particular, our objective is to develop a Knowledge Extraction and Management Component (KEMC) as part of a comprehensive infrastructure for e-Participation. To achieve this goal, we construct two technical artefacts – (1) a Lexicon of public service names and (2) a Named Entity Recogniser based on the lexicon and integrating generic NER solutions through dedicated APIs. The development of the lexicon is based on the national public service catalogues. The two datasets were employed as input into a process which automatically related public service names based on a set of semantic similarity and relatedness measures including Explicit Semantics Analysis (ESA) [36] and WordNet-based measures. The resulting graph of Public Service Names is subsequently employed to develop a NER or spotter using an open source dictionary based spotter framework. In line with the DSR process model described in [35].

4 Knowledge Extraction and Management Component (KEMC)

In this section we elaborate on Knowledge Extraction and Management Component implementation encapsulating two core building blocks: the public service lexicon and the NER solution leveraging the generated language resource. First we present the comprehensive infrastructure for e-Participation design to provide the context for KEMC development. Then we present the domain-specific lexicon creation process

---

[10] https://wordnet.princeton.edu/.

algorithm followed by application of the language resource to dedicated NER solutions combining the output of the generic NER solutions.

4.1 e-Participation Infrastructure Design

The infrastructure for e-Participation [5] presented in Fig. 1, is a comprehensive design resulting from extensive works on identifying and consolidating the duality of e-Participation requirements. The black and white components represent the tool-containers while arrows represent the interfaces. The central component – Knowledge Extraction and Management (marked with the red dashed line) is primarily responsible for all Social Media participation data retrieval and processing. The component extracts and analyses the discussion data, i.e., posts, user profiles, discussion topics, threads and performs continuous data quality improvement by filtering and linking related concepts as well as linking data from external sources such as other e-Participation systems, governmental portals or any other places holding valuable e-Participation information. The work presented in this paper attempts to provide an approach and implementation for realising this core e-Participation infrastructure component.

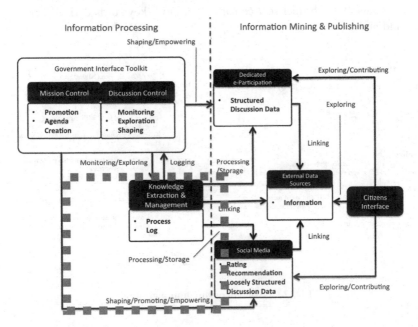

Fig. 1. Infrastructure for e-Participation design

4.2 Lexicon

In order to construct the lexicon we drew from the existing catalogue of services and the Core Public Service Vocabulary[11] – a simplified reusable and extensible data model

---

[11] https://joinup.ec.europa.eu/asset/core_public_service/description.

that captures the fundamental characteristics of a service offered by public administrations. We leveraged the Core Public Service Ontology as the basis for creating the
initial language resource. Two major datasets were employed as input resource to the
development of the lexical resource – United Kingdom and Irish Government Public
Service Catalogues. Given that the recall potential of the resource is directly linked to
the diversity of its entries, continued update to the lexical resource based on other
government public service catalogues is important. Using this language resource in the
information extraction task is aimed at enabling the automatic population of the public
service ontology using the information extracted from governmental public service
documents (different from public service catalogues) available in the form of standard
PDF documents or as web documents. We describe the lexicon construction algorithm
in Fig. 2. In summary, the construction starts with acquisition of the first list of the
Public Services Names and unique identifiers in a form of URLs from the first catalogue. Then the following public service catalogues are aligned to the existing index
based on similarity measures. The resulting structure is a simple tree in which parent
nodes are the automatically generated generic service name and child or leave nodes
are semantically related concrete service names obtained from the different public
service catalogues. The alignment procedure is repeated for consequent service catalogues. The generated abstract service names comprise keywords derived from names
of the child nodes.

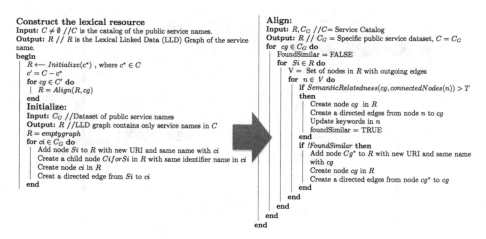

Fig. 2. Lexicon construction algorithm

4.3 Named Entity Recogniser

In this section we briefly explain our NER solution. The JAVA-based basic tool
developed incorporates the implementation of the "Public Services Spotter" for Social
Media with the domain-specific lexicon (represented in RDF) for Public Services
Names as the input dictionary. As shown in the results from initial validation (or
evaluation) of the tool in "spotting" public services related information (see example
Table 1), the dedicated solution outperforms the generic NER tools (Dbpedia

Table 1. NER performance comparison

Tweet	LEX NER	DBpedia	Alchemy
Ireland issuing passport cards for EU travel, like US/Canada. Can take photo from smartphone	Passport issuing: https://egov.deri.ie/PublicServices/Service/UK_PASSPORT_ISSUING Passport: https://egov.deri.ie/PublicServices/Service/CA_goc_passport	Passport cards: http://dbpedia.org/resource/Passport_card EU: http://dbpedia.org/resource/European_Union Canda: http://dbpedia.org/resource/Canada smartphone: http://dbpedia.org/resource/Smartphone	US/Canada: Country EU: Organization Ireland: Country
Why Rwanda Plans to Issue Biometric Passport - Rwanda will start issuing biometric passports to her citizens which	Passport: https://egov.deri.ie/PublicServices/Service/CA_goc_passport	Rwanda: http://dbpedia.org/resource/Rwanda biometric passports: http://dbpedia.org/resource/Biometric_passport	Rwanda: Country
@SenatorLesniak No hunting licence for ANYONE that hasn't completed a gun safety course.	https://twitter.com/christwords199/status/553672403046240256	hunting licence: https://egov.deri.ie/PublicServices/Service/UK_HUNTING_LICENCE	gun safety: http://dbpedia.org/resource/Gun_safety

Spotlight[12] and Alchemy API[13]) which hardly identified any public services. However, off-the-shelf solutions supply rich, contextual information for instance: location, organisation, persons (and more). The tools are also capable of providing statistics-based data, like "hot" topics and keywords. We argue that the final output of KEMC as a combination of Public Services names linked with miscellaneous information in a single semantic graph can deliver a very powerful tool for political Social Media data analytics. In particular, this enables creation of rich data stories with detailed information on where particular Public Services are being discussed and which certain political figures or organisations are usually mentioned around the topics in specific locations. Moreover certain main topics and keywords can be supplied together with sentiment analysis and popularity statistics. To visualise better the range of possibilities we consider a use case scenario in next section.

4.4 Scenario

The goal of this section is to demonstrate the use of KEMC solution through a use case scenario: John Smith (hypothetical character) is an Irish politician promoting

---

[12] https://github.com/dbpedia-spotlight/dbpedia-spotlight/wiki.

[13] http://www.alchemyapi.com/.

legislation introducing restrictions on medical card applicants' eligibility. John opens the e-Participation Analyser supported by KEMC. Based on his specific request, the interface generates a dynamic report of places in Ireland from which it appears that citizens express negative sentiment towards the healthcare services. From the information mined from Twitter (public service tweets detected by our NER solution) it is apparent that Galway City (location detected) has the highest rate of negative opinions (sentiment analysis) oscillating around the institution of University Hospital – UH and Merlin Park Hospital – MPH (organisation entities detected). Moreover common topics found are (through topic analysis): prenatal care, physiotherapy and medical card. John tries to identify the key arguments against his policy project therefore he explores the posts and discussions of highest popularity rank with negative sentiment associated with the medical card and public healthcare. After following selected discussions (represented in semantic web format - every posts and discussion is distinguished by unique URL) he realises that the negative opinions come mainly from UH and MPH not accepting the medical card for particular services (prenatal care and physiotherapy) therefore he engages into discussion with citizens on Twitter and explains that the issues mentioned by citizens are of local character (but will be addressed) and ensures citizens that the upcoming legislation will not bring any harm but rather improve the current set of services covered. Moreover now, since John knows that the "hot" topics detected around Public Healthcare Services in Ireland are closely related medical card (similarity measures and graph distance), he suggests relevant common strategy that should be developed in order to facilitate a solution for these problems. The use case scenario presented will be leveraged for real-world experimentation for KEMC deployment. We believe that the direct implication of the use of KEMC will be to enable government to interact with citizen-spaces on Social Media in a more selective, topic-relevant, efficient way and long-term, can contribute significantly to enhancing the delivery of the public services as a result of better understanding of citizen's needs and concerns; hence directly supporting the duality of e-Participation.

5 Discussion

In this paper we have briefly introduced the state-of-the-art use of social software (in particular Social Media) for e-Participation, focusing on the main trends. The last decade has seen a shift in e-Participation from simple Web 2.0 forums to more advanced platforms integrating Social Media like Facebook or Twitter. Social Media are by many folds more widely used by citizens than any e-Participation solution. Moreover, many people incorporated them into everyday activities as they are very easy to use [37] and indeed they became a spontaneous place for, every-day political discussions. Nevertheless, we argue that to date, the current e-Participation solutions do not unleash the full potential of Social Media analytics in the context of e-Government, essential to deal with significant channel-specific obstacles like information overload and varying content quality. The main challenge, which is the lack of dedicated analytical tools for e-Participation, renders most of the contemporary e-Participation solutions' performance insufficient to fully support the duality of e-Participation. Results from our work, in creating Knowledge Extraction and Management component as part of a holistic infrastructure for e-Participation, in a form a domain-specific NER solution powered by a Public Service Lexicon, provides first significant step towards building explicit connection between the sphere of government and citizen spontaneous discussions on Social Media, thus delivering the base to support duality of e-Participation. We show that dedicated solution outperforms the generic, of-the-shelf analytical solutions; therefore further development of custom solutions (that can follow our universal methodology) is a viable option for the advancement of e-Participation domain. We claim better universality and scalability of the automatically generated lexical resources (based on similarity measures) in comparison to Supervised-Learning-based solutions, which demand significant manual efforts on creating relevant resources. Moreover we claim better alignment of the resource delivered to specific e-Participation need. Nevertheless, we emphasise on the limitation of the resource, created explicitly for Irish and UK context. We demonstrate, through a specific use case scenario that a combination of the dedicated NER, supplied with rich contextual information provided by generic NER solutions can be a very powerful tool for e-Participation information analytics. The example use of KEMC for identifying Social Media discussions and posts related to concrete public services opens up a possibility for completely new set of capabilities for public services' citizen-perception evaluation, hence supporting future improvement and public service integration. Apart from the extensive works carried under WeGov project [13], we are not aware of any other significant attempt at applying advanced Social Media analytics to e-Participation. We acknowledge innovative work by Hagen et al. [38] on leveraging NLP technologies to analyse e-Petitioning content. However, we haven't found any approach that would try to combine and apply dedicated, scalable NER, supported by rich, automatically annotated domain-specific lexical resources, Semantic Web and Natural Language Processing technologies to address the duality of e-Participation.

6 Conclusion

Motivated by the need to provide the necessary step towards supporting the duality of e-Participation, we have presented a technical component – KEMC for extracting, consolidating and enriching (by linking) information from spontaneous discussions on Social Media as part of the comprehensive infrastructure for e-Participation design implementation, advancing the existing e-Participation methods and tools. Results from our work show immediate opportunities for developing and consolidating the domain-specific lexical resources, Semantic Web and NLP technologies into an analytical infrastructure for application to the context of e-Participation. While we have demonstrated theoretically the usefulness of the KEMC component, on the example of public healthcare service information matching supported by miscellaneous contextual information, more detailed and formal evaluations in different contexts are yet to be conducted. Next steps for the research include the implementation of special, information-visualisation-rich dashboards building upon developed analytical component to explain better the capabilities of the comprehensive infrastructure for e-Participation. This will be followed by a set of interviews with politicians and citizens in order to determine the usefulness of presented solution in reaching out the information about public services and potentially supporting the process of public services improvement. Future steps should also bring series of design and development iterations of the solution with applications of the component to other contexts of e-Participation to advance the domain of Social Media analytics for e-Government.

Acknowledgement. This work has been funded by EU Commission - Grant 645860 (ROUTE-TO-PA).

References

1. Sæbø, O., Rose, J., Skiftenesflak, L.: The shape of eParticipation: characterizing an emerging research area. Gov. Inf. Q. **25**, 400–428 (2008)
2. Chadwick, A.: Bringing e-democracy back in: why it matters for future research on e-governance. Soc. Sci. Comput. Rev. **21**, 443–455 (2003)
3. Porwol, L., Ojo, A., Breslin, J.: On the duality of e-participation – towards a foundation for citizen-led participation. In: Kö, A., Leitner, C., Leitold, H., Prosser, A. (eds.) EDEM 2013 and EGOVIS 2013. LNCS, vol. 8061, pp. 211–225. Springer, Heidelberg (2013)
4. Grishman, R.: Message understanding conference-6: a brief history. In: Proceedings of COLING 1996 (1996)
5. Porwol, L., Ojo, A., Breslin, J.: Harnessing the duality of e-participation. In: Proceedings of the 7th International Conference on Theory and Practice of Electronic Governance - ICEGOV 2013, pp. 289–298 (2013)
6. Reuter, C., Marx, A.: Social software as an infrastructure for crisis management - a case study about current practice and potential usage. In: Proceedings of 8th International ISCRAM Conference, pp. 1–10 (2011)
7. O'reilly, T.: What is web 2.0: design patterns and business models for the next generation of software. Commun. Strateg. **65**, 17–37 (2007)
8. Macintosh, A., Coleman, S., Schneeberger, A.: eParticipation: the research gaps. In: Macintosh, A., Tambouris, E. (eds.) ePart 2009. LNCS, vol. 5694, pp. 1–11. Springer, Heidelberg (2009)
9. Chang, A.: Leveraging Web 2.0 in Government. E-Government/Technology Series Leveraging Web 2.0 in Government
10. Panopoulou, E., Tambouris, E., Tarabanis, K.: eParticipation initiatives in Europe: learning from practitioners. In: Tambouris, E., Macintosh, A., Glassey, O. (eds.) ePart 2010. LNCS, vol. 6229, pp. 54–65. Springer, Heidelberg (2010)
11. Charalabidis, Y., Loukis, E.: Transforming Government Agencies' Approach to eParticipation through Efficient Exploitation of Social Media. In: ECIS 2011 (2011)
12. Agichtein, E., Castillo, C., Donato, D., Gionis, A., Mishne, G.: Finding high-quality content in social media. In: Proceedings of the 2008 International Conference on Web Search and Data Mining - WSDM 2008, p. 183 (2008)
13. Claes, A., Sizov, S., Angeletou, S., Taylor, S., Wandhoefer, T.: WeGOV project: where eGovernment meets the eSociety. In: Initial WeGov toolbox, pp. 1–65 (2010)
14. Effing, R., Van Hillegersberg, J., Huibers, T.: Social media and political participation: are Facebook, Twitter and YouTube democratizing our political systems? Electron. Participation **6847**, 25–35 (2011)
15. Moreira, A.M., Ladner, A.: E-Society and e-democracy. Media (2009)

16. Kuzma, J.: Asian Government Usage of Web 2.0 Social Media. Sites J. 20th Century Contemp. French Stud. 1–13 (2010)
17. Ashley, H., Corbett, J., Jones, D., Garside, B., Rambaldi, G.: Change at hand: web 2.0 for development. In: Participatory Learning and Action, vol. 59, pp. 8–20. IIED (2009)
18. Makinen, M., Kuira, M.W.: Social media and postelection crisis in Kenya. Int. J. Press/Polit. **13**, 328–335 (2008)
19. Gao, H., Barbier, G., Goolsby, R.: Harnessing the crowdsourcing power of social media for disaster relief. IEEE Intell. Syst. **26**, 10–14 (2011)
20. Berners-Lee, T., Hendler, J., Lassila, O.: The semantic web. Sci. Am. **5**, 28–37 (2001)
21. Schreiber, R., Swick, G.: Semantic web best practices and deployment working group (2006)
22. Frank, M., Eric, M.: RDF primer
23. Wimmer, M.A.: Ontology for an e-participation virtual resource centre. In: Proceedings of the 1st international conference on Theory and practice of electronic governance - ICEGOV 2007, p. 89 (2007)
24. Loutas, N., Lee, D., Maali, F., Peristeras, V., Tarabanis, K.: The semantic public service portal (S-PSP). In: Antoniou, G., Grobelnik, M., Simperl, E., Parsia, B., Plexousakis, D., De Leenheer, P., Pan, J. (eds.) ESWC 2011, Part II. LNCS, vol. 6644, pp. 227–242. Springer, Heidelberg (2011)
25. Ojo, A., Estevez, E., Janowski, T.: Semantic interoperability architecture for Governance 2.0. Inf. Polity **15**, 105–123 (2010)
26. Embley, D.W., Campbell, D.M., Smith, R.D., Liddle, S.W.: Ontology-based extraction and structuring of information from data-rich unstructured documents. In: Proceedings of the Seventh International Conference on Information and Knowledge Management - CIKM 1998, pp. 52–59. ACM Press, New York (1998)
27. Alani, H., Kim, S., Millard, D.E., Weal, M.J., Hall, W., Lewis, P.H., Shadbolt, N.: Web based Knowledge Extraction and Consolidation for Automatic Ontology Instantiation. In: proceedings of the Workshop on Knowledge Markup and Semantic Annotation at the second International Conference on Knowledge Capture (K-Cap 2003) (2003)
28. Bikel, D.M., Miller, S., Schwartz, R., Weischedel, R.: Nymble. In: Proceedings of the Fifth Conference on Applied Natural Language Processing, pp. 194–201. Association for Computational Linguistics, Morristown (1997)
29. Etzioni, O., Cafarella, M., Downey, D., Popescu, A.-M., Shaked, T., Soderland, S., Weld, D.S., Yates, A.: Unsupervised named-entity extraction from the web: an experimental study. Artif. Intell. **165**, 91–134 (2005)
30. Soderland, S.: Learning information extraction rules for semi-structured and free text. Mach. Learn. **34**, 233–272 (1999)
31. Dalvi, B., Cohen, W., Callan, J.: Websets: Extracting sets of entities from the web using unsupervised information extraction. In: Proceedings of the Fifth ACM International Conference on Web Search and Data Mining. ACM (2012)
32. Alfonseca, E., Manandhar, S.: An unsupervised method for general named entity recognition and automated concept discovery. In: Proceedings of the 1st International Conference on General WordNet, Mysore (2002)
33. Mccrae, J., Aguado-de-Cea, G., Buitelaar, P., Cimiano, P., Asunci, D., Gracia, J., Hollink, L., Tobias, M.D.S.: Interchanging lexical resources on the semantic web. Lang. Resour. Eval. **46**, 701–719 (2012)
34. Hevner, A., Chatterjee, S.: Design Research in Information Systems. Integrated Series in Information Systems, pp. 9–23. Springer, Boston (2010)
35. Peffers, K., Tuunanen, T., Rothenberger, M.A., Chatterjee, S.: A design science research methodology for information systems research. J. Manage. Inf. Syst. **24**, 45–77 (2007)

36. Gabrilovich, E., Markovitch, S.: Computing semantic relatedness using wikipedia-based explicit semantic analysis. In: IJCAI International Joint Conference on Artificial Intelligence, pp. 1606–1611 (2007)
37. Lane, M., Coleman, P.: Technology ease of use through social networking media. Technology 1–12 (2012)
38. Hagen, L., Harrison, T.M., Uzuner, Ö., Fake, T., Lamanna, D.: Introducing textual analysis tools for policy informatics: a case study of e-petitions. In: Proceedings of the 16th Annual International Conference on Digital Government Research, pp. 10–19 (2015)

Towards Continuous Collaboration on Civic Tech Projects: Use Cases of a Goal Sharing System Based on Linked Open Data

Shun Shiramatsu[1]([✉]), Teemu Tossavainen[1,2], Tadachika Ozono[1], and Toramatsu Shintani[1]

[1] Graduate School of Engineering, Nagoya Institute of Technology, Nagoya, Japan
{siramatu,ozono,tora}@nitech.ac.jp
[2] School of Science, Aalto University, Espoo, Finland
teemu.tossavainen@aalto.fi

Abstract. Civic hackathon is a participatory event for prototyping of innovative services through collaboration between citizens and engineers towards addressing social issues. Although continuous contributions are needed for improving the prototypes and for applying them to social issues, participants frequently stop contributions after the hackathon due to their day job. To address this problem, we applied our Web system, called GoalShare, which gathers linked open data (LOD) of hierarchical goals to address social issues, to civic hackathons held in the city of Nagoya in Japan. We compared goal structures between two situations. The results showed that goal structures input by team members themselves with enough instruction time were relatively detailed but varied widely among teams, and those input by a single GoalShare user with limited time remained at a simple overview level but had uniform level of detail. A more user-friendly interface usable without instruction is required for real-world situations.

Keywords: Linked open data · Civic tech · Hackathon · Public collaboration · Open innovation

1 Introduction

Coverage of local government services in Japan is at risk of shrinking due to ongoing social issues that threaten the sustainability of regional societies, e.g., the aging population, disaster risks, and dilapidated infrastructure. In this context, public collaboration between broad citizens, local government officers, local companies, experts, and engineers has become more important to address social issues. Actual instances have arisen of addressing social issues by utilizing open data and mobile applications [1] with smartphones, which are now widely used by citizens. *Civic Tech* refers to an activity for applying information technology to addressing social issues through collaboration between engineers, citizens, and local governments [2]. In Japan, the Civic Tech movement has been rapidly growing since around 2013.

© IFIP International Federation for Information Processing 2015
E. Tambouris et al. (Eds.): ePart 2015, LNCS 9249, pp. 81–92, 2015.
DOI: 10.1007/978-3-319-22500-5_7

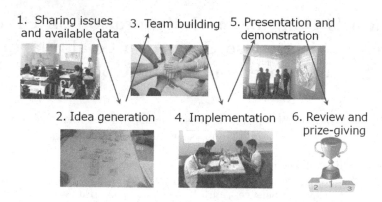

1. Sharing issues and available data   3. Team building   5. Presentation and demonstration

2. Idea generation   4. Implementation   6. Review and prize-giving

Fig. 1. Typical flow of civic hackathon

Collaboration between a wide range of citizens is needed for addressing social issues using a civic-tech approach because engineers alone cannot design solutions without background context and because stakeholder citizens alone cannot utilize information technology. For example, local community managers and local IT companies are desired to participate in civic tech projects. Public outreach of contextual information on project activities is indispensable for getting a broad range of citizens to participate. The outreach of visions and approaches to addressing social issues facilitates collaboration with newly-arrived participants.

We have been developing a Web application called GoalShare for sharing such contextual information about collaborative activities by using linked open data (LOD) consisting of social issues and their solutions as goal hierarchies [3,4]. In this paper, we describe our application of GoalShare to civic hackathons organized by civic tech communities. A hackathon, a coined term consisting of "hack" and "marathon," refers to a participatory event for prototyping services or applications in a short period such as over the weekend or for several hours. Civic hachathon [5] is a type of hackathon that is for prototyping civic tech applications. Figure 1 shows the typical flow of civic hackathons. Because outcomes of a civic hackathon in a short period tend to be an early prototype, continuous development is needed for applying the outcome to addressing real-world social issues. However, initial members frequently drop out of their project after a hackathon event due to the busyness of their day job. Contextual information on project activities needs to be disclosed and new participants need to be found to continue a project for improving the prototype as an outcome of a hackathon. Data on progress management and information sharing between project members should be reused for disclosing such contextual information to the public.

We applied GoalShare to two civic hackathons held in Nagoya city in Japan. This paper presents our qualitative analysis of difference in goal hierarchy data between a case of inputting by members of hackathon teams and a case of inputting by an audience who listens to the final presentation of hackathon teams. We seek improvement in GoalShare for collaborating on Civic Tech projects. Concretely, we consider a function for a tagging skill set to goal data and person data for matching a goal and a person.

2 Context of This Study

2.1 Civic Tech Organizations in Japan

Code for Japan[1], which is inspired by Code for America[2], was launched in 2013 [6]. Code for Japan collaborates with local organizations called "brigades" around the country. As of March 2015, 28 official brigades of Code for Japan have been registered. In this study, as we will describe later, GoalShare is used in civic hackathons organized by Code for Nagoya[3], which is one of the official brigades of Code for Japan. The Open Knowledge Foundation Japan[4] and Open Street Map Foundation Japan[5] are also active in Civic Tech in Japan.

On March 2015, Civic Tech Forum 2015[6] was held in Tokyo, and over 300 people participated. The invited speakers of the forum were from the brigades of Code for Japan, research institutes, local non-profit organizations, and local companies that are related to Civic Tech.

2.2 Systems for Sharing Issues and Ideas

Civic Tech Issue Finder[7] is a system for sharing civic tech issues and for supporting collaboration provided by Code for America. Issues in this service are stored as GitHub Issues with the tag "Help Wanted." GitHub[8] is a widely used Web repository for source code.

Knowledge Connector[9] provided by the Ministry of Economy, Trade and Industry of Japan and LinkData [7] is a Web platform for supporting commercialization of ideas that utilize open data [8]. It has a functionality for structuring events, organizations, ideas, datasets, issues, and subsidy programs.

Code for Kobe[10] and Code for Japan are also planning to develop a Web system consisting of a "person finder" and "project finder" for Civic Tech activities in Japan.

Although the focus of this paper is close to the purpose of these systems, the originality of GoalShare is goal hierarchies as scenarios for addressing issues linked with existing SNSs and geographical datasets based on the LOD framework. The interoperability of the LOD framework can provide the possibility to link the dataset of GoalShare with those of the aforementioned systems in the future.

---

[1] http://code4japan.org/.
[2] http://www.codeforamerica.org/.
[3] https://www.facebook.com/code4nagoya and http://code4.nagoya/.
[4] http://okfn.jp/.
[5] http://www.osmf.jp/.
[6] http://wired.jp/special/ctf2015/.
[7] https://www.codeforamerica.org/geeks/civicissues.
[8] https://github.com/.
[9] http://idea.linkdata.org/.
[10] https://www.facebook.com/codeforkobe.

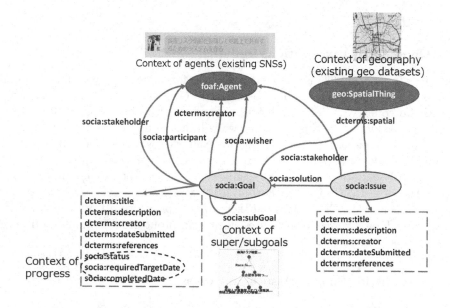

Fig. 2. Data model for public goal hirarchies as solutions of social issues

2.3   Our Previous Study: Data Model of Goal Hierarchy

We have developed a Web application called GoalShare[11], which has a backend dataset based on the data model shown in Fig. 2. The class socia: Issue represents the social issue, and socia: Goal represents the public goal as the solution of issues in this figure. The prefix "socia," which corresponds to the namespace http://data.open-opinion.org/socia-ns, is prepared for the data model that we designed. This data model is designed to satisfy the following requirements.

Context of Agents: Represented by the link to people or organizations, e.g., those who wish for the goal or who participate in it. URIs of existing social networking services (SNSs), such as Facebook and Twitter, are used for linking to agents.

Context of Geography: Represented by the link to geographical regions. URIs of existing geographical datasets, such as GeoNLP LOD[12] and GeoNames.jp[13], are used for linking to geographical regions.

Context of Super/Subgoals: Represented by the goal hierarchy consisting of the link to subgoals. Concrete subgoals close to actions are linked with abstract final goals.

Context of Progress: Represented by the properties for the deadline date and current status.

---

[11] http://radish.ics.nitech.ac.jp/goalshare/.
[12] http://geolod.ex.nii.ac.jp/.
[13] http://geonames.jp/.

The context of super/subgoals was represented by the property socia: sub-Goal enabling users to organize a goal hierarchy and to break down each goal into subgoals close to concrete actions. Concrete subgoals also enable citizens to consider which subgoal they can participate in or contribute to. Moreover, when concrete subgoals are not agreed on by multiple participants even if a final abstract goal is generally agreed on by them, visualizing their goal hierarchies has the potential to support building a consensus about their differences and to compromise on their collaboration. Furthermore, the properties socia: status and socia: completedDate for the context of progress enable users seamless reuse of data across managing progress and sharing the current status of the project with new participants or potential collaborators because the values of socia: status ("NotStarted," "InProgress," "Aborted," and "Completed") represented by colors of goal nodes can support grasping which subgoals are currently in progress, which ones are not started yet, and which ones are already completed. These features enable new participants to grasp a current context of projects easily.

3   Facilitating Collaboration on Civic Tech Project

There are two types of participation in Civic Tech: one is voluntary participation such as with aforementioned brigade organizations, and the other is participation with fellowship programs. The voluntary participants, in particular, sometimes drop out of their project due to the busyness of their day job. For continuous progress of civic tech projects based on voluntary participation, we need to open a gate for new participants with the transparency of contextual information about "what the project members are trying to do" and "which subgoals the new participant can contribute to." Such transparency enables new project members to make a match between themselves and partial subgoals of the project.

Here, we deal with the possibility of match making between new participant a and a concrete goal g, where g is a partial subgoal of an abstract supergoal g_0. In this situation, a and g could collaborate when they satisfy one or more of the following conditions.

(a) **Similarity of Goals.** Goals or issues focused on by agent a are similar to goal g.

(b) **Complementarity of Resources.** Agent a can provide resources (including skills as human resources) required to archive g.

In this study, we developed a function for matching a and g based on (a) the similarity of goals [3]. Many prototypes implemented in civic hackathons could have slept without brushing up because many civic hackathons have been held since around 2013 in Japan. If such a situation is true, the matchmaking function based on (a) can enable hackathon participants to reorganize their team for continuous acitivity. Moreover, we need to consider the matchmaking function based on (b) the complementarity of resources that was not dealt with in this study. In particular, we will consider the complementarity of skill sets for civic tech in a later section.

Table 1. Differences in situations between two hackathons

Hackathon	Barrier-free hackathon	ODD hackathon
Event period	Two days	One day
Time for instructing usage	About 15 min	Cannot be ensured (0 min)
Inputter	Team members themselves	A single participant trained in the usage of the GoalShare
Way to structure goal hierarchies	Structuring collaboratively between team members using sticky notes before inputting data to GoalShare	Structuring by a single inputter only with the GoalShare during five minutes of an outcome presentation for each team
Time for structuring goal hierarchies	About 45 min	5 min (except for a team participated in by the inputter)
Level of detail of goal hierarchies	Relatively detailed but vary widely among teams	Simple overview level but uniform level of detail (expect for the inputter's team)
Maximum and minimum count of goal nodes for each team	Max: 13, Min: 1	Max: 4, Min: 2 (expect for the inputter's team)

4   Trial Use in Civic Hackathons

We tried to apply the GoalShare to two actual civic hackathons; the Hackathon on Barrier-free Underground Mall at Nagoya Station[14] held at October 2014 and the Hackathon on International Open Data Day 2015 in Nagoya[15]. These hackathons were organized by the Code for Nagoya and the non-profit organization Lisra. Hereafter, the former one is called the barrier-free hackathon, and the latter one is called the ODD hackathon. The barrier-free hackathon was held on both days of a weekend. The goal hierarchies were input in a debate between members of each participating team themselves. On the other hand, the ODD hackathon was held on just one day. The goal hierarchies were input by a member of the audience for the final presentation of each team. These situations are summarized in Table 1.

Figures 4 and 5 show goal hierarchies accumulated in each hackathon. The blue nodes represent ongoing goals, and the orange ones represent not-yet-started goals. Both of the goal hierarchies have top goals that correspond to a given theme of the hackathons and the direct subgoals of the top goals that correspond to the final goals of participating teams in the hackathons.

4.1   Case of Barrier-Free Hackathon

In the barrier-free hackathon, members of four participating teams input goal hierarchy data of each team by themselves. After idea generation and team

---

[14] http://nagoya-bfree-hackathon.peatix.com/ (in Japanese).
[15] http://opendata-nagoya2015.peatix.com/ (in Japanese).

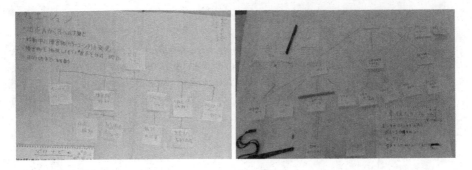

Fig. 3. Goal hierarchies written and structured by participants in the barrier-free hackathon

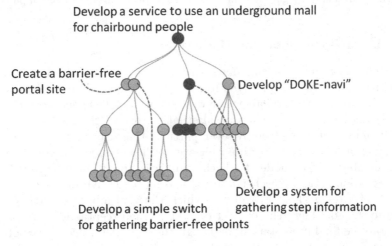

Fig. 4. Goal hierarchy gathered in barrier-free hackathon (translated from Japanese)

building, team members first wrote their goals for development on sticky notes and organized them into a hierarchy on a paper. Figure 3 shows examples of goal hierarchies created through debate between team members participating in the barrier-free hackathon. After creating the goal hierarchies consisting of sticky notes, they input the data into GoalShare. With consideration for ensuring time for development, an organizer of the barrier-free hackathon announced that subgoals after the fourth layers of the goal hierarchies on a paper could be omitted when inputting the subgoals into GoalShare.

As shown in Fig. 4, the minimum count of goal nodes for each team was one, and the maximum count was thirteen. Although this difference was affected by the context thats the team inputting minimum nodes consisted of foreign students and that the instruction about GoalShare was spoken in Japanese, this result indicates that data input by hackathon participants themselves tended not to be uniform in quality.

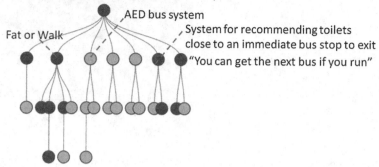

Fig. 5. Goal hierarchy gathered in ODD hackathon (translated from Japanese)

4.2 Case of Open Data Day Hackathon

In the ODD hackathon, the time for instruction of GoalShare and for inputting of goal hierarchies was not provided to avoid reducing time for implementation. The reason was that the available time was less in the ODD hackathon than that in the barrier-free hackathon. As an alternative, one of the audience members for the final presentation given by seven participating teams input the goal hierarchies of each team. This goal inputter was proficient in the use of GoalShare.

The number of goal nodes for each team was about three or four because the presentation time for each team was short (about five minutes), with the exception of a team "Fat or Walk" in which the goal inputter participated. It is because the goal hierarchy of "Fat or Walk," the exceptional team, was created before the final presentation. Although the goal hierarchies of the other six teams were commonly abstract and their socia: wisher properties tended to be anonymous, such outline information can be used for considering the participation in the project by new candidate participants. Moreover, the blue nodes, which represent the ongoing subgoal with the property socia: state, in the ODD hackathon were more numerous than those in the barrier-free hackathon. This result indicates that data gathering from the final presentation of the hackathon by a proficient user can be the second best solution in cases where hackathon events cannot provide time for discussion and planning.

5 Discussion: Towards Application to Real-World Situations

The aforementioned cases of trial use of the GoalShare indicate that a more user-friendly interface usable without instruction time is desired for real-world operations because organizing multiple days such a civic hackathon event is generally difficult. Because the main purpose of the civic hackathon is generally prototyping of an innovative service for social issues, the time for sharing goals

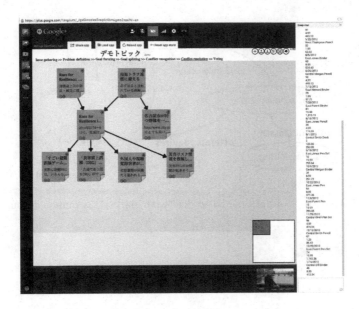

Fig. 6. The user interface designed using the metaphor of sticky notes

should not interfere with the time needed for development more than necessary. We are currently implementing a more intuitive user interface, shown in Fig. 6. This interface is designed using the metaphor of sticky notes, which is familiar to citizen participants in public workshops. This design of the user interface also considers remote and realtime co-authoring being implemented using the Google Hangout API.

Alternatively, a hybrid approach to inputting goal data through an interaction between team members and a proficient user in structuring goal hierarchies after the presentation time can be considered for improving data quality. Although goal hierarchies input only by team members themselves are not uniform, the process for structuring goals by themselves is valuable for sharing detailed scenarios for addressing social issues. To attract new collaborators into a team after an event, concrete subgoal trees as a scenario to address a socia issue should be shared with potential collaborators. An interaction between team members and a proficient user in structuring goal hierarchies can improve the quality of goal hierarchies, and it does not disrupt development if the interaction is conducted after the final presentation. Moreover, a function for generating summary text of a goal hierarchy is desired to be provided to enable potential collaborators to understand the team's approach.

Furthermore, recruiting new participants in the team building process (including after a hackathon event) needs complementarity of resources, e.g. a dataset or skill set, although we used GoalShare only just after team building in the aforementioned hackathon. We need to extend the data model shown in Fig. 2 to enable us to describe a skill set as human resources. Figure 7 shows an extension of the properties connected to socia: Goal class and foaf: Agent class. The class socia:

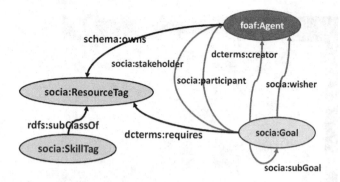

Fig. 7. Extension of data model to deal with skill set as human resources

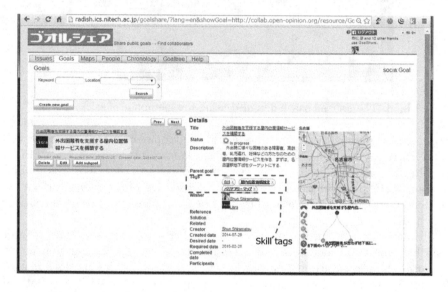

Fig. 8. Web interface of GoalShare extended to append skill tags

SkillTag represents the skill, and its super class socia: ResourceTag represents the general resource. The property dcterms: requires[16] connects with socia: Goal, and the aforementioned classes correponding to resources. Resources or skills owned by agents are represented by the property schema: owns[17].

Figure 8 shows our extended Web interface of GoalShare to enable users to add skill tags to each goal node, and Table 2 shows an example of the inheritance relationship between skills. Such interface and data structure can be used for matchmaking algorithms if a skill ontology can be prepared. Therefore, we need to consider how to build a skill ontology. For example, we will consider a subgraph extraction from general-purpose ontologies such as DBpedia[18] to build a skill ontology.

---

[16] http://purl.org/dc/terms/requires.
[17] http://schema.org/owns.
[18] http://dbpedia.org/.

Table 2. Examples of skill tag

Tag	Super concept
Android programming	Programming
GIS	Programming
Google maps	GIS
Open street map	GIS
Sensor	Android programming
Acceleration sensor	Sensor
Geomagnetic sensor	Sensor

6 Conclusion

We presented four requirements for designing a linked data model of goal hierarchies to facilitate collaboration in Civic Tech projects. We applied GoalShare to two actual civic hackathons held in Nagoya in Japan and qualitatively analyzed the differences in goal hierarchies between a case of inputting by members of hackathon teams and a case of inputting by an audience that listens to the final presentation of hackathon teams. These cases indicate that a more user-friendly interface usable without instruction time is desired for real-world situations. We presented a prototype of a more intuitive user interface designed using the metaphor of sticky notes, which are familiar to citizen participants in public workshops. Alternatively, to improve data quality, we considered a hybrid approach to inputting goal data through an interaction between team members and a proficient user in structuring goal hierarchies after the presentation time. Moreover, we considered an extension of our data model to deal with complementarity of skill sets that is important for Civic Tech, and we extended our Web interface for adding skill tags to each goal node.

In the future, we plan to integrate the similarity of goals and the complementarity of resources for improving the function to match citizens and Civic Tech projects. Moreover, we will apply a new intuitive user interface to goal input in the short final presentation of civic hackathons. The realtime co-authoring mechanism of the new user interface will be applied to an interaction between team members and a proficient user in structuring goal hierarchies after the presentation time.

Acknowledgments. This work was partially supported by a Grant-in-Aid for Young Scientists (B) (No. 25870321) from JSPS and a grant by the Nippon Foundation. We greatly appreciate the support by Prof. Nobuo Kawaguchi, Mr. Shinji Ichien, Mr. Takemi Nohara, partcipants in the hackathons, members of the NPO Lisra, and members of the Code for Nagoya.

References

1. Sandoval-Almazan, R., Gil-Garcia, J.R., Luna-Reyes, L.F., Luna, D.E., Rojas-Romero, Y.: Open government 2.0: citizen empowerment through open data, web and mobile apps. In: Proceedings of the 6th International Conference on Theory and Practice of Electronic Governance, pp. 30–33 (2012)
2. Pyrozhenko, V.: Implementing open government: exploring the ideological links between open government and the free and open source software movement. In: The 11th Annual Public Management Research Conference (2011)
3. Shiramatsu, S., Tossavainen, T., Ozono, T., Shintani, T.: A goal matching service for facilitating public collaboration using linked open data. In: Tambouris, E., Macintosh, A., Bannister, F. (eds.) ePart 2014. LNCS, vol. 8654, pp. 114–127. Springer, Heidelberg (2014)
4. Tossavainen, T., Shiramatsu, S., Ozono, T., Shintani, T.: Implementing a system enabling open innovation by sharing public goals based on linked open data. In: Ali, M., Pan, J.-S., Chen, S.-M., Horng, M.-F. (eds.) IEA/AIE 2014, Part II. LNCS, vol. 8482, pp. 98–108. Springer, Heidelberg (2014)
5. Johnson, P., Robinson, P.: Civic hackathons: innovation, procurement, or civic engagement? Rev. Policy Res. **31**(4), 349–357 (2014)
6. Takagi, S.: Research note: an introduction to the economic analysis of open data. Rev. Socionetwork Strat. **8**(2), 119–128 (2014)
7. Shimoyama, S., Gifford, D., Yoshida, Y., Toyoda, T.: http://Linkdata.org synergistically associating rdf data repository and application repository stimulates positive feedback of mutual developing data applications. In: The 2nd Joint International Semantic Technology Conference, December 2012 Poster and Demonstration Proceedings, JIST 2012 Nara, Japan, pp. 19–20 (2012)
8. METI: Supporting business creation with utilizing open data: Launch of knowledge connector (β version) (2014). http://www.meti.go.jp/press/2014/11/20141107002/20141107002.html (in Japanese)

Evaluation

Citizen-to-Citizen vs. Citizen-to-Government eParticipation in Uganda: Implications for Research and Practice

Wairagala Wakabi(✉) and Åke Grönlund

Department of Informatics, Örebro University, Örebro, Sweden
{wairagala.wakabi,ake.gronlund}@oru.se

Abstract. The use of Information and Communication Technologies (ICT) is growing globally, as is interest in the use of digital technologies to improve citizens' participation in governance. In African countries, where ICT use remains low and where there is a democratic deficit, the nature and extent of citizens' participation via ICT is unknown. Based on a print questionnaire with 322 internet users in Uganda, this paper compares citizen-to-citizen (C2C) participation and citizen-to-government (C2G) participation, examines the factors that hinder greater C2C and C2G online participation, and explores the implications for greater eParticipation in future. For effective eParticipation, the majority of Ugandan internet users need to become more active as creators of online content, as well as conversationalists and critics. Results show that regardless of whether it is engagements among citizens or between citizens and leaders, most citizens are spectators.

Keywords: Uganda · eParticipation · Citizen participation · Online participation

1 Introduction

Growing recognition of the role that Information and Communication Technologies (ICT) can play in social, political and economic transformation is not always matched by research on the utility of digital technologies, notably in African countries. The state of the art of e-government in Africa is poorly documented, and only such research has only been conducted in a quarter of the countries on the continent [1]. Likewise, empirical evidence on the use of ICT in governance in East Africa is limited despite growing interest and investment in this area [2]; and throughout sub-Saharan Africa, there are few examples of direct political action facilitated by mobile devices and networks [3].

Similarly, a review of literature on ICT and participation in Africa concluded that although there was much excitement and optimism about the role of ICT in governance, the evidence of actual impact was thin [4]. In America and Europe, research abounds on how ICT is enabling citizens to participate in various governance processes. The growing ICT use in Uganda could offer an avenue for addressing aspects of the country's democracy deficit. However, numerous obstacles to eParticipation in Uganda have been identified by previous research such as [3, 5, 6]. This creates the

© IFIP International Federation for Information Processing 2015
E. Tambouris et al. (Eds.): ePart 2015, LNCS 9249, pp. 95–107, 2015.
DOI: 10.1007/978-3-319-22500-5_8

need for research to understand the nature and extent of, and obstacles to, online participation becomes imperative. This paper investigates the differences between the ways ordinary citizens engage online with other citizens and with political leaders, as well as the primary impediments to greater use of ICT by citizens to engage with political leaders and with other citizens. The research fills a gap concerning the nature of and challenges to eParticipation in a developing country with a democracy deficit, distinguishing between citizen-to-citizen and citizen-to-government engagements. It is important to make this distinction because with the emergence of Web 2.0 platforms supporting eParticipation, citizens have the potential to become the main actors of eParticipation activities, which necessitates a research shift of focus from government to citizens and other stakeholders [7]. Moreover, in authoritarian countries, citizens tend to have scarce connections to their government and mostly interact with other citizens on political matters [5].

2 Background and Motivation

Internet access in Africa stands at 20 %, while mobile access is 69 %, according to 2014 numbers from the International Telecommunications Union. Growing use of ICT makes it worth exploring its role as a tool for participation. eParticipation is defined as the use of ICT to support information provision and "top-down" engagement i.e. government-led initiatives, or "ground-up" efforts to empower citizens, civil society organizations and other democratically constituted groups to gain the support of their elected representatives [8]. The purpose of eParticipation is to increase citizens' abilities to participate in digital governance [9]. Governance processes that comprise participation may concern administration, service delivery, decision making and policy making [10] and can take place within the formal political process by means such as voting, or outside it by means of political activism [11]. A literature review of various models on eParticipation [9, 11–14], shows that common features of participation include Informing, Consulting, Involving, Engagement, Empowerment, and Collaboration. Seeking news and information, joining online networks and political conversations also constitute eParticipation activities [15]. In drawing the link between media use and participation, the role of ICT as a communications channel and an enabler of online networking has been noted [16], while social network sites (SNS) have been noted as a great source for political news and a way of influencing contacts for the politically-inclined individuals [17].

  With 27 African countries under an authoritarian regime, 13 under regimes that have both democratic and autocratic elements, and a further nine characterized as flawed democracies [18], the possibility to advance democratic governance and citizen participation through eParticipation becomes compelling. However, there is a paucity of literature on the nature and utility of eParticipation in Africa. Equally, there is a grey area regarding security concerns in using ICT in political processes. Given the poor state of democracy in many African countries, there is widespread self-censorship by citizens due to fear of reprisals for expressing opinions that state authorities find objectionable [5, 19, 20]. Freedom House's *Freedom on the Net Report* 2013 report ranks Uganda, the focus of this study, as 'partly free'. An example of the limits of freedom is that in 2013 a cabinet minister announced that the country would establish a social media monitoring centre "to weed out those who use [the web] to damage the government and people's reputation". Moreover, citizens in Uganda have become skeptical about their ability to impact political change, as seen in a decline in voter turnout [3]. President Yoweri Museveni, who grabbed power via a guerrilla war in 1986, has been president for 29 years, and is accused of condoning corruption, stifling the opposition, and harassing independent media. The Government has in the past ordered service providers to block access to SMS services, Facebook and Twitter in order to deny the opposition an opportunity to mobilize supporters for anti-government protests.

Indubitably, ICT is increasingly being used in political processes in Africa, including for promoting human rights monitoring [4], in election campaigns and for monitoring elections [3, 21], and for promoting transparency and accountability in government operations [6, 22]. ICT is helping to amplify citizens' voices, increasing civic awareness and empowering citizens to monitor the delivery of services [23–25]. The spread of mobile phones, crowdsourcing technologies, and social networks have particularly enabled messages to be amplified, information flows to be accelerated, and new spaces to be opened up for the involvement of individuals and communities [26]. In Kenya, social networks act as communication spaces that promote democracy through individuals' "articulation of democratic ideas" [22]. Research has found that in Uganda and East Africa, some social accountability initiatives that use ICT are giving voice to individuals who otherwise would not participate in community affairs, improving citizens' civic skills and helping to hold local leaders and service providers accountable [4, 27, 28].

Many obstacles stand in the way of meaningful eParticipation in Africa, including low levels of literacy (both informational and ICT), high costs of accessing ICT, shortages of electricity. In Uganda, where the present study was conducted, only 23 % of the population uses the internet relative to 19 % for sub-Saharan Africa, 65 % in the Americas, 75 % in Europe, 41 % in Arab States, 32 % in Asia and the Pacific [29]. Information illiteracy hampers the efficient adoption and utilization of ICT on the continent [30].

However, Gagliardone et al. noted that in spite of the refrain common in literature on eParticipation in Africa that access to ICT will spur particular democratic behaviours and political and democratic outcomes, it evades to evaluate how particular cultural and sociological contexts drive ICT use [4]. A study has found that Kenyan citizens had no trust or confidence in using mobiles for communicating with government and service providers [31]. In Uganda, citizen-to-citizen participation is the predominant form but still at low levels, while citizen-to-government participation is negligible [5]. This is primarily due to perceived risks of retribution and intimidation for expressing a particular opinion or supporting a political cause. An analysis of citizens' motivations for utilising ICT in citizen participation and democracy showed that despite widespread awareness of ICT-based tools for participation, a significant proportion of Ugandan citizens preferred non-ICT spheres for engaging in democratic processes [32].

There is under-utilization of ICT for the provision of efficient government services in Africa [33], while bandwidth is insufficient to spur efficient online service delivery. Also, most eGovernance initiatives in many countries are largely dependent on external funding, which put their sustainability into question [34]. Lack of financial sustainability, as well as bad design, poor implementation, and political interference were noted as primary factors that prevented ICT-for-governance projects in Kenya, Tanzania and Uganda from moving beyond the pilot phase [6]. A study on the participation platform Uganda Watch found that user concerns that hindered greater use by citizens were related to costs, trust, and safety [3].

In South Africa, too, the public has a generally poor opinion of government services [35]. An analysis of the Facebook pages of South Africa's two leading political parties found that the parties did not participate in political discussions online and when they posted information on the sites, it was to impart knowledge and information, and not to engage in a conversation with the public [36]. Meanwhile, a survey of 1,044 South African students found that although they had a considerable social relation engagement online, they did not engage politically online [37].

Ochara argues that under the alienating conditions of digital exclusion in Africa, there is an evolution of public administration towards a technocracy and increasing the efficiency of government bureaucracy through "managerialization", which reinforces digital exclusion and thus hinders effective eParticipation [38]. Drawing on data from 20 African countries, Isaksson argued that the "lack of resources" hypothesis does a poor job at explaining (the lack of) political participation in Africa, as poorer citizens and people with little time on their hands were more likely to participate [39].

This brief literature review shows that the nature of eParticipation in Africa is not well studied. It also shows that many factors hamper eParticipation in Africa, and that in countries where there is a democracy deficit, the activities which citizens participate in are likely to be constrained. Generating knowledge on these issues is the focus of this paper. It is particularly concerned with Uganda, as the nature of participation and the role of social media in enabling participation in authoritarian, developing country contexts remains an under-studied issue. The Arab spring, for one, provided some evidence of the role social media such as Facebook, Twitter and YouTube can play in creating safe communication channels for citizens to coordinate collective opposition, to express their dissent in the public sphere [40–42], and to gather and spread information to counter the propaganda and apparatus of the repressive state [43, 44]. Social media generally serve to reduce transaction costs for protest organizers and present rapid and powerful channels for disseminating messages and images [45]. Nonetheless, it has been suggested that the role of ICT in instigating, organizing and reporting on socio-political change in the Arab uprising may have been overstated [46–48].

3   Research Questions and Methodology

In order to understand the nature of participation and the factors that motivate engagement among citizens and with public officials, this research sought to answer the following questions:

1. What is the difference between the way individuals engage online with other citizens and with political leaders?
2. What are the key impediments to greater use of ICT by citizens to engage with political leaders and with other citizens?

A survey was conducted between June and October 2014 through physical administration of a pre-tested questionnaire among 322 internet users in nine districts of Uganda – Lira, Gulu, Iganga, Mayuge, Mbale, Mpigi, Masaka, Kabarole and Kasese. The questionnaire consisted of 20 questions, which were based on the review of participation models and the various activities they entail. Respondents, who included both people who were members of online political groups and those who were not, were asked about their informational and ICT skills and needs; and frequency of use of different ICT tools and services. These included Google and other search engines, Email (including for sharing photos and documents as attachments), contributing to online discussion groups/chats, use of social media such as Twitter, Whatsapp, Facebook, and MySpace, SMS on mobile phone, blogging, downloading documents and media, and video conferencing.

There were also questions on the perceived usefulness of ICT for monitoring of government programmes and public services delivery and whether respondents used ICT to monitor or report on public services delivery. Other questions related to the ways and frequency with which respondents use ICT to engage with other citizens and with duty bearers (government officials, public services organisations) on issues of community or national concern (social, political, economic).

Interviewer-administered questionnaires have the advantage that unclear questions can be clarified to the respondent and open-ended questions can be used to collect a range of possible responses [19]. Furthermore, since our research was about a subject many people found sensitive, having face-to-face interviews helped create trust about the identity and intentions of the researchers, which may have been difficult if the research was conducted through email, Skype or online survey tools. However, in a society where citizens fear that expressing certain political opinions could attract reprisals, and since the research was about a politically related issue, this may have affected the nature of some of the responses relative to those that could have been provided via a more anonymous survey. This was minimised by assuring survey respondents about the anonymity of their contributions.

Responses to survey questions were coded to generate statistical descriptions of the different datasets representing the various responses received. Qualitative responses were analyzed and interpreted with a focus on what was specific to the question, unique to the respondent or deviant from the other responses received for the same question. The subjective descriptions given by respondents in the open-ended questions provided a deeper contextual picture of the statistical data generated from quantitative responses.

4 Results

Profile of Respondents and Proficiency in Using ICT. Fifty-nine percent of the respondents were male, 41 % female. Ages 18-24 comprised 41 % of the sample while 38 % were in the 25–34 age bracket. The majority (66 %) were educated to university level holding either diplomas or degrees. The mobile phone was the primary tool for access to the internet for 45 % of those surveyed, followed by desktop and laptop computers at home or work (29 %).

Respondents were asked about their knowledge of ICT tools and services and proficiency in using them. Social media emerged as the top tool most survey participants (79 %) had good or excellent knowledge and proficiency in using, followed by Short Messaging Services (SMS) at 76 %, and search engines at 73 % (Table 1).

Table 1. Rate the level of your knowledge and proficiency in using the following technology tools and services

Tool/service	Knowledge and proficiency in use				
	None	Poor	Workable	Good	Excellent
Google and other search engines	3 %	9 %	15 %	41 %	32 %
Email (including sharing photos and documents as attachments)	3 %	8 %	17 %	44 %	28 %
Contribute to online discussion groups/chats	11 %	10 %	21 %	38 %	20 %
Use of social media (Twitter, Whatsapp, Facebook, Myspace, etc.)	5 %	4 %	12 %	40 %	39 %
SMS on mobile	3 %	8 %	13 %	35 %	41 %
Blogging	38 %	18 %	19 %	17 %	8 %
Downloading files (documents and media)	7 %	12 %	18 %	38 %	25 %
Video conferencing (Skype, Google plus etc.)	20 %	20 %	19 %	29 %	12 %

Usefulness of ICT for Social Accountability. Eighty eight percent of respondents agreed that it was faster, effective and more productive to use ICT for monitoring government programmes. In a separate question about the use of ICT to contact government officials, 68 % of respondents agreed that ICT would make it easier to communicate with public officials; only 15 % disagreed. These results showed a high perception about the potential of ICT to enhance interactions between citizens and leaders. It followed then that when respondents were asked whether the "use of ICT makes monitoring of public services easier and simple", 78 % agreed. However, only a third of respondents (31 %) were actually involved in social accountability, which indicated a disconnect between the positive perceptions most respondents held of ICT use and whether they went ahead to engage in ICT-enabled social accountability.

How Citizens Use ICT to Engage with Other Citizens. Forty-three per cent of the respondents engaged with other citizens on issues of community and national concern through posting social media updates on Facebook and Twitter. This was followed by 39 % who shared concerns through text messages and seeking information and news (Table 2).

Table 2. In what ways and how often do you use ICT to engage with other citizens on issues of community or national concern (social, political, economic, etc.)?

Form of engagement with fellow citizens	Frequency of engagement				
	Always	Often	Sometimes	Rarely	Never
Emailing information (including forwarding documents)	23 %	20 %	25 %	15 %	17 %
Posting social media updates (Facebook and Twitter)	43 %	18 %	21 %	9 %	9 %
Participating in politics-related online discussions	13 %	14 %	20 %	25 %	29 %
Mobilizing via SMS	26 %	16 %	21 %	19 %	19 %
Participating in radio/TV debates (live call ins, SMS strips)	13 %	8 %	21 %	24 %	34 %
Writing in the local press or community newsletters	9 %	10 %	13 %	22 %	46 %
Seeking information and news	39 %	21 %	22 %	11 %	8 %
Commenting on other's posts	33 %	26 %	25 %	8 %	9 %
Sending/Receiving text messages	39 %	19 %	20 %	12 %	10 %

Table 3. In what ways and how often do you use ICT to engage with duty bearers on issues of community or national concern (social, political, economic)?

Form of engagement with duty bearers	Frequency of engagement				
	Always	Often	Sometimes	Rarely	Never
Email requesting information/documents	18 %	17 %	25 %	17 %	25 %
Following duty bearers on social media (Facebook and Twitter)	22 %	18 %	26 %	18 %	16 %
Engaging via social media (Facebook and Twitter)	26 %	17 %	29 %	13 %	15 %
Participating in online discussion forums with leaders/public officials	11 %	10 %	21 %	27 %	31 %
Participating in radio/TV debates (live call ins, SMS strips)	11 %	9 %	22 %	24 %	34 %
Commenting on political websites	9 %	8 %	26 %	24 %	32 %
Seeking information and news	33 %	21 %	24 %	11 %	12 %

How ICT is Used to Engage with Political Leaders. Table 3 shows that seeking information and news was the most frequent form of engagement with duty bearers (54 %). Social media was the second most commonly used form of engagement with duty bearers at 43 %. Among the least forms of engagement were participating in live call-in and SMS strips on radio and TV debates, commenting on political websites, and participating in online discussion forums.

Factors Hindering Greater Use of ICT to Engage with Citizens and Duty Bearers. The main factors that most hindered greater use of ICT to engage with fellow citizens included literacy (66 %), language (62 %), cost (59 %), and lack of awareness of availability of tools. 69 % of respondents stated that security concerns did not hinder use of ICT for engagement with citizens. Regarding hindrances to greater use of ICT to engage with duty bearers, security concerns emerged top at 61 %, followed by low confidence in receiving feedback and responses (45 %). Cost emerged as the third factor (38 %).

5 Discussion and Conclusions

The results showed a high belief in the utility of ICT to make it easier and simple for citizens to engage with leaders and with citizens, with nearly half of the respondents (88 %) agreeing that ICT could enable swift and more effective social accountability. This was because most respondents had experience of using ICT and had first-hand experience of its potential to improve the ease, speed and efficiency of interactions between scattered individuals and groups. But most respondents feared reprisals for expressing political opinions, particularly those against a president in power for 29 years, and whose government has stifled freedom of expression online and offline. This fear factor, combined with the widespread perception that leaders are extremely unresponsive to issues raised by citizens, worked greatly against eParticipation.

There was markedly high proficiency in using technologies, with 79 % reporting good or excellent proficiency in using social media, plus very frequent use of Facebook, in particular. Relative to other social media such as Instagram and Twitter, Facebook has a longer legacy in Uganda, which partly explains its position as the most popular SNS in Uganda. Another factor that works in its favour is that subscribers on two of Uganda's biggest telecom services providers – MTN and Orange Telecom – can use the so-called 'Facebook Zero' which allows a subscriber free access to a text-only version of this social network, update their status, and read and comment on posts. The user is only charged if they make downloads, stream audio or video, or upload pictures. Facebook and Twitter were the most used tools for eParticipation.

There were notable differences in the way individuals related with other citizens and with leaders. For citizen-to-citizen communication, posting social media updates was the most pursued activity, followed by seeking information and news, emailing information (including forwarding documents), and commenting on other citizens' posts. The least interest was paid to participating in politics-related online discussions, participation in radio and TV debates, and writing in the local press or in community newsletters. There was much less engagement between citizens and leaders. Seeking information and news, following leaders on Facebook and Twitter, and engaging via social media were the most prominent activities. Worth noting is that the first two activities are unlikely to expose one to reprisals or even to show their stand on a political issue. Many citizens therefore had trust that they could engage in them without compromising their safety. It was also telling that commenting on political websites was the least engaged in of the activities respondents were asked about, followed by participating in online discussion forums with leaders, and participation in radio and

TV debates. Thus, where in C2C we see more actively engaged citizens (postings SNS updates, seeking and sharing information, commenting on other citizens posts), in C2G the citizens tend to be spectators or followers, engaging on fewer ICT platforms and in less active areas.

These results show a desire to engage with the leaders on the one hand and, on the other, a detachment from them and from politics. The reasons for not engaging were telling too: with leaders it was security concerns first, then lack of trust in the engagement resulting into any change or citizens receiving a response to issues they raised; and third, was cost. With C2C, security concerns were less prominent – in fact, 69 % stated that security concerns did not hinder their engagement with other citizens. The implication here is that for as long as leaders remain unresponsive to issues raised by citizens, and provided citizens have a fear of reprisals for expressing opinions online, eParticipation will remain minimal, in particular as concerns the citizen-to-government relation.

The major reasons cited by previous research, such as by Hellström [3], Grönlund and Wakabi [5], and Zanello and Maassen [6], such as high cost and low trust, were validated by this research. Other common factors cited in the literature that are related to accessibility, affordability, and illiteracy were also borne out by this research. The place of unresponsive government officials, fear of reprisals and self-censorship are not well articulated or studied in the previous literature but emerged as the major impediment to eParticipation in this study, notably by those for whom access and ICT skills were not problematic. A fear of reprisals was entrenching a widespread culture of self-censorship (as previously found by Gagliardone et al., CIPESA, and Laverty [5, 19, 20]) and this was further negating participation in both the C2C and C2G contexts. Moreover, the engagement of ordinary citizens with leaders depends not only on the citizens' wish to do so but also on the availability of engagement mechanisms (not just lack of awareness of their existence). With Ugandan political leaders having a negligible, and often perfunctory, online presence, C2G engagement cannot go far.

For effective eParticipation, the majority of Ugandan internet users need to become more active as creators of online content, and as conversationalists and critics. These results show that regardless of whether it is engagements among ordinary citizens or between citizens and leaders, most citizens are inactive, and either they are spectators or engage in passive activities. Only a few citizens fall in the active participation category yet these would be the ones to push most of the needed citizen-to-government participation that would enhance good governance.

6   Conclusion

This research has found that ICT has enabled only a fraction of connected Ugandans to participate and they are doing this in a few domains, and rarely with political leaders. The much-touted benefits of eParticipation in amplifying voices and raising civic awareness as advanced by Subhajyoti [23], Arpit [24] and Woro and Supriyanto [25] or enabling citizens to "articulate democratic ideas" as was found by Ochara's study in Kenya [38], are hardly visible in the Ugandan case. And with few citizens engaging with political leaders, ICT is not living up to its potential to raise government transparency and accountability, to promote human rights monitoring, and to accelerate information flows between citizens and leaders.

This research has produced empirical evidence on the nature of eParticipation in Uganda, a developing country with a democratic deficit. It has developed an understanding of both citizen-to-citizen and citizen-to-government participation. The results tell us that citizens see more benefit in engaging with other citizens than with leaders. It is safer, more fulfilling in terms of the gratifications which citizens derive from engaging with other citizens, as opposed to the non-responsiveness of leaders and other duty bearers to concerns raised by citizens. There is also citizens' perceived inability to change the status quo even if they engaged public officials, which has dulled citizens' appetite for C2G engagements.

Furthermore, this research has produced empirical results on the factors that make citizens shun eParticipation even when they are aware of the benefits which could result from their online participation. On the balance, the fears and frustrations that citizens have outweigh the benefits of eParticipation. In most instances, these fears are not lived but are based on perceptions or the experiences of others. The sum total of this is that if these fears are not addressed, the great majority of Ugandans, including those with ample access to ICT, and who are aware of the benefits of online participation, will for many years remain out of the fold of eParticipation. Citizen-to-citizen participation will likely grow, as it faces fewer hurdles that are also easier to navigate in the short term relative to the hurdles to engagements between citizens and the government. In the circumstances, what are the implications for eParticipation in Uganda? More efforts are needed to deepen citizen-to-citizen engagements because if citizens' skills, trust and experience in this area is cultivated, in future these skills and experience will form the basis for their eParticipation with government.

Going forward, there is need for more research to understand better the needs and motivations of the more active citizens, particularly those who, in spite of the factors ranged against C2G engagement, still participate. That could help find ways to bring into the actives fold many citizens who currently are inactive. Other research that helps to bring more citizens to participate, in spite of the obstacles observed in Uganda, would be welcome. Larger scale studies in Uganda and similar countries to develop a keener understanding of how citizens use ICT more gainfully with other citizens and with government officials, in low-income countries with a democracy deficit is equally needed.

Acknowledgements. We wish to thank the Collaboration on International ICT Policy in East and Southern Africa (CIPESA) for supporting this research. We are also grateful for Ashnah Kalemera's support in analysing the data.

References

1. Dombeu, F., Vincent, J., Nelson, R.: African e-government research landscape. Afr. J. Inf. Syst. **6**(3), Article 2 (2014)
2. Sika, V.: Promoting citizen participation using low-tech. Upcoming presentation to the Conference for Democracy & Open Government, Danube Krems University, Austria, May 2015

3. Hellström, J.: Crowdsourcing as a tool for political participation? The case of Uganda watch. Int. J. Public Inf. Syst. **2015**, 1 (2015)

4. Gagliardone, I., Kalemera, A., Kogen, L., Nalwoga, L., Stremlau, N., Wakabi, W.: In search of local knowledge on ICTs in Africa. CGCS, University of pennyslvania. http://www.global.asc.upenn.edu/app/uploads/2015/01/In-Search-of-Local-Knowledge-on-ICTs-in-Africa1.pdf (2015)

5. Grönlund, Å., Wakabi, W.: Citizens' use of new media in authoritarian regimes: case study of Uganda. Electron. J. Inf. Syst. Dev. Countries **67**(1), 1–23 (2015)

6. Zanello, G., Maassen, P.: Strengthening citizen agency and accountability through ICT. Public Manage. Rev. **13**(3), 363–382 (2011)

7. Medaglia, R.: eParticipation research: a longitudinal overview. In: Tambouris, E., Macintosh, A., de Bruijn, H. (eds.) ePart 2011. LNCS, vol. 6847, pp. 99–108. Springer, Heidelberg (2011)

8. Macintosh, A., Whyte, A.: Towards an evaluation framework for eParticipation. Transf. Gov. People Process Policy **2**(1), 16–30 (2008)

9. Sæbø, Ø., Rose, J., Flak, L.: The shape of eParticipation: characterizing an emerging research area. Gov. Inf. Q. **25**(3), 400–428 (2008)

10. Avdic, A., Hedström, K., Rose, J., Grönlund, Å. (eds.): Understanding eParticipation: Contemporary PhD eParticipation Research in Europe. Örebro University, Örebro (2007)

11. Sanford, C., Rose, J.: Characterizing eParticipation. Int. J. Inf. Manage. **27**(6), 406–421 (2007)

12. Grönlund, Å.: ICT is not participation is not democracy – eParticipation development models revisited. In: Macintosh, A., Tambouris, E. (eds.) ePart 2009. LNCS, vol. 5694, pp. 12–23. Springer, Heidelberg (2009)

13. Kalampokis, E., Tambouris, E., Tarabanis, K.: A domain model for eParticipation. In: Third International Conference on Internet and Web Applications and Services, pp. 25–30 (2008)

14. Grönlund, Å.: Connecting eGovernment to real government - the failure of the un eParticipation index. In: Janssen, M., Scholl, H.J., Wimmer, M.A., Tan, Y.-H. (eds.) EGOV 2011. LNCS, vol. 6846, pp. 26–37. Springer, Heidelberg (2011)

15. Tambouris, E., Liotas, N., Kaliviotis, D., Tarabanis, K.: A framework for scoping eParticipation. In: Proceedings of the 8th Annual International Conference on Digital Government Research, pp. 288–289 (2007)

16. Cullen, R., Sommer, L.: Participatory democracy and the value of online community networks: an exploration of online and offline communities engaged in civil society and political activity. Gov. Inf. Q. **28**(2), 148–154 (2011)

17. Gustafsson, N.: The subtle nature of Facebook politics: Swedish social network site users and political participation. New Media Soc. **14**(7), 1111–1127 (2012)

18. The Guardian: Power in Africa: democracy mapped. http://www.theguardian.com/global-development-professionals-network/ng-interactive/2015/feb/25/democracy-africa-maps-data-visualisation (2015)

19. CIPESA: State of Internet Freedoms in East Africa. http://www.cipesa.org/?wpfb_dl=76 (2014). Accessed 25 Oct 2014

20. Laverty, A.R.: The Missing Connection: ICTs and Democracy in Africa. UCLA: African Studies 0044 (2012)

21. Kretchun, N.: Will Kenya's digitally engaged have an effect on this election? (2013). http://www.intermedia.org/will-kenyas-digitally-engagedhave-an-effect-on-this-election/

22. Ndavula, J.O., Mberia, H.K.: Social networking sites in Kenya: trigger for non-institutionalized democratic participation. http://www.ijbssnet.com/journals/Vol_3_No_13_July_2012/37.pdf (2012)

23. Subhajyoti, R.: Reinforcing accountability in public services: an ICT enabled framework. Transf. Gov. People Process Policy **6**(2), 135–148 (2012)
24. Arpit, B.: E-Government and social media as openness and anti-corruption strategy. Res. J. Manage. Sci. **1**(1), 48–52 (2012)
25. Woro, J.S., Supriyanto, S.: Enhancing trust, transparency and accountability in the local development process. Int. J. Adm. Sci. Organ. **20**(1), 36–43 (2013)
26. Coyle, D., Meier, P.: New technologies in emergencies and conflicts: the role of information and social networks. http://www.unfoundation.org/news-and-media/publications-and-speeches/new-technologies-emergencies-conflicts.html (2009)
27. Asiimwe, E., Wakabi, W., Grönlund, Å.: Using technology for enhancing transparency and accountability in low resource communities: experiences from Uganda. In: ICT for Anti-Corruption, Democracy and Education in East Africa. Spider ICT4D Series No. 6 (2013)
28. Wamala, C.: Empowering local people and communities to monitor districts services delivery through ICTs: results and lessons learned. http://spidercenter.org/polopoly_fs/1.162451.1389618325!/menu/standard/file/Results%20WOUGNET%20December%202013.pdf (2013)
29. ITU: The world in 2014: facts and figures. http://www.itu.int/en/ITU-D/Statistics/Documents/facts/ICTFactsFigures2014-e.pdf (2014)
30. Tilvawala, K., Myers, M.D., Andrade, A.D.: Information literacy in Kenya. Electron. J. Inf. Syst. Dev. Countries **39**(1), 1–11 (2009)
31. Moraa, H., Salim, A., Nduati, L.: Technology in solving society's water problems in Kenya. iHUB Research. http://research.ihub.co.ke/uploads/2012/july/1343057495__796.pdf (2012)
32. CIPESA: Uganda: user and non-user profiles and their [de] motivations for utilizing ICTs in citizen participation and monitoring of democracy. http://www.cipesa.org/?wpfb_dl=64 (2012)
33. Asogwa, B.E.: The state of e-government readiness in Africa: a comparative web assessment of selected African countries. J. Internet Inf. Syst. **2**(3), 43–57 (2011)
34. Waiswa, R., Okello-Obura, C.: To what extent have ICTs contributed to e-Governance in Uganda? Library Philosophy and Practice, paper 1125 (2014)
35. Bagui, L., Bytheway, A.: Listening to the ground: key indicators of e-Participation in government for Africa. In: Bwalya, K., Zulu, S. (eds.) Handbook of Research on E-Government in Emerging Economies: Adoption, E-Participation, and Legal Frameworks, pp. 474–495. Hershey, PA (2012)
36. Steenkamp, M., Hyde-Clarke, N.: The use of Facebook for political commentary in South Africa. The use of Facebook for political commentary in South Africa. Telematics Inform. **31**(1), 91–97 (2014)
37. Oyedemi, T.: Participation, citizenship and internet use among South African youth. Telematics Inform. **32**, 11–22 (2015)
38. Ochara, N.M.: An organizing vision for e-Participation projects in Africa. In: Aikins, S. (ed.) Managing E-Government Projects: Concepts, Issues, and Best Practices, pp. 100–130. Information Science Reference, Hershey (2012)
39. Isaksson, A.: Political participation in Africa: the role of individual resources. Electoral. Stud. **34**(2014), 244–260 (2014)
40. Tufekci, Z., Wilson, C.: Social media and the decision to participate in political protest: observations from Tahrir Square. J. Commun. **62**(2), 363–379 (2012)
41. Aman, M., Jayroe, T.J.: ICT, social media, and the Arab transition to democracy: from venting to acting. Dig. Middle East Stud. **22I**(2), 317–347 (2013)
42. Howard, P.N., Duffy, A., Freelon, D., Hussain, M., Mari, W., Mazaid, M.: Opening Closed Regimes: What Was the Role of Social Media During the Arab Spring? Project on

Information Technology and Political Islam. Department of Communication, University of Washington, Seattle (2011)

43. Manrique, M., Mikail, B.: The role of new media and communication technologies in Arab transitions. FRIDE Policy Briefing No. 106. http://fride.org/publication/965/the-role-of-new-media-and-communication-technologies-in-arab-transitions (2011)

44. Allagui, I.: Waiting for spring: Arab resistance and change. Int. J. Commun. **8**, 983–1007 (2014)

45. Lynch, M.: After Egypt: the limits and promise of online challenges to the authoritarian arab state. Perspect. Polit. **9**(2), 301–310 (2011)

46. Reuter, O.J., Szakonyi, D.: Online social media and political awareness in authoritarian regimes. Br. J. Polit. Sci. **45**, 29–51 (2015)

47. Wojcieszak, M., Smith, B.: Will politics be tweeted? New media use by Iranian youth in 2011. New Media Soc. **16**(1), 91–109 (2013)

48. Wojcieszak, M., Smith, B., Enayat, M.: Finding a way: how Iranians reach for news and information. The Iran Media Program, University of Pennsylvania. http://www.iranmediaresearch.org/en/research/pdffile/990 (2012)

49. Williams, A.: How to write and analyse a questionnaire. J. Orthod. **30**(3), 245–252 (2003)

Identification in E-Participation: Between Quality of Identification Data and Participation Threshold

Peter Parycek, Judith Schossböck, and Bettina Rinnerbauer[✉]

Danube University Krems, Dr. Karl Dorrek-Straße 30, 3500 Krems, Austria
{peter.parycek, judith.schossboeck,
bettina.rinnerbauer}@donau-uni.ac.at

Abstract. E-participation projects have to consider a low participation threshold while maintaining security and data quality standards. While users often perceive complex regulations and logins as hurdles for participation, providers of solutions want to avoid misuse and in some cases have identified the participants uniquely. Not all levels of e-participation require the same quality of identification and authentication to produce reliable outcomes. Based on the first results of an Austrian e-participation project, the paper presents a model that tries to match these complex relations and examines which identification methods are seen as appropriate on which levels of e-participation based on the dimensions of quality of identification data and low participation threshold.

Keywords: E-participation · Identification · Authentication · Data quality

1 Introduction

Whenever an e-participation process is designed, a decision about the modes of user identification is mandatory. For decision- makers and citizens who are initiating an e-participation process (top-down and bottom-up setting) some guidance would be helpful. Such efforts are complicated by the complexity of e-participation processes and the large number of participation areas [1].

As part of the nationally funded research project "e-participation – authentication in democratic online participation", that aims at developing an e-participation ecosystem, questions like "Which levels of e-participation ask for what sort of identification method? How can the tension between the desired low participation threshold and the need for security be conceptualized?" arose. The model in this paper builds on the idea that a matching of the levels of e-participation with electronic identification methods can be a useful orientation for future initiators of e-participation processes and that the modelling of e-participation processes with a focus on identification options can be helpful for the scientific community.

In the following the levels of e-participation (Sect. 2.1) and a selection of electronic identification methods (Sect. 2.2), which the model is based on, are introduced. After describing the methodology (Sect. 3) and the relevant dimensions (Sects. 4.1, 4.2), authors will present the model (Sect. 5) before describing limitations and suggestions on further research (Sect. 6).

© IFIP International Federation for Information Processing 2015
E. Tambouris et al. (Eds.): ePart 2015, LNCS 9249, pp. 108–119, 2015.
DOI: 10.1007/978-3-319-22500-5_9

2   Theoretical Framework

2.1   Levels of E-Participation: Definitions, State of the Art and Legal Aspects

When classifying e-participation processes, a useful framework, which is based on Glass' (1979) classification of the objectives of participation, was proposed by Phang and Kankanhalli [2]. By distinguishing four objectives of e-participation and matching them with the process of policy making, Phang and Kankahalli map e-participation as described in extracts as follows (Fig. 1).

stage in process of policy making	e-participation objective	appropriate means (e.g.)
agenda setting	input probing	online-survey questionnaires
formulating policy	information exchange	web portal with online discussion
	decision-making supplement	visualization tools
implementation phase	education and support building	online chat
after implementation	information exchange	

Fig. 1. Mapping of e-participation objectives with stages of policy making

   Another model includes performance indicators for each level [3]. Drawing on levels as presented by the Organization for Economic Cooperation and Development (OECD), Al-Dalou and Abu-Shanab emphasise that three basic levels (*information provision, citizen-consultation* and *citizen active participation*) would leave the final decision under the responsibility of the government [4, 5]. However, they also mention *"codetermination"* as proposed by Medimorec et al. [6] as a new level. Another classification is described by Ergazakis et al. [7], referring to the DEMO-net Excellence Network on e-Participation. They differ applied forms and areas of e-participation: *consultation* is distinguished from *deliberation, polling, voting, campaigning, electioneering, petitioning, decision making, service delivery, spatial planning, information provision, mediation and community building.* [7]. Further aspects relevant for examining participation threshold in e-participation processes are the role of mobile solutions as found in Wimmer et al. [8], and the effect of e-participation on the trust of citizens as examined by e.g. Kim and Lee [9]. An Austrian model conceptualizing (e-) participation is the one proposed in the standards for public participation. This model distinguishes *informative public participation, consultative public participation* and *cooperative public participation* [10] and was amended by the working group e-democracy of the Federal Chancellery [11] as follows: At the *information* level citizens are informed about a plan or decision without the opportunity to further influence it. *Consultation* refers to citizens stating their opinion. The third level is further divided into *cooperation (3a)*, where citizens can influence the decision, and *co-decision (3b)*, understood as a decision made commonly by participants and decision-makers.

2.2   Electronic Identification and Authentication

According to Art 3 paragraph 1 Regulation (EU) No 910/2014[1], *'electronic identification'* is defined as the process of using person identification data in electronic form
uniquely representing either a natural or legal person, or a natural person representing a
legal person. Art 3 paragraph 5 of the aforementioned regulation regulates *authentication* as an electronic process that enables the electronic identification of a natural or
legal person, or the origin and integrity of data in electronic form to be confirmed.

This understanding does not correspond with how identification and authentication
are currently defined by the Austrian legal framework (for more detailed information
see [12]). As the project consortium consists of technical as well as legal experts and
the technical understanding of those terms is not equal to the legal definitions, it has
agreed on defining authentication and identification as is done by the Austrian
E-Government-Act: Identification is understood as the process necessary to validate or
recognize identity, while identity is the designation of a specific person by means of
data which are particularly suitable to distinguish persons from each other, such as
name, date of birth and place of birth. "Unique identity" enables the unmistakable
distinction of one data subject from all other data subjects.[2] The process, which is
necessary to validate or recognize authenticity is called authentication, while authenticity is understood as the genuine nature of a declaration of intent in the sense that the
purported author of that declaration is in fact its actual author.[3]

Unique identification in Austria is possible through the state-implemented
citizen-card or mobile-phone-signature: Independent of technology, the so-called
"link to a person" assures unique *identification* of a natural person[4] by a derivation of
the number assigned to a person within the central register of residents. *Authentication*
of the declaration of intent is made possible through an electronic signature.[5]

To summarize, unique electronic identification is the process equal to identification
with an official document and the qualified electronic signature serves[6] as a means (of
authentication) equal to a handwritten signature.

---

[1] Regulation of the European Parliament and of the Council of 23 July 2014, published in OJ L 257/73
on 28 August 2014; this regulation shall apply from 1 July 2016 (Art 52 describes the entry into force
further).

[2] These definitions are regulated in § 2 Nr. 4 (identification), Nr. 1 (identity) and Nr. 2 (unique
identity) of the Austrian Federal Act on Provisions Facilitating Electronic Communications with
Public Bodies (E-Government-Act), Austrian Federal Law Gazette (BGBl), part I, Nr. 2004/10,
version BGBl I 2013/83; accessible in English: https://www.ris.bka.gv.at/Dokumente/Erv/ERV_
2004_1_10/ERV_2004_1_10.pdf.

[3] § 2 Nr. 5 and Nr. 6 E-Government-Act, Austrian Federal Law Gazette (BGBl), part I, Nr. 2004/10,
version BGBl I 2013/83.

[4] § 4 Nr. 2 E-Government-Act, Austrian Federal Law Gazette (BGBl), part I, Nr. 10/2004, version
BGBl I 2013/83.

[5] Other means, which can guarantee authentication are e.g. log files or a mobile TAN. The latter serves
as a second factor of authentication through the Austrian mobile-phone-signature.

[6] apart from certain exceptions, see § 4 Federal act on Electronic Signatures, Austrian Federal Law
Gazette (BGBl) I Nr. 1999/190 BGBl. I Nr. 2010/75.

3 Methodology

Our central goal was to examine the appropriateness of e-ID options at the different levels of e-participation processes and how these can be mapped in a model based on already existing classifications and expert opinions. A qualitative approach was pursued: After a desk research, focus groups were held both with interested citizens (external focus group 1, November 2014) and experts (internal focus group 2, March 2015). As a part of the requirement analysis for the e-participation ecosystem to be developed, 10 expert interviews were held until March 2015.

The first focus group was a one hour moderated discussion starting with the clarification of basic definitions of identification and authentication, with around 20 participants (practitioners and activists with an interest in ICT and governance) in Vienna in November 2014. The goal of this focus group was to access the user perspective and to define areas of conflict and high interest.

Guided expert interviews with open questions [13] have been conducted with 10 experts in e-participation, e-governance and e-voting in Austria and the EU. Experts were defined as those with knowledge in the field of e-participation due to their profession [14], i.e. whose research interests were relevant for the topic or who had been running projects of this sort. The role of the expert interviews was to evaluate and further elaborate the findings from desk research for the requirement analysis of the project. Interview guidelines were set up in accordance with the project consortium. The interviews lasted from 40 to 60 min and were done in person (3), in written form (2) or by Skype recording (5). Interviewees are quoted anonymously (as interviewee A – J).

Focus group 2 consisted of the interdisciplinary scientific partners of the consortium with a strong legal and technical specialization, as well as three representatives of the Austrian Federal Ministry of the Interior (e.g. the leader of the Austrian Election Commission). The results of this focus group lead to a depiction of relating six selected identification methods to seven forms of e-participation. Therefore, the dimensions risk/security and practicability/reasonability/low participation threshold were suggested in a first attempt. In a second step, these were amended to the following sub-questions:

- How strong is the link to a specific person? The quality of identity data is considered higher if an authority validated the identification data.
- How low-levelled or high-levelled can the electronic identification method possibly be without forming a too high participation threshold with regard to a particular form of participation?

4 Results

4.1 Citizen Perspective

With view to the citizen perspective, in focus group 1, it became clear that the topic e-IDs in e-participation is controversial and often polarizing. Two major areas of conflict could be identified: Firstly, in order to reach a big and diverse amount of participants, access to an e-participation process should be as low as possible (low participation threshold). Secondly, the level of risk resp. security often seems to contradict high participation rates from a user perspective. These dimensions are also reflected in the two perspectives of the model. The focus group showed that high quality ID are perceived as a hurdle for participation, and e-ID management can reduce manipulation, but could also be used to control citizens' activities. Compared to offline participation, there is a lack of trust in e-ID providers or organizations that run e-participation projects. Anonymous e-participation is not seen as a solution; however specific user groups are very critical regarding data security standards. The potentials of a comprehensive e-ID management are seen in the increasing reliability of results and the possibility to lower participation threshold by using different e-ID solutions. This was also reflected in the interviews, which point towards the importance of user empowerment by offering transparent processes (e.g. regarding data collection) and different e-ID options (cp. Interviewees F, D, B, J).

In the following, we describe the analytical dimensions used to create a two-dimensional model and how they were selected, based on desk research, interviews and focus groups.

4.2   Vertical Dimension: Levels of E-Participation

The levels of e-participation express the intensity of the influence of citizens during a participation process, based on the distinction proposed by Arbter [10] and amended by Parycek [11]. At the third level, Parycek distinguishes *cooperation* from *co-decision*. These levels of e-participation were amended and further divided into sub-categories reflecting more concrete e-participation processes:

- The first step is information, meaning the provision of information to be accessed by participants.
- Participants are provided with more influence at the second step, consultation, divided into three subcategories: the statement of ideas, the addition of content and opinions (one-way-communication), annotation/commenting/discussion (two-way-communication) and the evaluation of content (e.g. to "like").
- Cooperation, defined as a collaborative preparation of results, builds the third step.
- Co-decision is understood as a possibility to vote on results or implementations.
- Decision is defined as a legally binding decision made solely by the participants.

4.3   Horizontal Dimension: Identification Methods

On this axis we focused on the following selected e-IDs relevant for Austrian citizens and according to technical requirements:

1. Unique identifications provided by the state (unmistakable distinction of citizens);
2. Application specific user management (like LDAP, Active Directory etc. used, f.i. in an enterprise for the identification of employees);
3. The number of an official document (e.g. passport), which is saved in a register; (A link to the corresponding register would not enable verification of the user, but at least verify if there is a document with this number at all.)

4. A reputation based processes of identification (a login with e.g. username and password and a confirmation of other users in the sense, that the user's real identity is equal to the one used in the participation process); similarly to a social media login, this is risky due to the lack of verification of the identity data.
5. "Social IDs"; this category summarizes identification methods like OpenID, Facebook Connect, Google Connect, Twitter, Amazon, LinkedIn etc. (username and password).
6. No identification.

Regarding the quality of identification data, interviewees point towards the bindingness of a decision as a main factor speaking for high quality of identification data. For some e-participation cases, e.g. youth participation, some experts are in favour of a lower participation threshold at the cost of security standards to ensure participation (I, J). Youth also seems to be more prepared to use real names for political participation (I). The integration of target group specific IDs plays a big role in e-participation. In particular practitioners emphasize a multidimensional solution on most e-participation levels to empower citizens (B, J), which is also reflected in the description of minimum standards in our model. In particular youth and citizens living abroad can be reached well through e-participation (I). Independent from target groups, it is almost impossible to separate the bindingness of a process from secure identification tools (B, D, E, J, K.). If decision making relies on an output based on participant numbers, the importance of the quality of identification data is increased.

4.4   Context of E-Participation

As it is difficult to detach e-participation from its context, we address the aspects e-participation is embedded in.

4.4.1   Anonymous Participation and no Identification

Anonymity and pseudonymity play a big role as a general option for users, in particular for a more critical target group (cp. interviewees I, B, F). Interviewee A points to the fact that identical solutions can be linked to different participation thresholds in different countries, depending on cultural factors, marketing and the recognition value of a solution. Often, there is a difference between the anonymity experienced by users and the technical possibilities. An advantage of anonymity might be that the content is more focused and personalization becomes less relevant. On the contrary, anonymity may lead to lower inhibition by users up to aggressive tones of a discussion. Nagiller [15] investigated news portals with comment functions, showing a high amount of abusive postings. She concludes that the use of real names results in less offences. The working group E-democracy of the Austrian Federal Chancellery mentioned the danger of "flamewars" because of the perceived distance between users in an anonymous setting [11]. However, the thesis that the use of real names automatically minimizes offensive comments could not be proved either. In contrast, interviewees state that offensive behavior plays a minimal role in official e-participation projects (B, I, J). Another advantage of anonymity is that peer pressure might become less relevant in online communication [11]. Interviewees emphasized the importance of anonymity, if a project allows for that option (D, F, I, J). A study conducted by Bernstein et al. [16] outlines that a large majority of users (over 90 % of posts were anonymous) tend to choose anonymity if they have the choice to either enter no name, use any name or use a cryptographic identity mechanism on a discussion board. The question whether a huge amount of participants shall be reached is crucial (J, F). In any case, the declaration of a name and registration processes will form a participation hurdle. Technical advancements are often in favor of user privacy, although they have to be both known and implemented and usually lead to a more complicated process. Recent research on identity management has, for instance, concentrated on protecting user data [20]. Generally, anonymization and pseudonymization are complex categories. When speaking of anonymity, it should be clarified whether this refers to identification towards a system or the participants.

4.4.2   Strategies to Lower Participation Threshold

As strategies to lower participation threshold for users, the use of solutions that are known from e-business cases as well as the use of widely accepted e-IDs were mentioned. Drawing on existing e-business cases might decrease participation threshold for particular IDs (cp. interviewee A), as users are already used to that sort of online identity management and tend to trust those things they already know. The implementation of basic e-government technologies like IDs guaranteed by the state into the corporate sector can lead to more acceptance of such technologies [17]. Increasing availability of such technologies in the private sector (like electronic signatures, online registration based on secure identity data or electronic RSa-delivery) could encourage citizens to also use those for e-government services. One example would be the transnational online opening of an account as implemented in the EU large scale pilot project STORK 2.0.[7] In particular experts from the practitioner domain were very open towards integrating social IDs in e-participation processes. Offering such IDs in addition to other e-ID options was seen as a valid option that empowers users by providing them with alternative solutions (B, I, J). However, if many levels of the e-participation process are reflected in a particular solution (multi-level approach), due to the complexity of the system, one e-ID for all processes might be more applicable (B). Nevertheless, there seems to be a big potential for multi-level, flexible e-participation processes with voting options (in particular for a tech-savvy and politically interested target group) that can be used by smaller administrative communities or communes. Germany builds on such models in close cooperation with associations and the lessons learned from such projects should be further considered in the Austrian, but also European context (B, D).

4.4.3   Legal Framework vs. Standards

Identification methods have to meet legal requirements, e.g. those of data protection law. There is a tendency against more legal regulations regarding the implementation of e-participation processes (cp. interviewees F, I, D, E, H), however, a better

---

[7] https://www.eid-stork2.eu/ (accessed 31 March 2015).

standardization in the e-participation field is seen as advantage (F). Other experts criticize the lack of a unified access to e-government services for the general public (one-stop-shop) as well as a lack of a legal framework for e-participation [18]. EU Regulation No 211/2011[8] e.g. regulates the European Citizens' Initiative (ECI) and has been critically reviewed by Stein and Wenda [19].

5 Model

The following model originates from two tables created within the internal focus group. It is an attempt to conceptualise the use of e-IDs along the two perspectives quality of identification data and participation threshold and shall serve as a basis for further defining use cases, best practices and recommendations: Which e-ID options can or cannot be recommended as a minimum standard on a specific level of participation? Not all aspects of online identification and e-participation shall be comprehensively captured in one model, but this depiction shall be used as a basis for further verification by experts and the scientific community. The internal focus group discussed the model along the following two questions: Is the quality of the investigated identification data good enough to be used for a particular level of participation? How high-levelled can the e-ID possibly be without being regarded as a too high participation threshold for a particular form of e-participation?

stepmodel of e-participation	information	consultation				cooperation	co-decision	decision
e-identification-methods	information access	to state ideas, add content, opinions (one-way-communication)	to comment and discuss (give feedback interaction, two-way-communication)	to evaluate content or intermediate results ("to like")		to prepare results in a collaborative way	to vote on results or implementations	to decide in a legally binding way (e.g. election concerning an institution, which aims at representing interests)
unique identifications implemented by the state (like the Austrian citizen card or STORK)								
applicationspecific user-management (LDAP, Active Directory, etc.)								
number of an official document saved in a register								
reputation based processes of identification								
Social IDs (OpenID, Facebook Connect, Google Connect, Twitter, Amazon, LinkedIn, etc.)								
no identification at all								

Fig. 2. Matching of quality of identification data and participation threshold (Colour code: white: the quality of the identification data and the e-identification method are considered as appropriate for its use on the corresponding step of participation; light grey: the identification method on the corresponding level of e-participation depends on the individual case and cannot be unconditionally recommended; dark grey: the use of this identification method on the corresponding level is – as a tendency – seen as resulting in a too high participation-threshold (H) or the quality of identification data is regarded as too low (L)) (Coloured figure online)

---

[8] Regulation (EU) No 211/2011 of the European Parliament and of the Council of 16 February 2011, published in OJ L 65/2 on 11 March 2011.

As mentioned, the model describes minimum requirements on the ID level. In favour of a wide distribution of e-identification methods, it is not advised against the use of eID methods with higher quality of identification data in general, in order to include users who prefer using these forms of e-ID over of methods with lower quality of identification data. Those e-ID methods can often be technically included, depending on their availability and dissemination. In the following we summarize experts' opinion and reasoning that lead to the depicted model (Fig. 2).

For accessing information all identification methods would possibly prevent citizens from participating. Therefore it is recommended to design the participation process without the need of any identification of participants. However, the possibility to identify themselves can be provided to participants. The same applies to the step of consultation seen as an option to state ideas and add content in a one-way-communication-process.

For an interactive discussion process in the form of a two-way communication, it is recommended to use a form of identification, as the counterpart of a discussion is of interest. At this point the model shows a breaking point, from that it is recommended to make use of an identification method. It will depend on the individual case whether social IDs, a number of an official document saved in a register or an application specific user management will be the appropriate method of identification in such processes. This will further depend on the topic as well as the necessity to identify participants. In this process, the possibility of owning more than one social media account has to be taken into account, as well as the fact that the real identity of the user and his/her social ID do not necessarily have to correspond. There is no possibility of a secure verification in this case. A reputation based process of identification contains the additional component of other participants confirming that the identity of the user corresponds with the identity he or she participates with. On the level of consultation as a discussion, it is recommended to use reputation based processes of identification. If the use of a number of an official document saved in a register or an application specific user management is seen as more complex than other identification options, the decision should be made individually according to each case. The voluntary use of an electronic identification method implemented by the state should be possible.

The use of identification methods implemented by the state could hold back participants from participating in a discussion or evaluating content. Moreover, a unique identification is not necessary in a consultation. Therefore there is no need to only use identification methods implemented by the state on this level. Due to the insecurity of social IDs, which also applies to other levels of participation, their use is not recommended in general, but seen as a possibility on the steps of consultation in a discussion, for evaluation and on the level of cooperation, especially with regard to specific target groups. The use of a number of an official document saved in a register as well as the use of identification methods implemented by the state is considered as a potential participation hurdle. To keep participation threshold as low as possible, the mandatory use of such systems is not recommended on the level evaluation. It is recommended to use application specific user management or reputation based processes of identification as they provide a higher probability that the alleged author of a statement is the actual author.

On the level of cooperation, which basically means a collaborative elaboration of content or solutions, it may be appropriate to make use of e-ID methods that identify participants uniquely. Social IDs may be appropriate for decision makers not considering unique identification as greatly important, but preferring a high participation rate. Dependent on the requirements of the initiator of the cooperation, it is recommended to either use application-specific user management, a number of an official document saved in a register or reputation based processes of identification.

At the step of co-decision (and above all at the decision-level), it will most likely not suffice to aim for a high participation rate without knowing the identity of participants. Thus, for the processes codecision and decision, not implementing an identification method or using social IDs is not advisable. Apart from this, all identification methods are seen as appropriate.

On the decision level, participants are provided with the most influence. Therefore, the use of secure identification methods providing a unique identification method is highly recommended. Application-specific user management is also an appropriate solution. The use of a number of an official document saved in a register or reputation based processes of identification can be appropriate, dependent on the individual case, and is thus not excluded.

6 Limitations and Further Research

On the basis of these results, we conclude that the integration of target-group specific e–IDs, the creation of exciting and motivating use cases for existing e-ID models as well as building on already well received and known solutions can significantly lower participation threshold. However, the right method mix in e-participation will always depend on the scope of the project and the specific target group. Emphasis of further research will be on the development of use-cases, additional options for different e–participation levels (new forms of online identification may arise or gain more popularity) and on digital inclusion, on further evaluation and review of the model proposed through expert opinions. A workshop at the International Conference for E-Democracy and Open Government 2015 was held in May 2015. A quantitative survey is planned.

Limitations of the model can be seen in its dedicated focus on top-down processes. Some relevant and promising e-participation models like the supranational European Citizens' Initiative [20], despite some issues regarding stochastic elements and certification [21], work well on the basis of just mentioning a passport number without further validation of the identity document, are not mentioned separately. User assessment and usability testing are still necessary once specific projects are put into practice. The model proposed shall be seen as a first expert based depiction for categorizing and choosing e-ID options for specific e-participation processes.

Acknowledgement. The project "E-Partizipation" ("E-Participation") is funded by the Austrian security research programme KIRAS of the Federal Ministry for Transport, Innovation and Technology (bmvit). We would like to thank our project partners: the Austrian Institute of Technology, the Austrian State Printing House, the Centre for Computers and Law (University of Vienna), the Federal Ministry of the Interior and Rubicon.

References

1. Fraser, C., et. al: DEMO_net: Demo_net Deliverable 5.1: Report on current ICTs to enable participation (2006). http://www.academia.edu/2737661/DEMO_net_Deliverable_5.1_Report_on_current_ICTs_to_enable_Participation. Accessed 15 March 2015
2. Phang, D., Kankanhalli, A.: A framework of ICT exploitation for e-participation initiatives. Mag. Commun. ACM **51**(12), 128–132. New York (2008) based on Glass, J.J.: Citizen participation in planning: the relationship between objectives and techniques. Am. Plan. Assoc. J. 45, 180–189 (1979)
3. Al-Dalou, R., Abu-Shanab, E.: E-Participation levels and technologies. In: Proceedings of the ICIT 2013 The 6th International Conference on Information Technology (2013), 8 May 2013. http://sce.zuj.edu.jo/icit13/images/Camera%20Ready/E-Technology/656.pdf. Accessed 15 March 2015
4. Machintosh, A.: Characterizing e-participation in policy-making. In: The Proceedings of the Thirty-Seventh Annual Hawaii International Conference on System Sciences (HICSS-37) (2004), 5–8 Jan 2004
5. Ahmed, N.: An overview of e-participation models. UN Department of Economic and Social Affairs (UNDESA) (2006). http://unpan1.un.org/intradoc/groups/public/documents/un/unpan023622.pdf. Accessed 15 March 2015
6. Medimorec, D., Parycek, P., Schossböck, J.: Vitalizing democracy through e-participation and open government: An Austrian and Eastern European perspective (2010). Bertelsmann Verlag. http://www.fundacionbertelsmann.org/cps/rde/xbcr/SID-853E53E9-9B1F1F76/bst/Daniel%20Medimorec.pdf. Accessed 15 March 2015
7. Ergazakis, K. Metaxiotis, K, Tsitsanis, T.: A state-of-the-art review of applied forms and areas, tools and technologies for e-participation. Int. J. Electron. Gov. Res. **7**(1) (January–March 2011). www.researchgate.net/profile/Teta_Stamati/publication/220526926_Electronic_Transformation_of_Local_Government_An_Exploratory_Study/links/53f463ae0cf2888a7490eae3.pdf. Accessed 15 March 2015
8. Wimmer, M.A., Grimm, R., Jahn, N., Hampe, J.: Mobile participation: exploring mobile tools in e-participation. In: Wimmer, M.A., Tambouris, E., Macintosh, A. (eds.) ePart 2013. LNCS, vol. 8075, pp. 1–13. Springer, Heidelberg (2013)
9. Kim, S., Lee, J.: E-participation, transparency, and trust in local government. Public Adm. Rev. **72**(6), 819–828 (2012)
10. Arbter, K.: Standards for public participation (2008). http://www.partizipation.at/fileadmin/media_data/Downloads/Standards_OeB/standards_der_oeffentlichkeitsbeteiligung_2008_druck.pdf. Accessed 15 March 2015
11. Parycek, P.: Positionspapier zu E-Democräy und E-Participation in Österreich. AG EDEM, Wien (2008). http://www.ref.gv.at/uploads/media/EDEM-1-0-0-20080525.pdf. Accessed 15 March 2015
12. Böszörmenyi, J, Hötzendorfer, W, Rinnerbauer, B.: Identitätsmanagement bei demokratischer Online-Beteiligung. In: Schweighofer/Kummer/Hötzendorfer, Tagungsband des 18. Internationalen Rechtsinformatik Symposions, IRIS 2015: S. 361, Österreichische Computer Gesellschaft, Wien (2015)
13. Atteslander, P.: Methoden der empirischen Sozialforschung, 12th edn. Schmidt Verlag, Berlin (2008)
14. Gläser, J., Laudel, G.: Experteninterviews und qualitative Inhaltsanalyse. VS Verlag für Sozialwissenschaften, Wiesbaden (2004)
15. Nagiller, J.: Das deliberative Potenzial von Online-Diskussionen auf Nachrichtenportalen; In: Dander, V., Gründhammer, V., Ortner, H., Pfurtscheller, D., Rizzolli, M. (Hg.) Medienräume: Materialität und Regionalität, Innsbruck University Press (2013)

16. Bernstein, M.S., Monroy-Hernández, A., Harry, D., André, P., Panovich, K., Vargas, G.G.: 4chan and/b: an analysis of anonymity and ephemerality in a large online community. In: Proceedings of the Fifth International AAAI Conference on Weblogs and Social Media (ICWSM) 2011 (2011)
17. Stranach, K., Rössler, T.: Bürgerkarte und Handy-Signatur in der Privatwirtschaft. In: eGovernment review no. 15, Jan 2015, pp. 20–21 (2015)
18. Ringler, P., Parycek, P., Schossböck, J., Sturmberger, W., Schönherr, D., Oberhuber, Fl., Aichberger, I., Hacker, E.: Internet und Demokratie in Österreich. Grundlagenstudie. SORA (Institute for Social Research and Consulting), Wien (2013)
19. Stein, R., Wenda, G.: Reviewing the regulation: the future of European citizens' initiatives. In Proceedings of ceeeGovDays 2015 (in print; 2015)
20. Stein, R., Wenda, G.: Implementing the ECI: challenges for the member states. In: Proceedings of EDEM 2011 (2011), p. 45
21. Müller-Török, R., Prosser, A.: The European citizens' initiative – a supranational approach towards eparticipation. In: Eixelsberger, W., Stember, J. (eds.) E-Government – Zwischen Partizipation und Kooperation, pp. 89–108. Springer, Wien (2012)
22. Wu, L., Zhou, S., Zhou, Z., Hong, Z., Huang, K.: A Reputation-based identity management model for cloud computing. Mathematical Problems in Engineering (2015). http://www.hindawi.com/journals/mpe/. May 2015

Social-Economic Approach
to an eParticipation Experience
Based on eCognocracy

Cristina Pérez-Espés[(⊠)] and José María Moreno-Jiménez

University of Zaragoza, Gran via 2, 50005 Zaragoza, Spain
{perezesp,moreno}@unizar.es

Abstract. Most eParticipation initiatives have social, economic and environmental costs, financed in most cases with public funds, so it would be convenient
to evaluate them in order to be transparent and consistent with the strategic
objectives pursued. Thus, it is necessary to quantify, monetarily, both the economic, social and environmental aspects, and the value added generated by the
practical application of this type of eParticipation initiatives. The main objective
of this paper is to value, in monetary terms, the social and economic aspects of
the implementation and development of an eParticipation experience based on
eCognocracy. This evaluation will allow us to obtain the social and economic
information as to the true value added that these initiatives contribute to society
in general, and to give an appropriate answer to the new challenges and neces-
sities in the sphere of public decisions that arise within the Knowledge Society.

Keywords: eParticipation · eCognocracy · Social return on investment
(SROI) · Social-economic approach

1 Introduction

The concept of eGovernment appeared, its evolution has led to the search for multiple
attempts at modernization and innovation in the field of public management [1, 2]. The
activities of the public sector in the following years have focused, among other things,
on citizen involvement in the political process through eParticipation.

The presence of the citizenry in institutional environments in which the management
and design of public policies are defined and specified introduces a capacity of control
that helps to reduce one of the fundamental imbalances in the relations between the State
and civil society. In effect, citizen participation not only enables citizens to propose
initiatives, carry out consultations, improve their level of information, and participate in
certain decision processes but also to control and monitor institutional activity.

Building this context it should be enabled experiences of eParticipation that exploit
the potential of the knowledge society and respond to its new challenges and needs. In
this way, eCognocracy [3, 4] is a new cognitive democracy that combining the representative and the direct democracy pursues the creation and social diffusion of
knowledge relative to the scientific resolution of public decision making problems.

All these participative experiences and processes, in which the citizen is directly
involved, have a clear impact on material, social and economic questions. The analysis

© IFIP International Federation for Information Processing 2015
E. Tambouris et al. (Eds.): ePart 2015, LNCS 9249, pp. 120–131, 2015.
DOI: 10.1007/978-3-319-22500-5_10

of the economic and social component of an eParticipation experience is considered fundamental and necessary in order to be able to study its final impact on society.

Taking into account the great efforts of public administrations to maintain a high degree of transparency in the implementation of eGovernment services projects, they justify their budgets through studies that describe comparative analyses of cost information between the traditional way of serving citizens and the IT-based solutions. Nevertheless, due to the lack of established methodologies for calculating the costs and assessing the benefits of implementing eGovernment services, these studies often contain analyses that do not reflect the reality of the costs [5].

Moreover, in accordance with new social requirements and with the properties of transparency and accountability recommended for any process financed through public funds, as habitually occurs in eParticipation experiences, the public powers have to take decisions as to where to invest resources. An economic-social analysis is a useful tool to evaluate and study the value created by the implantation of projects and initiatives and can serve as a guide in public decisions to channel resources towards the experiences that provide greater net benefit to society.

In this paper, we carry out an analysis, in monetary terms, of the economic and social aspects of the implementation and development of an eParticipation experience based on eCognocracy (the Cadrete case), using an advanced management tool called Social Return on Investment (SROI). This analysis, allows us, through the comparison of the economic and social benefits with the investment made, to obtain a global vision of the true value added that eParticipation initiatives provide for society.

This article is structured as follows: after this brief introduction, Sect. 2 covers the economic-social valuation of the eParticipation experiences; Sect. 3 presents the tool SROI and its application in our case of study. And Sect. 4 shows the main conclusions that can be drawn from the work and the future research lines.

2 Economic-Social Valuation of the eParticipation Experiences

This section presents a review of the literature on the economic and social valuation of projects and initiatives carried out by the government and the possible methodologies that can be applied to evaluate an eParticipation experience in monetary terms.

2.1 Background

The work of Matusuda and others [6] evaluates, through AHP, the importance of carrying out social programs that contribute to the social welfare of elderly people belonging to the community of Fukuoka (Japan).

Bhatnagar [7], as well as identifying the goals and objectives to be achieved in different initiatives of electronic government, establishes how to attain the objectives fixed so that they have an impact. To do so, the author focuses on a compilation of various examples of eGovernment applications in different countries including Korea, Mexico, India and the Philippines.

Gupta and Jana [8] study the evaluation of eGovernment through a framework that suggests choosing a strategy to measure the tangible and intangible benefits of the application of eGovernment initiatives in society.

Hadzila [5] proposes a structured framework for calculating the cost of eGovernment services, based on the complementary application of the IDEF0 modelling tool and the Activity-Based Costing technique.

Other papers, such as Ajilian and Crameri [9] analyze the possible economic and social impact of an effective and efficient electronic administration on society. They show that the use of ICT not only improves the interactions between the administration, citizens, businesses and industries but also has positively affected the quality and delivery of services.

Loff [10] studies, using cost-benefit analysis (CBA), whether it is profitable, both in economic and social terms, to implement a participation project. This work was presented for the European Public Sector Award (EPSA). Another example that uses CBA as its evaluation tool is that of Cuenin [11]. The main aim of this study was to give a general idea about how the economic analysis of projects could aid the design, monitoring and evaluation of operations, focusing on the particular case of neighborhood improvement programs.

2.2   Methodologies

This section describes different tools that allow the evaluation of a project or an initiative in monetary terms.

The numerous references in the literature lead us to the conclusion that *Cost-Benefit Analysis (CBA), Multi-criteria Decision-Making (MCDM) Techniques, Icam DEFinition for Function Modeling (IDEFo), Activity-based costing (ABC)* and *Social Return on Investment (SROI)* are among the most widely-used tools in decision making, especially in the public sector.

Cost-Benefit Analysis is one of the methods most used in the sphere of Public Administration to analyze its own behavior. CBA is, basically, the rationalization of a daily practice: weighing up the advantages and disadvantages of any decision or alternative, whether by itself or in comparison with others [12]. CBA is a tool that permits the evaluation of the costs and benefits of a project (program, intervention or political measure) with the aim of determining whether the project is desirable from the social welfare point of view and, if it is, to what extent.

On occasions, the analyst is faced with a double-edged problem that impedes the use of CBA [12]: (i) some of the costs and benefits identified cannot be reduced to the number previously established and (ii) the decision maker, or some of the social groups that take part in the process of collective decision, consider that this reduction should not be carried out, that is, they reject the use, for example, of the economic value of statistics.

In both cases, the analyst is deprived of the possibility of reducing all the costs and benefits to a single figure that permits direct comparison. To resolve this type of problem, one of the tools proposed are the Multi-criteria Decision-Making (MCDM) Techniques. The origin of these techniques is the same as the conventional BCA: the necessity of maximizing a function that depends on a series of well-specified objectives but with the difference that, now, they can present conflicts among themselves. The methods of multi-criteria evaluation and decision-making consist of selecting, from among a set of feasible alternatives, the optimization with various simultaneous objective functions and just one decision maker, and procedures of rational and consistent evaluation [13].

IDEF0, a compound acronym (*Icam DEFinition for Function Modeling*, where 'ICAM' is an acronym for *Integrated Computer Aided Manufacturing*), is a function modeling methodology for describing manufacturing functions which offers a functional modeling language for the analysis, development, reengineering, and integration of information systems, business processes, or software engineering analysis[1]. IDEFo was developed by the US Air Force under its ICAM program. The key principle of IDEFo is that complex systems can be explained in terms of the activities performed in the system and in such a way as to present details progressively through a hierarchical decomposition [14].

Another evaluation method is that of Activity Based Costing (ABC). This method was first clearly defined in 1987 by Kaplan, Robert S. and W. Bruns as a chapter in their book *Accounting and Management: A Field Study Perspective* [15]. According to CIMA (Chartered Institute of Management Accountants), ABC can be defined as an approach to the costing and monitoring of activities which involves tracing resource consumption and costing final outputs. Resources are assigned to activities, and activities to cost objects based on consumption estimates. The latter utilize cost drivers to attach activity costs to outputs.

Lastly, it is necessary to refer to one of the methods most employed to measure the social, environmental and economic impacts in public decision making, the Social Return on Investment (SROI), which is dealt with in detail in the next section.

3   Social Return on Investment

Social Return on Investment is a methodology created in the mid-1990s in San Francisco and intended to evaluate investments in social organizations. It was later revised in 2000 by New Economics Foundation with the collaboration of public administrations in the United Kingdom.

SROI is a participative approach that permits the monetary calculation of the value of a wide range of results, whether they have a market value or not. It is a tool with which both the managers of and the investors in a project can take decisions based on the optimization of the social and environmental impacts of the project.

It is a method that adds principles of measurement of extra-financial value with respect to the resources invested, that is, the social and environmental value that, at present, is not reflected in conventional financial accounts. SROI also incorporates the concept of return, which, in financial terms, simply refers to the benefits received as a result of an investment.

---

[1] *Systems Engineering Fundamentals*. Defense Acquisition University Press, 2001.

The use of this tool illustrates how an organization, program, project, initiative, etc., creates value and a coefficient that indicates how much total value in euros is created for each euro invested.

This SROI coefficient is a comparison between the value generated by an initiative and the investment necessary to achieve this impact. SROI seeks more than to obtain a simple number because the method describes the process for reaching the final ratio and contextualizes the information to permit its correct interpretation. Furthermore, it presents a framework to explore the social and environmental impacts of an organization in which monetization plays an important, but not exclusive, role.

There are two types of SROI analysis: (i) evaluation, that is carried out a posteriori and on the basis of the real results already obtained (measurement of the impact of finished projects) and (ii) forecasting, that predicts the social value that will be created if the activities achieve the foreseen results (especially useful in the planning stages of an initiative). The two types of SROI can be combined to include both the results already attained and future ones [16].

The SROI methodology has been widely used for the calculation of the impact of the triple dimension -social, environmental and economic-, containing all externalities, whether they have market value or not. SROI, as has been commented previously, is a participative approach that permits the capture, in monetary terms, of the value of a wide range of results, whether they have economic value or not. The effects derived from the implementation and development of an e-Participation experience are not only economic but, in most cases, social and environmental. The need to quantify, in monetary terms, the contribution of the whole participation process, as well as the value created, leads us to carry out a SROI analysis that will be useful in the sense that it generates relevant information for decision making. Moreover, SROI helps us to understand, manage and communicate the social value that our work creates in a clear and consistent way for customers, beneficiaries and funders. It will bring out potential improvements to services and information systems. A consistent approach to understanding and accounting for social value means that you can communicate clearly where and how you create value in a credible way[2]. All the above has let us to apply this methodology in our case study.

3.1 SROI Analysis for the Cadrete Experience

This section presents each of the steps carried out to calculate the SROI coefficient of the Cadrete initiative based on eCognocracy.

3.1.1 Description of the Experience

In April 2010, the Cadrete Municipal Council, in collaboration with Zaragoza Multicriteria Decision Making Group (GDMZ), implemented a citizen participation project (https://participa.cadrete.es) aimed at giving the residents of the municipality a voice in public policy decisions. The issue in question was the design of cultural and sporting

---

[2] http://www.thesroinetwork.org/117-home/all-regions/167-why-should-i-use-sroi10.

policies. There was one objective for the GDMZ: the validation of the methodological and technological tools and two main objectives for the City Council: (i) that decisions on the budget assigned to the aforementioned policies would be conjointly made by the politicians and the citizenry; (ii) that citizens would be encouraged to involve themselves in the debate and take part in the decision making process, and more specifically, that the arguments that supported the decisions would be publicly disseminated.

This eParticipation experience consisted of the following phases, which correspond to the basic structure of the model of democracy known as eCognocracy [17]: (i) problem formulation, (ii) information and training, (iii) modeling the problem, (iv) first round of voting, (v) discussion, (vi) second round of voting and (vii) presentation of the results.

3.1.2   Determining the Scope

1. Proposal

   The objective of this analysis is to measure the impact that the Cadrete experience has had on society, as well as the value created by the practical application of this initiative.

   This is an evaluation analysis because it is carried out a posteriori and is based on the real results obtained 4 years after putting the experience into practice.

2. Public/Receivers

   The receivers of our SROI analysis are all those to whom we must be held accountable (being, above all, transparent) for the project financed mainly by public funds: (i) Citizens and society in general; (ii) Financing entities: Council of Cadrete, Government of Aragón and the University of Zaragoza; (iii) Promoter of the initiative: the Zaragoza Multi-criteria Decision Making Group.

   This analysis is also addressed to the "science of research" to serve as a guide and to be improved in other experiences.

3. Context

   There are more and more eParticipation experiences carried out in society in which, among other things, citizen participation in public decision making is fomented. As a consequence, a need arises to measure the economic, social and environmental impact of these initiatives as well as the value added they generate.

4. Resources

   To carry out the SROI analysis, we had, as personnel resources, all the members of the Zaragoza Multi-criteria Decision Making Group. The expenditure arising from the carrying out of this report was financed by the GDMZ.

5. Analysis team

   The personnel that carried out the SROI analysis are the members of the Zaragoza Multi-criteria Decision Making Group, who were the promoters of the initiative.

6. The range of activities to be included

   The topic of the Cadrete experience was the design of cultural and sporting policies. There were two main objectives for the research group: the implementation of the experience and the validation of the methodological and technological tools; and the three objectives for the City Council: (i) that decisions on the budget assigned to the aforementioned policies would be conjointly made by the politicians and the citizenry; (ii) that citizens would be encouraged to involve themselves in the debate and take part in the decision making process; and (iii) that the arguments that supported the decisions would be publicly disseminated.

The activities to be included in the SROI analysis are all those that were necessary for implementing the experience. Therefore, most of them coincide with the stages, grouped into 4 blocks, of the methodology followed by eCognocracy [17].

7. Time range to analyze
   The Cadrete experience was carried out in 2010. This report was drawn up in 2014, but the period to be analyzed is of 1 year (from 2010-short term).

3.1.3   Identification and Incorporation of the Actors Involved

The actors or groups of interest (stakeholders) that we have taken into account for carrying out the SROI analysis are all those directly affected by the experience: the municipal council, the citizens of Cadrete and its surroundings and the promoter of the experience, the GDMZ.

3.1.4   Identification Inputs

Table 1 shows, in detail, all the inputs used to carry out the Cadrete experience.

Research and development (R&D) expenditures are understood to be "current and capital expenditures (both public and private) on creative work undertaken systematically to increase knowledge, including knowledge of humanity, culture, and society, and the use of knowledge for new applications. R&D covers basic research, applied research, and experimental development." (World Bank[3]). We have accounted for this type of expenditure through the number of researchers who participated in this experience as well as the number of meetings and the time employed in each of them.

Material resources are the goods and/or physical and tangible means necessary to achieve an objective, for example, installations, computer equipment (hardware), software, documentation etc.

Human resources include all the people who contribute work to an organization (whether profit-motivated or not and from any type of association).

The time factor encompasses the time invested in the implementation and development of the initiative.

The item "other expenditure" includes all the other expenditure incurred by an organization in achieving its objectives. In the case of the Cadrete experience, it includes allowances and travel expenses between Zaragoza and Cadrete.

All the inputs used and expenditures incurred in the experience were quantified, in monetary terms, for each of the stages that form part of the methodology followed by eCognocracy. In this way, we individually accounted for the implementation cost of each stage of the Cadrete experience. The total cost was 42046.73€.

---

[3] http://datos.bancomundial.org/indicador/GB.XPD.RSDV.GD.ZS/countries/1W?display=graph.

Table 1. Inputs of the Cadrete experience

INPUTS
INTELLECTUAL CAPITAL (R&D expenditure)
- Use of intellectual capital: N° of researchers participating (4 people in the Council and 15 from GDMZ), meetings and weekly debates during 1 year (35).
MATERIAL RESOURCES
- **Installations:** 4 rooms
- **Computer equipment (hardware):** 12 computers
- **Software:** Voting Applet in Java 6.18
- **Technological tools:** 1 projector
- **Web browsers:** Mozilla and Internet Explorer 8
- **Documentation:**
- 1600 leaflets
- 1949 letters sent to citizens
- 15 letters sent to associations
- 20 posters
- 1 online guide
- 1 questionnaire
- 1 final report
- **Web pages:** 1 web page for the experience
- **Other materials:**
- 1 bracelet for fairground
- 1 cultural excursion
- 2 quarterly gym season tickets
- 3 inscriptions in sporting activities
- 4 swimming pool season tickets
- 20 USB memories
- 30 electronic ID readers
HUMAN RESOURCES
- **Council personnel:** 4 people: Mayoress, Secretary and 2 technicians
- **Personal del GDMZ:** 15 people
- Head Researcher (HR): Professor (P)
- Mathematical modeling (3 people): Associate Professor (AP), 1 Graduate (G) and 1 Fellow (F).
- Intelligent Data Analysis (3 people): 1 Associate Professor (AP) and 2 Assistant Lecturers (AL)
- Informatics developments (3 people): 2 Associate Professors (AP) and 1 technician (G)
- Communications Technology Group (1 person/Engineer): Graduate (G)
- 4 Political Scientists: Graduates (G)
- **Collaborators** (1 person): Associate Professor (AP)
- Evaluation of the experience: 1 person (AP) (design of the questionnaire)
TIME FACTOR
Time is also a resource used in this experience.
OTHER EXPENDITURE
- **Other allowances:** Meal tickets (14)
- **Travel allowances (Zaragoza-Cadrete-Zaragoza_ 24km):** 12

3.1.5 Identification Outcomes

This section presents the quantification, in monetary units, of the results through the use of financial proxies for each of the stakeholders (see Tables 2, 3 and 4). The total outcomes were 115623.50€.

For the outcomes "knowledge of new e-Participation experiences", "acquiring technological knowledge" and "social and individual learning through the discussion forum", the proxy "savings on the cost of training courses" has been used. To quantify them in monetary terms, the following have been taken into account: (i) an estimation of the hours that each of the stakeholders would have had to dedicate to training/education, (ii) the price per hour that an Associate Professor would charge for giving each of these courses and (iii) an estimation of the number of students that would attend these courses. In the case of the council, the 3 people that worked in the council and were responsible for the implementation and the development of the Cadrete experience were taken into account. In the case of the citizens of Cadrete, the people that participated in the voting process were considered. As there were two

Table 2. Proxies for the indicators of outcomes (council)

	OUTCOMES	INDICATORS	PROXIES	Total €: 42622.5	
COUNCIL	Knowledge of new e-Participation experiences	Time dedicated to learning the experience	Savings on the cost of training courses	Hours dedicated to training/education: 15 hours	
				Number of people: 3	
				Price AP: 34€/h	
				Total € savings: 1530	
	Improvement of image through good practice	Number of advertisements published, talks and lectures given, and certificates or prizes received	Savings on the cost of an advertising campaign	Price of advertising spot 20": 900€	
				Price of advert 2500€	
				Total spots and adverts: 10 each	
				Total €: 9000+25000=34000	
	Fostering of citizen participation and involvement	Number of people that participated and degree of involvement in the activities	Time invested by each citizen and number of messages and comments in the discussion forum	Time dedicated to each round of voting: 15 min	
				Price min: 5€	
				Total people 1st vote: 43	
				Total people 2nd vote: 41	
				Total messages in the discussion forum: 61	
				Total comments in the discussion forum: 195	
				Price of message: 5€	
				Price of comment: 2.5€	
				Total €: 6300+792.50=7092.50	

Table 3. Proxies for the indicators of outcomes (citizens of Cadrete)

	OUTCOMES	INDICATORS	PROXIES	Total €: 55200	
CITIZENS OF CADRETE	Knowledge of new e-Participation experiences	Time dedicated to learning the experience	Savings on the cost of training courses	Hours dedicated to training/education: 20 hours	
				Number of people: 40	
				Price AP: 34€/h	
				Total € savings: 27200	
	Acquiring technological knowledge	Time dedicated to learning	Savings on the cost of training courses	Hours dedicated to training/education: 15 hours	
				Number of people: 40	
				Price AP: 34€/h	
				Total € savings: 14400	
	Social and individual learning through the discussion forum	Time dedicated to learning	Savings on the cost of training courses	Hours dedicated to training/education: 10 hours	
				Number of people: 40	
				Price TU: 34€/h	
				Total € savings: 13600	

Table 4. Proxies for the indicators of outcomes (GDMZ)

	OUTCOMES	INDICATORS	PROXIES	Total €: 17801	
GDMZ	Increase in the value of the methodology applied by the GDMZ	Number of tools created	Cost of each tool used	Cost of Software: 1920€	
				Cost of Forum: 790€	
				Total €: 2710	
	Social Recognition	Number of prize received	Amount received from each prize	Total prizes received: 2 (EPSA and UNPS)	
				Total €: 2000	
		Number of conferences	Price of each congress	Number of congresses: 8	
				Average price: 300€	
				Total €: 2400	
		New projects awarded	Amount received from projects awarded	Zaragoza Multi-criteria Decision Making Group	
				Total €: 10691	

rounds in which 43 and 41 people, respectively, participated, in the calculation of the proxy, we have used 40 people as the characteristic sample.

For the outcome "improvement of the council's image through good practice", the proxy "savings on the cost of an advertising campaign" has been used. The Cadrete experience has given the council a good image, leading to a social benefit which, in order to quantify it in monetary terms, has been considered the equivalent of the cost of carrying out an advertising campaign. To estimate this cost, the price of advertising spots and advertisements and the number of adverts have been taken into account.

To quantify the outcome "foster citizen participation and involvement" the following has been taken into account: (i) the time spent by each participant in the voting process (voting) and discussion (sending messages and comments) and (ii) the price assigned to each minute spent on both processes (€5/min). It was estimated that a citizen dedicated about 30 min to voting (15 min per round), 1 min sending the message and 30 s to write a comment associated with a message. The price per minute used (€5/min) was calculated as follows: a total of three hours (prior training, accreditation, 1st round of voting, discussion forum, 2nd round of voting, survey and closing) was the estimated time needed for each citizen to conduct the experiment. These hours were valued at €60/h. bearing in mind the activities carried out and the amount an external consultant would be willing to charge if they were to participate in the initiative. These €180 have been distributed over the 36 min which on average have been evaluated in the experiment (30 voting and 6 discussion), resulting in €5/minute.

To quantify the outcome "increase in the value of the methodology applied by the GDMZ", the cost of both the software used in the experience and that of the tool of the forum has been taken into account.

Lastly, to quantify the outcome "social recognition" the following have been taken into account: (i) the amount received from the two prizes obtained by the GDMZ for the development of the experience (ii) the price paid for attending congresses to make known the research projects awarded through the development of the initiative and (iii) the number of new projects that have been awarded as a result of the investigation carried out in the implementation of the Cadrete experience.

3.1.6   Calculation of the SROI Coefficient

This section presents the calculation of the SROI coefficient, that is, the division between the value of the social benefits (value of the outcomes) and the value of the investment (value of the inputs) (Table 5).

The coefficient has a value of 2.75, which means that, for each monetary unit invested in the Cadrete experience, a return of 2.75 monetary units of social value has been obtained.

Table 5. SROI coefficient

Calculation of the SROI coefficient	
Social benefits	115623.50€
Value of the investment	42046.73€
Coefficient	**2.75**

4 Conclusions and Future Work

Carrying out this SROI analysis has allowed the identification and quantification in monetary terms not only of the inputs that were necessary for the implementation and development of the eParticipation experience, based on eCognocracy, that took place in Cadrete but also of the outcomes obtained (social benefits). The relation between the social benefits and the total value of the investments of the experience has allowed us to calculate the SROI coefficient. The value of this coefficient was 2.75 units. This means that, for each monetary unit invested in the Cadrete experience, a return of 2.75 monetary units of social value has been obtained. Furthermore, it leads us to the conclusion that, in the development of an initiative based on eCognocracy, not only economic but also social and environmental value is created.

The carrying out of this SROI analysis shows a social-economic approach to the eParticipation experience, based on eCognocracy, that took place in Cadrete. This approach has allowed to measure the social, environmental and economic impact of an initiative. As its name indicates, this is an approach and, as such, it has its limitations. Besides, the Cadrete experience is a pilot experience and presents some limitations. This SROI analysis has not taken into account the evaluation of some outcomes, especially the intangible ones. The transparency of the process of participation, stakeholder satisfaction from feeling involved in the experience, cohesion, freedom, and equity are outcomes that have not been evaluated in the carrying out of this analysis due to their intangible nature and to the limitations of the experience. Thus, an immediate future research line will be to establish a methodology that allows the measurement, in monetary terms, of the intangible effects derived from carrying out an eParticipation experience. For this purpose, multi-criteria decision-making techniques will be employed.

Furthermore, in the item of *intellectual capital*, and in the development and elaboration of the software, the capital received by the GDMZ for the hiring of technical personnel during 2009, 2011 and 2012 has not been taken into account. The total quantity received amounted to 29,183 euros. It is intended that these limitations will be addressed and remedied with the application of the SROI analysis to other eParticipation experiences.

References

1. Jaeger, H.: Adaptive nonlinear system identification with echo state networks. In: Proceedings of NIPS 02, 2002, p. 8 (2002)
2. Wimmer, M.A.: A European perspective towards online one-stop government: the eGOV project. Electron. Commer. Res. Appl. **1**(1), 92–103 (2002)
3. Moreno-Jiménez, J.M.: E-cognocracia: Nueva Sociedad, Nueva Democracia. Estudios de Economía Aplicada **24**(1–2), 559–581 (2006)
4. Moreno-Jiménez, J.M., Polasek, W.: E-democracy and knowledge. A multicriteria framework for the new democratic era. J. Multicriteria Decis. Anal. **12**, 163–176 (2003)
5. Hadzilias, E.A.: A methodology framework for calculating the cost of e-Government services. In: Böhlen, M.H., Gamper, J., Polasek, W., Wimmer, M.A. (eds.) TCGOV 2005. LNCS (LNAI), vol. 3416, pp. 247–256. Springer, Heidelberg (2005)
6. Matusuda, S., Tsutsui, Y., Takashima, Y.: Evaluation of factors associated with well-being of elderly in an aged society by analytic hierarchy process analysis. Nihon Koshu Eisei Zasshi **45**(8), 704–712 (1998)
7. Bhatnagar, S.: Transparency and corruption: does egovernment help? DRAFT Paper prepared for the compilation of CHRI 2003 Report Open Sesame: looking for the Right to Information in the Commonwealth, Commonwealth Human Rights Initiative (2003). http://www.iimahd.ernet.in/~subhash/pdfs/CHRIDraftPaper2003.pdf#search=%27can%20egovernance%20curb%20corruption%20in%20tax%20departments
8. Gupta, M.P., Jana, D.: EGovernment evaluation: a framework and case study. Gov. Inf. Q. **20**(4), 365–387 (2003)
9. Ajilian, S., Crameri, C.: The economic & social impact of e - governance (2011). https://diuf.unifr.ch/main/is/sites/diuf.unifr.ch.main.is/files/documents/student-projects/eGov_2011_Ajilian_Stefanie_&_Crameri_Claudio.pdf
10. Loff, J.: Public return on investment: how to determine costs and benefits of EPSA participation and other reform projects. EPSA Trends in Practice Driving Public Sector Excellence to Shape Europe for 2020, pp. 105–115 (2011). http://issuu.com/eipa-epsa/docs/researchreport_web
11. Cuenin, F.: Patrimonio cultural y desarrollo socio económico: la recuperación de áreas centrales históricas. Banco Interamericano de Desarrollo (BDI), Notas Técnicas # IDB-TN-201, pp. 28–29 (2009)
12. Azqueta, D.: Introducción a la economía ambiental (2° edición), McGraw-Hill (2007)
13. Martínez, E., Escudey, M.: Evaluación y Decisión Multicriterio – reflexiones y experiencias. Editorial Universidad de Santiago/UNESCO, Santiago de Chile (1998)
14. O'Sullivan, D.: Project management in manufacturing using *IDEFO*. Int. J. Proj. Manag. **9**(3), 162 (1991)
15. Kaplan, R.S., Bruns, W.: Accounting and Management: A Field Study Perspective. Harvard Business School Press, Cambridge (1987). ISBN 0-87584-186-4
16. Millar, R., Hall K.: Social Return on Investment (SROI) and performance measurement. Public Management Review, pp. 1–19. ISSN 1471-9037 (in Press) (2012)
17. Moreno-Jiménez, J.M., Pérez-Espés, C., Velázquez, M.: ECognocracy and the design of public policies. Gov. Inf. Q. **31**, 185–194 (2014)

Policy Formulation and Modelling

Modeling for Policy Formulation:
Causal Mapping, Scenario Generation,
and Decision Evaluation

Aron Larsson[1,2](✉) and Osama Ibrahim[1]

[1] Department of Computer and Systems Sciences, Stockholm University,
Stockholm, Sweden
{aron, osama}@dsv.su.se
[2] Department of Information and Communications Systems,
Mid Sweden University, Sundsvall, Sweden

Abstract. In this paper we present a work process with associated operational research modeling and analysis tools for the policy formulation stage of the Lindblom policy cycle process model. The approach exploits the use of causal maps for problem structuring and scenario generation of policy options together with decision analysis for evaluating generated scenarios taking preferences of decision makers and stakeholders into account. The benefits of interest when exploiting this integrated modeling approach is to enable for; (i) problem structuring and facilitating understanding and communication of a complex policy problem, (ii) simulation of policy consequences and identification of a smaller set of policy options from a possible very large set of possible options, and (iii) structured decision evaluation of the generated alternative policy options.

Keywords: Policy analysis · Impact assessment · Policy modelling · Problem structuring · Dynamic simulation · Causal mapping · Scenario planning · Decision analysis

1 Introduction

A large body of public policy analysis is devoted to retrospective analysis (evaluation), which tries to understand the causes and consequences of policies after they have been implemented (Tsoukiàs et al. 2013). Equally important in policy analysis is the role of ex ante evaluations, i.e. prescriptive analysis involving impact assessment carried out at the early stages of policy development, cf., e.g., (Turpenny et al. 2009). Ex ante evaluation encompasses forecasting of consequences if policies were to be implemented and prescriptions about which policies should be implemented. One important aim of ex ante decision support within the context of policy making therefore involve developing ways of facilitating for policy-makers to create policies that is consistent with their preferences while at the same time being accepted by other stakeholders, cf. (Bryson 2007). However, there is a lack of operational approaches for addressing the cognitive activity of designing or finding policy options. The long term implications of policy making imply the need to consider a vast range of possible futures, often

© IFIP International Federation for Information Processing 2015
E. Tambouris et al. (Eds.): ePart 2015, LNCS 9249, pp. 135–146, 2015.
DOI: 10.1007/978-3-319-22500-5_11

characterized by the presence of multiple stakeholders and sometimes characterized by large uncertainties as well.

Problem structuring are now widely acknowledged as an important feature of strategic decision support tools and there is a growing but still small body of research and practice on how to integrate such methods with other formal and/or quantitative methods for decision evaluation, see (Tsoukiàs et al. 2013). The aim of this paper is therefore to provide a basis for the selection and use of modeling and decision support tools from the operational research field in a common toolkit for ex ante policy analysis, such that there is a logical relationship between the tool used to the stage and sub-stage of the policy making process and how the modeling tools provide decision value in the policy making process.

2   Policy Making Process and Policy Formulation

Herein public policy is defined as a purposeful, goal-oriented action that is taken by government to deal with societal problems or to improve societal conditions for the wellbeing of its population. Decision making is the cognitive process of selecting a course of action from many possible ones which might be initially known or not known. According to Bero and Jadad (1997) policy making has some distinguishing features having an impact on the decision process:

(i)   A population level decision making context;
(ii) Explicit justification is required, as policies are formally and informally evaluated by government agencies, by outside consultants, by interest groups, by the mass media, and by the public;
(iii) Effect of the existing political ideology and governance; and
(iv) Evidence of systematic reviews on public policy decisions is hard to come by.

We relate to three-stage process model for policy-making conforming to the well-established policy cycle models of Lindblom (1968) and Howlett et al. (2009). The process model includes the following steps; (i) problem identification stage, (ii) policy formulation stage, and (iii) policy implementation stage, see Fig. 1.

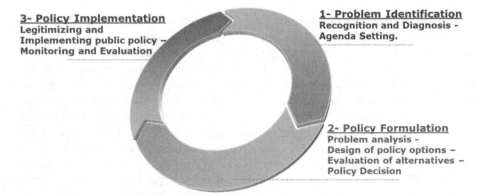

Fig. 1. Policy-making process model.

This process model acknowledges that policy-making is an ongoing, continuous process that requires continuous assessment, evaluation, and reaction. Each stage has a set of activities according to Table 1 below.

Table 1. Stages and sub-stages of the policy-making process model.

Stage	Activity
1. Problem identification	Recognition and diagnosis: Decision makers become aware of the fact that there is a problem and diagnosis is required to order and combine the information related to that problem Agenda Setting: Focusing attention, involving interest groups, setting targets, defining and documenting the long view and/or the short view of the policy
2. Policy formulation	Problem analysis: Identify elements of policy problem: actors, stakeholders, decision variables, parameters, links, goals, risks, limitations and associated technologies Identify problem environment: conflicting goals, inter- and intra-group negotiations. Specify decision dynamics: interrupts, feedback loops, delays, and speedups Design and generation of policy options: Formulate policy proposals through political channels by policy planning organisations, interest groups and government bureaucracies. Identify the feasible options that will or might lead to desired policy consequences, conduct impact assessments of different policy options Evaluation of policy options/alternatives: Compare the feasible options, considering that conflicting goals are likely to exist as well as differing acceptance levels for different stakeholders Policy Decision: Decide upon policy after evaluation of the options encompassing different viewpoints and perspectives, multiple objectives, and multiple stakeholders using integrated assessments
3. Policy implementation	Legitimizing and implementing a public policy: Policy is legitimized as a result of the public statements or actions of government officials at all levels. This includes: executive orders, rules, regulations, laws, budgets, appropriations, decisions and interpretations that have the effect of setting policy direction. Policy is implemented through the activities of public bureaucracies and the expenditure of public funds Monitoring and Evaluation: Record and control of the implementation. Analysis, evaluation and feedback of the results of implementation

Hence, a large part of the activities occurring within a policy cycle is about understanding, formulating and structuring "problems", see also (Mingers and Rosenhead 2004; Tsoukiàs 2007). Thus, problem structuring is a key element of the public policy making process and in particular for the policy formulation stage. Modeling for problem structuring in order to find feasible policy options and decision evaluation of these options is of prime concern in the policy formulation stage, since in this stage "policy makers must ensure that there is a meaningful definition of the problem" and "need a comprehensive understanding of the problem" in order to identify different policy options (Hamilton 2010). Having this said, in the next section we focus on operational research and the decision sciences within the context of supporting policy formulation and a selection of methods for an integrated modeling approach to policy formulation decision support is suggested.

3   Modeling for Policy Formulation

3.1   Problem Analysis

Problem analysis calls for problem structuring methods (PSM) which aim to enable a better understanding of unstructured problems characterized by the existence of multiple actors, multiple perspectives, incommensurable and/or conflicting interests, intangibles and key uncertainties. The methods rely heavily on engaging with policy makers, adopting a facilitative mode of engagement, and simple, often qualitative, models (Franco and Montibeller 2010). See (Mingers and Rosenhead 2001) for an overview of the characteristics of a wide range of PSM's.

The use of cognitive maps is among the early approaches to enable for problem understanding, originally intended for representing social science knowledge, see (Axelrod 1976). A cognitive map is a directed graph where nodes represents societal concepts or variables (such as subsidy size, traffic intensity, CO_2 emission rates) and links represent causal connections between these concepts. With respect to the simple example, two nodes "car traffic" and "emissions" and a link from the former to the latter would then mean that the former causally has an impact on the latter, negative or positive.

Multiple perspectives of the problem from different actors can be represented and debated for improving the policy-makers' understanding of the problem situation and sharing it with associates. Several "dialects" of cognitive maps have emerged, which share focus on the qualitative aspects of problem structuring, see, e.g., (Acar and Druckenmiller 2006).

Although a cognitive map serves its purpose as a problem structuring method, its content is too informal to be used as an underlying model for simulation of how changes in one node affects other nodes through causal relations. A causal map in the sense of Acar (1983) is a diagram that maps problem variables, or factors, and defines their interdependencies in a quantitative manner. Goals for different actors of the problem can be defined to facilitate group decision making and negotiation analysis. The primitive elements used in the causal mapping method are: Independent variables (sources of change), dependent variables (intermediate and outcome/goal variables), change transmission channels, change transfer coefficients, time lags, minimum thresholds (minimum change to be transferred), status-quo level of the map (the initial state of the system, considering 0 % relative change), and goal vector representing the targeted changes in goal variables relative to status-quo values.

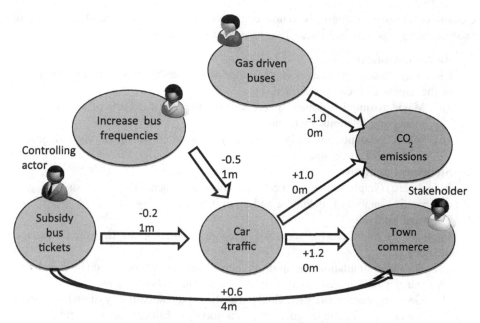

Fig. 2. Causal map model of bus ticket price subsidy policy problem with four actors, three controlling resources on the left hand side and one actor having an interest in the town commerce factor. The goal vector consists of that the three controlling actors want to reduce CO_2 emissions by 20 % while the third actor wants to increase town commerce with 5 %. Each link has a change transfer coefficient and a time lag. For instance, the link from "Subsidy bus tickets" into "Car traffic" has a coefficient of -0.2 and a time lag of 1 month.

As a simple example, consider a local government wanting to reduce CO_2 emissions in order to contribute to climate targets and improve central town air quality. The upfront objectives are focused on the environmental issue. One policy option is to increase the subsidy of bus tickets, where the underlying hypothesis in terms of causality is that higher subsidies (lower ticket prices) will cause more people to take the bus instead of cars when going into town, thereby reducing emissions also enabling for more citizens to access the central town area increasing town commerce, which is the main concern of an influential stakeholder group. However, there is also a positive causal relationship between car traffic and town commerce, increasing the complexity of the policy option making. In the problem analysis, it becomes clear that for many citizens it is not the bus ticket price that cause them to avoid taking the bus, but rather the frequency of buses. Further, reducing emissions can also be done by increasing the proportion of gas driven buses. A causal map of the policy problem can then be illustrated in Fig. 2 above.

The richer computational semantics of the causal mapping approach support simulation in ways that other varieties of cognitive mapping and causal mapping do not, see (Druckenmiller and Acar 2009). The method includes indications not only of the signs of the presumed causal influences, but also of their intensities, minimum threshold values and the time lags. Still, it is possible to utilize the non-quantitative elements of the map analogously to how cognitive maps are employed. Three classes of analyses are supported, see (Acar 1983) for detailed description:

1- **Backward analysis:**
   Clarifying, testing and reassessing assumptions about the cause-effect relationships of the situation. It can be divided into:
   (a) Major assumptional analysis (validity of the major aspects of the graph elements and relationships); and
   (b) Minor assumptional analysis (validity of detailed qualifications and quantifications of the graph).

2- **Structural analysis:**
   It includes: Graph scope, connectivity analysis, reachability analysis and goal comparative analysis (qualitative and quantitative).

3- **Forward analysis:**
   Implications of a "change scenario" through simulating the transfer of change, includes:
   (a) Scenario simulation: running change scenarios on the graph – simulating transfer of change over time from origins throughout the map.
   (b) Goal negotiation analysis: Goal feasibility and compatibility of goals, identify scenarios realizing a goal or goals jointly). Effectiveness or efficiency – expression of outcomes in comparison with objectives and relative to change needed at origins.

Within policy formulation, a policy option would be represented by a change scenario. Feasible scenarios would be the ones who satisfy the actors by reaching their goals in different ways, and in this way scenarios can be generated/discovered (Bryant and Lempert 2010). The method cannot capture all the intricacies of a situation to its minutest details, but can sufficiently map out its principal elements and their relationships.

3.2   Design and Generation of Policy Options

The identification and creation of new alternatives is one of the most important aspects of any decision support. If the decision alternatives under consideration are weak, it will lead to a poor choice (Brown 2005). Thus, support in the generation of feasible options is important for policy formulation.

A policy option is represented by a scenario of change from the status-quo level of the causal map. A base line scenario is defined with initial values for the problem's key variables with zero initial relative changes. The desired state of the system is represented by a goal vector (targeted relative changes in outcome variables compared to the base line scenario). The causal map allows triggering change transfer by a 'Pure scenario', a single change at one source, or a 'Mixed scenario', change in several sources all at once or with a time lag.

Graph change analysis allows us to investigate the dynamic consequences of entering a change in one of the graph origins, thus simulating the propagation of change throughout the causal map. Several decision analytic concepts are readily usable for scenario generation:

- "Optimality", relating scenarios to the level or degree to which the goal vector is realised.
- "Dominance", reducing the number of scenarios by discarding dominated ones.
- "Resource constraint", cost of input triggers of certain magnitude at a node. Triggering a scenario may impose on the controlling actor the supply of funds and resources.
- "Goal compatibility", goal vectors of different actors is compatible if a scenario can be found to realize them jointly.

The simulation is run upon the causal map modeled, whereas the set of objectives and their target values are used for identifying feasible scenarios. Based on the simulation results of an initially large sample of scenarios generated by, e.g., full factorial design or Latin hypercube sampling, unsatisfactory scenarios not realizing the goal vector or being dominated are filtered out, while scenarios deemed efficient and "interesting" according to some predefined decision rule based upon resource constraints and goal compatibility concepts mentioned above are suggested as policy options for further evaluation.

3.3 Evaluation of Policy Options

Arriving at a set of feasible options which are non-dominated, further discrimination between them will call for taking preference information into account. Although, the scenario-based dynamic simulation allows decision makers to identify alternative policy options and verify their effects over time, it does not provide the explicit decision evaluation of policy options. Multi-criteria decision analysis (MCDA) has been extensively used to support a wide variety of complex decision problems as a tool for evaluating options where decisions involve the achievement of multiple objectives and considering multiple decision makers and stakeholders, see, e.g., (Zavadskas et al. 2014). MCDA typically distinguish between a decision maker which has control of some decision variable, and stakeholders, which are affected by the consequences of a decision. This distinction is straightforwardly analogous to the actor representations of the causal map. Applying MCDA should thus provide the relative global performance of each alternative, and is particularly useful when selecting one out of a finite set of feasible alternatives.

When evaluation of policy options is guided by a decision analysis approach, a relevant MCDA model is required equipped with preference elicitation methods for capturing policy makers' and stakeholders' preferences. Given that we have identified feasible policy options from scenario generation, there are two main tasks remaining in structuring MCDA evaluation models; (i) representation of objectives in a structure, commonly a value tree, and (ii) the definition of attributes to measure the achievement of objectives (Franco and Montibeller 2011).

Traditionally in MCDA, the decision process starts by structuring the problem as an attribute tree hierarchically ordering the decision makers' aims at different abstraction levels, from fundamental objectives (such as "improved environment") to lower level attributes (such as "NO_x reduction") where the latter contributes to the former in a hierarchical value tree. It is generally assumes that each criterion can be operationalized by a set of measurable attributes allowing for assessing the consequences arising from the implementation of any particular alternative. In the next step preferential information is elicited. The relative importance of criteria is captured in weights for each criterion at each abstraction level. At the lowest level of the value tree these objectives are translated into attributes, with each one of them evaluating a given characteristic of the decision options (for example, an objective 'efficiency' may be measured by the attribute 'operating cost'). The performance of each decision option against each attribute is determined and weights reflecting acceptable trade-offs of performance among objectives are elicited from the decision-makers. Given the presence of many decision makers or stakeholders, for a group decision a decision has to be made and there might be disagreement with respect to what the best option is, but the group choice still has sufficient support from the group, i.e. there is a way of representing the collective preferences of the group. This differs from negotiation in that in such as process each stakeholder might simply abandon the decision process and there is no decision at all, see, e.g., (Kilgour et al. 2010).

There is no universal way of applying MCDA to group decision and negotiation processes, but the underlying use of a causal map and scenarios generated leads to that the features of interest are preference elicitation and preference aggregation. With respect to integrating multi-criteria decision analysis with causal maps and simulation of scenarios, Comes et al. (2011) presents the concept of "decision maps", integrating problem structuring and scenario planning using causal maps with multi-criteria decision analysis, but keeps the focus on operational decision making and to a lesser extent on policy making. However, the structure and content of the map informs the building of the value tree, in an ad hoc translation, in which, the causal map can be used to elicit preferences, cf. (Comes et al. 2011). For a simple example of this, see Fig. 5 showing a value tree model based upon the causal map of Fig. 4. Montibeller and Belton (2006) investigate various ways to use causal maps as the underlying problem structuring tool and extending it with decision evaluation features and/or using the map to effectively inform the decision analysis model in the form of a multi attribute value tree.

For simulation, in the SEMPAI[1] framework reported in Hansson et al. (2011), simulation results of flooding models are combined with multi-criteria decision analysis where multiple stakeholders are present. Elicitation or anticipation of stakeholder preferences is done or assessed in the form of utility statements for each stakeholder or stakeholder group regarding each specific policy option and criteria weights. Stakeholders give the different outcomes a ranking order if they are unsure of their preferred choice and methods for computational decision analysis with imprecise information is promoted in order to support such statements, see (Larsson et al. 2005, Danielson et al. 2007). The result is a preference assessment for each decision maker and/or stakeholder and the value tree is constructed with stakeholders as the lowest level of the tree, see Fig. 4 for the value tree corresponding to the causal map of Fig. 3 where each decision

---

[1] Simulation and Evaluation with Multiple Perspectives and Agents Integrated.

maker has a trade-off expressed as criteria weights between cost and their benefits of concern. With respect to the model in Fig. 4, we can consider the following simple preference scheme using value functions $V(S)$ of the scenarios for each criterion delimiting the decision evaluation to the status-quo scenario called S_0 and the generated scenario shown in Fig. 3 called S_1 (also in Table 2).

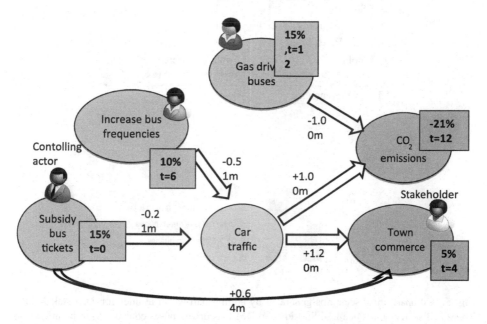

Fig. 3. Example of a generated scenario reaching both the emission and the town commerce target. The scenario consists of increasing the subsidy with 15 % at the initial timestep, increasing bus frequencies at the sixth, and increasing the proportion of gas driven buses at timestep 12.

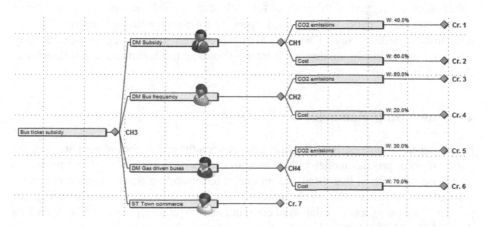

Fig. 4. Value tree counterpart of causal map in Fig. 3 in accordance to the SEMPAI framework. In this example, DM Subsidy's weight for CO_2 emissions is 40 % so for simplicity precise numerical weights are used here.

Table 2. Preference schema.

Decision maker	CO$_2$ emissions		Cost	
	$V(S_0)$	$V(S_1)$	$V(S_0)$	$V(S_1)$
DM Subsidy	0	1	1	0
DM Bus frequency	0	1	1	0
DM Gas driven buses	0	1	1	0

Stakeholder	Town commerce	
	$V(S_0)$	$V(S_1)$
ST Town commerce	0	1

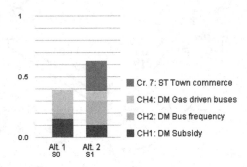

Fig. 5. Comparison of scenarios generated by adding part-worth utilities for each stakeholder. There is disagreement since DM Subsidy and DM Gas driven buses consider S_1 to be inferior to S_0 while the other actors have differing preferences.

Decision evaluation is then done stakeholder-wise. Each decision maker or stakeholder will receive a utility value for each scenario and the choice of selecting or discarding one scenario will be based upon its total utility through aggregating the stakeholders' utility values (see Fig. 5) together with group decision admissibility concepts such as maximum disagreement thresholds or minimum consensus thresholds (Fasth et al. 2013).

4   Concluding Remarks

In this paper we have outlined the linkages between the policy formulation stage of the policy making process model and contemporary decision analytic support methodologies and based upon that discussed an integrated modeling framework for computer assisted policy formulation. The approach suggested combines causal mapping for problem structuring and simulation of consequences together with identifying scenarios deemed feasible for further investigation in a multi-criteria decision evaluation. This sequence follows a logical work process conforming to the activities of the policy formulation process.

Scenario generation helps policy-makers in identifying feasible options from a possibly vast space of possible ones reaching stipulated targets, while the decision evaluation can supports an in-depth performance evaluation of policy proposals taking the preferences of stakeholders into account. The resulting integrated model for the policy problem situation can improve the process of reaching well-accepted scenarios and a transparent design of policy options while taking into account costs, benefits, resource constraints, different perspectives, and multiple objectives. In the context of policy-making the decision makers are often confronted with large and complex amounts of information, not seldom of a conflicting nature and reflect multiple interests. Problem structuring and decision analysis allows policy-makers to judge the performance of alternative policy options and from stakeholders' different points of view of what represents a positive or negative policy impact. Hence, policy impact assessment frameworks and tools have much to gain from implementing decision analytic support methodologies.

References

Acar, W.: Toward a Theory of Problem Formulation and the Planning of Change: Causal Mapping and Dialectical Debate in Situation Formulation. U.M.I, Ann Arbor (1983)

Acar, W., Druckenmiller, D.: Endowing cognitive mapping with computational properties for strategic analysis. Futures **38**, 993–1009 (2006)

Axelrod, R.: The cognitive mapping approach to decision making. In: Axelrod, R. (ed.) Structure of Decision, pp. 221–250. Princeton University Press, Princeton (1976)

Bero, L.A., Jadad, A.R.: How consumers and policymakers can use systematic reviews for decision making. Ann. Intern. Med. **727**(1), 37–42 (1997)

Brown, R.: Rational Choice and Judgment: Decision Analysis for the Decider. Wiley, New York (2005)

Bryant, B.P., Lempert, R.J.: Thinking inside the box: a participatory, computer-assisted approach to scenario discovery. Technol. Forecast. Soc. Chang. **77**, 34–49 (2010)

Bryson, J.M.: What to do when stakeholders matter. Public Manag. Rev. **6**(1), 21–53 (2007)

Comes, T., Hiete, M., Wijngaards, N., Schultmann, F.: Decision maps: a framework for multi-criteria decision support under severe uncertainty. Decis. Support Syst. **52**, 108–118 (2011)

Danielson, M., Ekenberg, L., Idefeldt, J., Larsson, A.: Using a software tool for public decision analysis: the case of Nacka municipality. Decis. Anal. **4**(2), 76–90 (2007)

Druckenmiller, D.A., Acar, W.: An agent-based collaborative approach to graphing causal maps for situation formulation. J. Assoc. Inf. Syst. **10**(3), 3 (2009)

Fasth, T., Kalinina, M., Larsson, A.: Admissibility concepts for group portfolio decision analysis. In: Proceedings of GDN 2013 (2013)

Franco, L.A., Montibeller, G.: Problem structuring for multicriteria decision analysis interventions. In: Cochran, et al. (eds.) Wiley Encyclopedia of Operations Research and Management Science. Wiley, New York (2011)

Hansson, K., Larsson, A., Danielson, M., Ekenberg, L.: Coping with complex environmental and societal flood risk management strategies: an integrated multi-criteria framework. Sustainability **3**(9), 1357–1380 (2011)

Hamilton, A.: Policy formulation – critique, analysis and strategic implications, in new voices: essays on the policy process. JSGS Student Working Paper Series, Johnson-Shoyama Graduate School of Public Policy (2010)

Franco, L.A., Montibeller, G.: Facilitated modelling in operational research. Eur. J. Oper. Res. **205**, 489–500 (2010)

Howlett, M., Ramesh, M., Perl, A.: Studying Public Policy: Policy Cycles & Subsystems. Oxford, New York (2009)

Kilgour, D.M., Chen, Y., Hipel, K.W.: Multiple criteria approaches to group decision and negotiation. In: Ehrgott, et al. (eds.) Trends in Multiple Criteria Decision Analysis. Springer, Berlin (2010)

Larsson, A., Johansson, J., Ekenberg, L., Danielson, M.: Decision analysis with multiple objectives in a framework for evaluating imprecision. Int. J. Uncertainty, Fuzziness Knowl. Based Syst. **13**, 495–510 (2005)

Lindblom, C.: The Policy-Making Process. Prentice-Hall, Englewood Cliffs (1968)

Mingers, J., Rosenhead, J.: Rational Analysis for a Problematic World Revisited: Problem Structuring Methods for Complexity, Uncertainty and Conflict. Wiley, New York (2001)

Mingers, J., Rosenhead, J.: Problem structuring methods in action. Eur. J. Oper. Res. **152**(3), 530–554 (2004)

Montibeller, G., Belton, V.: Causal maps and the evaluation of decision options – a review. J. Oper. Res. Soc. **57**, 779–791 (2006)

Tsoukiàs, A.: On the concept of decision aiding process: an operational perspective. Ann. Oper. Res. **154**(1), 3–27 (2007)

Tsoukiàs, A., Montibeller, G., Lucertini, G., Belton, V.: Policy analytics: an agenda for research and practice. EURO J. Decis. Process. **1**, 115–134 (2013)

Turnpenny, J., Radaelli, C.M., Jordan, A., Jacob, K.: The policy and politics of policy appraisal: emerging trends and new directions. J. Eur. Public Policy **16**(4), 640–653 (2009)

Zavadskas, E.K., Turskis, Z., Kildiene, S.: State of art surveys of overviews on MCDM/MADM methods. Technol. Econ. Dev. Econ. **20**(1), 165–179 (2014)

Opinion Mining and Sentiment Analysis in Policy Formulation Initiatives: The EU-Community Approach

Yannis Charalabidis, Manolis Maragoudakis,
and Euripides Loukis[✉]

University of the Aegean, 2 Palama Street, 83200 Karlovasi, Samos, Greece
{yannisx,mmarag,eloukis}@aegean.gr

Abstract. In the last decade there is extensive and continuously growing creation of political content in the Internet, and especially in the Web 2.0 social media, which can be quite useful for government agencies in order to understand the needs and problems of societies and formulate effective public policies for addressing them. So a variety of ICT-based methods have been developed for the exploitation of this political content by governments ('citizensourcing'), initially simpler and later more sophisticated ones. These ICT-based methods are increasingly based on the use of opinion mining (OM) and sentiment analysis (SA) techniques, in order to process the extensive political content collected from numerous sources. This paper describes a novel approach to OM and SA use, created as part of an advanced ICT-based method of exploiting political content created in the Internet, and especially in social media, by experts ('expertsourcing'), aiming to leverage the extensive policy community of the European Union, which is developed in the European EU-Community project. Furthermore, some first experimental results of it are presented.

Keywords: Opinion mining · Sentiment analysis · Public policy · Social media

1 Introduction

In the last decade there is extensive and continuously growing creation of political content in the Internet, and especially in the Web 2.0 social media, which has the form of numerous political postings, comments, articles and debates in various electronic spaces (e.g. web sites and social media accounts of political institutions and traditional or electronic media, political blogs, etc.). Citizens are increasingly using the above electronic media as efficient channels for the creation and exchange of extensive political content, and also for the quick organization of collective political action with large numbers of participants (Chadwick 2009; Shirky 2011; Bekkers et al. 2011). This political content can be quite useful for government agencies, as it can significantly assist them to understand the needs and problems of society, and the perceptions and feelings of the citizens, and to formulate effective public policies. The 'wicked nature' (Kunz and Rittel 1979; Conklin and Begeman 1989; Conclin 2003) and the continuously increasing complexity of social problems and needs makes this political content even more valuable,

© IFIP International Federation for Information Processing 2015
E. Tambouris et al. (Eds.): ePart 2015, LNCS 9249, pp. 147–160, 2015.
DOI: 10.1007/978-3-319-22500-5_12

as it contains extensive knowledge of citizens concerning social problems and needs, which can be quite useful for understanding and managing their complexity.

For the above reasons a variety of ICT-based methods have been developed for the exploitation of this political content by government agencies (aiming at conducting various forms of 'citizensourcing'), initially simpler and later more sophisticated ones. In this evolution we can distinguish four discrete 'generations'. The first generation includes the creation of websites and social media accounts of government agencies, which provide information about existing and planned policies of the latter and allow citizens to create political content on them (e.g. comments, suggestions, etc.). As this citizens-generated political content becomes massive, it becomes difficult to process it manually, and this gives rise to the development of a second generation of ICT based methods, which automatically retrieve this political content from various sources using (e.g. various social media accounts and websites of the particular government agency) their APIs, and then process it in order to generate various kind of 'analytics' (Kokkinakos et al. 2012; Wandhöfer et al. 2012; Charalabidis and Loukis 2012; Ferro et al. 2013). However, gradually it was realized that the most useful political content is generated beyond the websites and social media accounts, in numerous 'external' political forums, blogs, news websites, and also in various Twitter, Facebook, etc. accounts, without any stimulation from government; this gave rise to the development of a third generation of ICT based methods, which are oriented towards the automatic retrieval of this 'external' content using the APIs of the sources, and then its advanced processing (Bekkers et al. 2013; Loukis and Charalabidis 2014; Charalabidis et al. 2014a). The above three first generations of ICT tools were oriented towards the political content generated by the general public. This can provide valuable insights into the perceptions of the general public concerning important social problems and existing or planned public policies, which are definitely quite important for the formulation of effective policies. However, in order to collect higher quality content concerning social problems and public policies it is necessary to target specific communities having strong interest and knowledge on them. This leads to the development of a fourth generation of such ICT based methods, which focus on the retrieval and processing of high quality content about social problems and public policies created by experts ('expertsourcing'); some first research in this direction is conducted in the European project EU-Community (partially funded by the 'ICT for Governance and Policy Modelling' research initiative of the European Union (EU) - see http://project. eucommuni-ty.eu/), which aims to exploit and leverage the extensive policy community of EU (Charalabidis et al. 2014b, c).

These ICT-based methods are increasingly based on the use of opinion mining (OM) and sentiment analysis (SA) techniques (Maragoudakis et al. 2011; Wandhöfer et al. 2013), in order to automatically process the extensive political content collected from numerous sources, and extract from it useful elements (e.g. main topics discussed, sentiments (positive or negative), etc.), which enable better insights into social problems and needs, and provide substantial assistance for formulating public policies. However, the evolution of the ICT-based methods for the exploitation of the political content created in various web sites and social media accounts, creates new requirements with respect to OM/SA use, and necessitates the development of new ways of using OM/SA for meeting the particular needs and serving the objectives of each new method. This paper makes a contribution in this direction, by describing a novel approach to OM and SA use, created as part of the abovementioned fourth generation ICT-based method of exploiting political content created in the Internet, and especially in social media, by experts ('expertsourcing'), aiming to leverage the extensive policy community of the European Union. Furthermore, some first experimental results of it are presented.

In the following Sect. 2 the EU-Community project is outlined. In Sect. 3 the state of the art with respect to OM/SA use in similar project is discussed, together with the innovative features of the proposed OM/SA approach for the EU-Community project, which is described in Sect. 4. Some first experimental results of it are presented in Sect. 5, while the final Sect. 6 summarizes the conclusions.

2 Context: The EU-Community Project

As mentioned in the introduction, though the first three generations of ICT based methods for the exploitation of the political content created in the Internet, and especially in the Web 2.0 social media, were focusing on the general public, it was realized that in order to collect higher quality political content about the social problems and the public policies (existing and planned) it is necessary to adopt a more selective 'expertsourcing' oriented approach: to focus on content created by experts, who are highly knowledgeable on the specific topic/policy we are interested in and widely recognized. This is in line with previous research on policy networks (Skogstad 2005; Rhodes 2006, 2007), which has concluded that due to the growing complexity and of social problems and policy making, and also their dynamic nature (frequent changes), governments cannot design and implement public policies based only on their own information and knowledge resources; for this reason they are increasingly making use of 'external' information and knowledge resources of various non-state actors (initially economic actors and later other social and scientific actors as well), and cooperate with them, in order to design and implement effective public policies, and this has resulted in the generation of public policy networks.

The above lead to the development of a fourth generation of ICT based methods, which are focusing on the most knowledgeable and credible people on each topic/policy we are interested in. Such a method is developed in the European project EU-Community, which aims to exploit and leverage the extensive policy community of EU in order to support its policy making. An overview of this method is shown below in Fig. 1. It consists of three main processes: the first two of them crawl at regular time intervals the most relevant external sources of EU policies knowledgeable and credible people, and also of relevant documents of various types, update the corresponding databases, and also process the retrieved data, and assess their reputation/credibility of the former and the relevance of the latter. These databases are then used by the third process, which processes users' queries (e.g. concerning the most reputable/credible people, or the most relevant documents on a specific topic, etc.) and presents the results, making use of visualization/visual analytics techniques. More information about this ICT based expertsourcing method are provided by Charalabidis et al. (2014b, c). The research presented in this paper concerns the second of the above processes (shown in the right part of

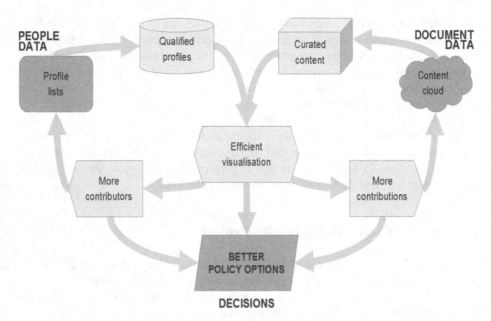

Fig. 1. An overview of the ICT-based expertsourcing method developed in the EU-Community project

Fig. 1), and focuses on the advanced processing of the retrieved documents through an innovative use of OM/SA techniques.

3 State of the Art

In order to design the OM/SA approach in the EU Community, we have studied the use of these technologies in related recent EU projects, which all aim at the exploitation of various types of political content created by citizens in the Internet, with main emphasis on the social media (in order to develop knowledge models, recommendations, intelligent services, etc.). A review of this OM/SA use approaches is initially provided in this section, and then are described the innovative features of the proposed OM/SA approach for the EU-Community project with respect to these recent related projects.

3.1 Related Projects

+spaces (2010–2012). +Spaces ("Positive Spaces") was a research project research aiming at supporting the formulation of effective public policies by assessing the impacts of prospective policies, using political content created in various Facebook and Twitter, alongside virtual spaces (VS), like Open Wonderland. Modern VSs can be viewed as micro-societies, with dynamics resembling those of real world societies, the most evolved ones having virtual economies as well as regulations analogous to real-life legislative frameworks. Moreover, VSs are controlled environments in which all parameters of users' reactions and interactions can be tracked, so they can be very useful for assessing impacts of various policy options. In this project, information retrieval mechanisms and ON/SA were applied in order to collect data from VS and process them. Structured data from polls and petitions as well as unstructured data from VS blogs and debate logs were incorporated, together with relational information like social networks from user tracing.

E-policy (2011–2014). The E-Policy ("Engineering the POlicy-making LIfe CYcle") project aimed at supporting policy makers for 'engineering' the policy making life-cycle, integrating both global and individual perspectives. Its objectives included assessment of social impacts through opinion mining on e-participation data from various thematic web sites and Web 2.0 platforms that allowed users to express their opinions on energy related topics through textual messages. In this project opinion mining identified social impacts that should be considered at both global and individual levels. At the global level, opinion mining aggregated individual opinions as trend line in order to conduct policy evaluation. Finally regression analysis was performed, in which text sentiment, estimated as a numeric score in the interval of $[-2; 2]$, with negative (positive) values indicating negative (positive) sentiment, was used as one of many independent variables in impact simulation modules.

Render (2010–2013). The Render ("Reflecting Knowledge Diversity") project targeted at leveraging diversity (viewed as a valuable asset and crucial source of innovation and adaptability) in information management, in order to allow for better communication and collaboration. Under this objective, they addressed the problem of sentiment analysis in multiple domains and several languages, such as English, French, German, Italian, and Spanish. They exploited domain knowledge in the form of different sentiment lexicons, as well as the influence of various lexical surface features. Experimental results showed that the improvement resulting from using a two-layer model, sentiment lexicons, surface features and feature scaling is quite important, especially in social media textual datasets. Also, in this project, a tool was developed that performs sentiment classification and visualization of Twitter short texts, which enables the analysis and visualization of diversity in tweets.

Arcomem (2011–2014). This project aims to enable memory institutions like archives, museums, and libraries to use and incorporate relevant social media content. A series of initial applications have been developed for opinion mining from social media using GATE, a freely available toolkit for language processing. Based on the work described in Maynard and Funk (2011), which focused on sentiments identification in tweets about political parties, their methodologies were extended to a more generic analysis of sentiment about any kind of entity or event mentioned, focusing on two specific domains: the current Greek financial crisis and the Rock am Ring rock festival in Germany in 2010. For both cases, first a basic sentiment analysis was performed, by associating a positive, negative or neutral sentiment to each relevant opinion target, together with a polarity score. As a next step, entity or event extraction was performed. A modified version of ANNIE, the default Named Entity (NE) recognition system in GATE, was used in order to identify mentions of persons, locations, organizations, dates, times and financial concepts. Sentiment analysis is performed by using a rule-based approach.

TrendMiner (2011–2014). TrendMiner dealt with large-scale, cross-lingual trend mining and summarization of real-time social media streams. This project was very similar to the abovementioned project ArcoMem, involving more or less the same OM/SA methodology and tools. Again, the use of sentiment lexicons, special purpose gazetteers and rule-based approaches, under GATE platform, comprised the overall strategy for performing OM/SA on social media.

Padgets (2010–2012). PADGETS ("Policy Gadgets Mashing Underlying Group Knowledge in Web 2.0 Media") focused on multilingual SA of citizens postings in government social media accounts, as a response to government policy campaigns and postings on specific topics/policies of interest. The main research objective of this project was to develop a methodology and a technological platform for the systematic and centrally managed exploitation of the emerging Web 2.0 social media by government organizations in their policy and decision making processes (Ferro et al. 2013). Citizens' postings (concerning opinions and comments) in government accounts in a variety of social media platforms, such as Twitter, Facebook, YouTube, Blogger, etc., were analyzed in order to identify citizens' sentiments. Since texts in social media tend to be very small, a machine learning approach was followed, in which limited linguistic resources were required. There was also a sentiment analysis module that incorporated sentiment lexicons, but this proved to perform significantly worse than machine learning models. Moreover, inclusion of emotional writing style attribute was taken into account in order to augment the performance of SA. From a technical point of view, feature selection was performed using a hybrid scheme of Support Vector Machines and Genetic algorithms. The system was implemented using RapidMiner®.

Nomad (2012–2015). The NOMAD project ("Policy Formulation and Validation through non-moderated crowd sourcing") aimed at enabling government agencies to exploit the extensive political content created in the social media beyond their own accounts, in multiple external sources (e.g. political blogs and forums, news websites, and various Twitter, Facebook, etc. accounts) (Loukis and Charalabidis 2014). For this purpose there is extensive use of sophisticated OM/SA techniques, such as semantically driven textual data acquisition, sentiment analysis, thematic analysis, topics extraction and arguments extraction, and summarization. The main technology used was polarity lexica with some learning algorithms that exploit name entities.

3.2   Innovative Features of the OM/SA of the EU-Community Project

The EU-Community project, in order to meet its particular objectives and requirements, has developed a novel approach to OM/SA (described in the following section), which includes some interesting innovative features with respect to the above similar projects, shown below in Table 1.

Table 1. Innovative Features of the OM/SA approach of the EU-Community project

Other Projects	EU-Community	Explanation
OM/SA is mostly performed on short-sized texts from social media opinion channels	OM/SA is functioning in a dual manner, both for short-sized opinions posted by users in various social media channels, and for larger documents, such as articles, positions and RSS feeds	While most existing projects focus on small texts, originating from social media platforms, our approach supports OM/SA in larger documents as well
Are based on rule-based systems and polarity lexicons	It is using a hybrid model that combines polarity resources and machine learning	The proposed approach is utilizing both rule-based systems and classification rules extracted from data
Provide a single polarity estimation for a whole document	It can support a dual mode of both document and sentence-level OM/SA	Usually, the sentiment score is a single number that describes the whole document. Our approach can support either a single score, or a detailed sentiment score for each sentence
Provide an OM/SA system that performs solely based on the sentiment of documents	It can support topic-based OM/SA applied on a collection of documents (=extraction of sentiment for each topic separately)	It allows extraction of sentiment for a document collection, based on the main topics are mentioned in them, for each topic separately. Users can focus on the documents posted by certain people, filter them according to their main topics, and see the corresponding sentiment of each

4   An Opinion Mining and Sentiment Analysis Approach

The EU-Community project, aligned with the recent trends in OM/SA, is seeking to exploit key ICT ideas in order to leverage the huge amount of user-generated political content existing in multiple external sources, beyond government websites and social media accounts, focusing on the high quality content generated by experts, in order to support the formulation of public policies. In particular, the general idea of the project is that EU policy stakeholders need to be better informed on the most knowledgeable and credible people for each specific topic/policy they are interested in, and also the most relevant documents. The OM/SA module is mostly concerned with the analysis of the documents retrieved from various sources (either large ones such as positions, RSS Feeds, articles, etc., or small ones such as comments and posts in various social media sources).

This section describes the proposed OM/SA approach, which initially performs information extraction from crawled documents, aiming at conducting sentiment analysis on the document as well as on the sentence level, based on filtering according to a topic modelling procedure. The linguistic pipeline followed is shown in Fig. 2.

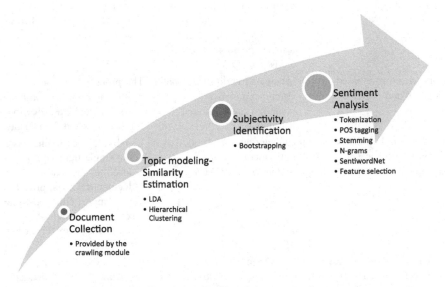

Fig. 2. The linguistic pipeline of the proposed approach.

The first component activated is the crawler, which fetches data from various sources, such as RSS feeds, comments on the **Euractory** platform, Tweets, LinkedIn articles, etc. Since one of the main tasks of the EU-Community project is to identify relevant documents, we process the fetched documents using a topic-modeling procedure, which can identify the main "concepts" of a document. Topic modeling refers to a family of machine learning algorithms, most of them consisted of a probabilistic nature, which infer the hidden semantic structure within a set of input documents. The main idea behind topic modeling lies to the fact that documents are comprised of some "concepts" (expressed through collections of terms). For the task at hand, we performed two different approaches. The former is the well-known Latent Dirichlet Allocation (LDA) method (Blei and Lafferty 2006) and the latter is an agglomerative hierarchical clustering approach.

Upon grouping the documents according to their topics, the third module deployed was the subjectivity identifier, namely, a tool for discovering whether a document contains subjective or objective text. Work in opinion mining often adopts the hypothesis that the incoming documents are opinionated. However, in real-world situations there is a need to decide whether a given document contains subjective information or not, since the subjective sentences are of high importance for our purposes as they contain sentiment. The implementation of our subjectivity classifier is centered upon the methodology proposed by Riloff (2004). In fact, it is a bootstrapping approach that learns linguistically-rich extraction patterns for subjective expressions. The main principle is that high-precision classifiers, trained by a small dataset of labeled instances, perform labeling of a larger set of unannotated data in order to automatically create a large training set, which is then given to an extraction pattern learning algorithm. The learned patterns are then used to identify more subjective sentences. The bootstrapping process learns many subjective patterns and increases recall while maintaining high precision (recall measures the ability of the module to find all available subjective parts of a document, while precision measures the ability of identifying correctly parts as subjective).

The final step involves the core component, which performs sentiment analysis. In our approach, the subjective sentences are transformed into a vector of weights, according to the TF-IDF (Term Frequency-Inverse Document Frequency) model. Prior to this transformation, a series of pre-processing steps is undertaken, as shown in Fig. 1. Tokenization includes the steps needed for removing any non-linguistic token and then taking care of contractions (e.g. didn't) and transforming all cases to lower for reducing the vocabulary size. Upon tokenization, the removal of non-informative, trivial tokens, called as "stopwords" was applied. Usually, these lists include tokens such as articles, personal pronouns, etc. In the present module, a custom list of stop-words was used as provided by RapidMiner®. Stemming is about keeping the core lexical form of a word from its various forms (e.g. *say*, *says*, *saying*, and *said* are all replaced by *say*). The next steps was about analyzing the part of speech of each token and keeping the most prone to contain sentiment such as adjectives, adverbs and verbs. In order to deal with text appearing in social media, which is characterized by idioms, abbreviations, emoticons, etc., a special gazetteer was tailored to identify them, and then replaced them by lexicons tokens (e.g. the emoticon ☺ was replaced by *happy*). The gazetteer also took punctuation marks into account and transformed them into tokens as well, since it is evident that there is a certain style when using such marks in social media texts (e.g. *!!!* was transformed as *frustration*).

Afterwards, a sliding window of N tokens was considered, in order to retain neighboring lexical content. N-grams are well known in computational linguistics and provide useful information about the context of a given term. For example, when we consider N-grams of $N = 2$ (i.e. bigrams) we could capture sentiment information such as "pretty stupid", while if we only consider single tokens then the word *pretty* would be assigned a positive sentiment and the word *stupid* a negative one. For our experiments, a value of $N = 2$ and $N = 3$ was respectively selected, with $N = 3$ providing the best classification results. The next step utilized SentiWordNet, a sophisticated resource that encompassed semantic information (Miller 1995). The motivation for this is based on the following idea: collection of affective words in a sentiment lexicon is tricky because such lexicons are limited to their domain and do not take into account the relation between words. Finally, due to the large amount of available features, generated by all the aforementioned pre-processing steps, we engaged a Support Vector Machine (SVM) classifier to weight each feature and eliminate those with lower weights.

5   Experimental Results

With respect to the data used in the experiments, initially we manually annotated some instances that were returned from the crawling component, upon removing non-English texts. As for evaluation, it was conducted for three different variations:

- Using Polarity Lexicon (PL) only.
- Using Machine Learning (ML) with all previous steps apart from the SentiWordNet feature;
- The hybrid ML method, i.e. the combined Polarity Lexicons and ML approach (HML).

In order to calculate the performance, a method of 10-fold cross-validation using stratification (i.e. keeping the ratio of the class instances in the training and test sets constant) was followed. The performance was measured using precision, recall and accuracy, using three ML algorithms (Naïve Bayes, Support Vector Machines and Multi-Layer Perceptron Neural Networks), also comparing with a baseline classifier (i.e. a majority vote classifier, which always replies by selecting the most represented class in the dataset). The distribution of classes in the data was as follows: 103 negative, 614 neutral and 118 positive. The equations of each metric are provided below:

$$Recall = \frac{t_p}{t_p + f_n} \tag{1}$$

$$Precision = \frac{t_p}{t_p + f_p} \tag{2}$$

$$Accuracy = \frac{t_p + t_n}{t_p + t_n + f_p + f_n} \tag{3}$$

Here, **tp** are the correct positive predictions (true positives), **fp** are the incorrect ones (false positives), **tn** are the correct negative predictions (true negatives) and **fn** are the incorrect ones (false negatives). In other words, recall is the relative number of the correctly classified instances that were actually classified, precision is the relative number of correctly classified instances among all those classified and accuracy is the proportion of the instances of the testing set that were classified correctly against all instances.

In the Figs. 3, 4 and 5 we can see the evaluation results for each metric (accuracy, precision and recall respectively). It is evident that the hybrid method HML of combining Polarity Lexicons with Machine Learning (Support Vector Machines) gives the best results.

5.1   Subjectivity Identification Results

In order to evaluate this task, a set of well-known datasets, also used by other relevant works, was adopted. Specifically, as a lexicon we used both the subjectivity lexicon

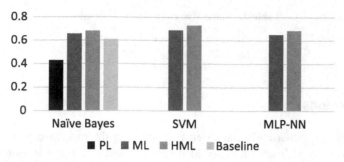

Fig. 3. Evaluation results of the proposed approach - accuracy

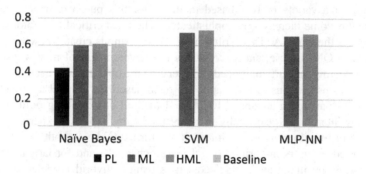

Fig. 4. Evaluation results of the proposed approach - precision

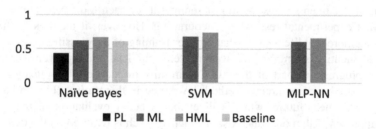

Fig. 5. Evaluation results of the proposed approach - recall

considered in Rodrigues et al. (2008), as well as a slang lexicon created by our team. The subjectivity lexicon consisted of about 8.000 words, stored in a form that retains the following information: Term, Subjectivity Type (*strongsubj* or *weaksubj*), POS tag and Polarity as returned by SentiWordNet. Furthermore, for our subjectivity and polarity classification we used the datasets of IMDb movie reviews used also in Pang et al. (2002) and Wiegand et al. (2013). In the following Table 2, we can see the results (accuracy, precision and recall metrics). By observing the outcome, the proposed system can predict subjective sentences quite satisfactory (79.1 %) however, it has some difficulties in identifying all of the existing subjective sentences in the dataset.

Table 2. Subjectivity identification results

Accuracy	Precision	Recall
66.3 %	79.1 %	58.6 %

6 Conclusions

Governments are increasingly interested in exploiting the extensive political content created in various web sites and social media accounts, in order to obtain a better understanding of the needs and problems of society, and also the perceptions and feelings of the citizens, and to formulate effective public policies. This has led to the development of a variety of ICT based methods for this purpose, which are rapidly evolving and become increasingly sophisticated. The most critical technology for their effectiveness is the OM/SA. The evolution of these methods creates new requirements with respect to OM/SA use, and necessitates the development of new ways of using OM/SA for meeting the particular needs and serving the objectives of each new method.

In the previous sections of this paper has been described a novel approach to OM and SA use, as part of an advanced ICT-based method of exploiting political content created in the Internet, and especially in social media, by experts ('expertsourcing'). It includes interesting innovative features: it performs OM/SA both for short-sized opinions posted by users in various social media channels, and for larger documents, such as articles, positions and RSS feeds; it is using a hybrid model that combines polarity resources and machine learning; it can support a dual mode of both document and sentence-level OM/SA; and also it can support topic-based OM/SA applied on a collection of documents (= extraction of sentiment for each topic separately).

The first experimental results are encouraging. However, it requires further evaluation using more real life data (so that a better training of the classifiers can be made), which will identify strengths and weaknesses, and lead to improvements. This is already in progress, as part of the EU-Community project: pilot applications of the whole ICT-based expertsourcing method developed in this project (Fig. 1) have been planned for the near future, which will enable a better evaluation of the proposed OM/SA approach with more data. Also, further research is required on the combination of such fourth generation methods (oriented towards expertsourcing) with the ones of the previous generations (oriented towards the general public), so that knowledge, perceptions, opinions and ideas from the general public on one hand and from experts on the other hand can be combined for the formulation of better public policies.

References

Bekkers, V., Edwards, A.R., Moody, R., Beunders, H.: Caught by surprise? Micro-mobilization, new media and the management of strategic surprises. Public Manage. Rev. **13**(7), 1003–1021 (2011)

Bekkers, V., Edwards, A., de Kool, D.: Social media monitoring: responsive governance in the shadow of surveillance? Gov. Inf. Q. **30**(4), 335–342 (2013)

Blei, D.M., Lafferty, J.D.: Dynamic topic models. In: Proceedings of the 23rd International Conference on Machine learning (ICML 2006), pp. 113–120. ACM, New York (2006)

Chadwick, A.: New challenges for the study of e-democracy in an era of informational exuberance. I/S J. Law Policy Inf. Soc. **5**(1), 9–41 (2009)

Charalabidis, Y., Loukis, E.: Participative public policy making through multiple social media platforms utilization. Int. J. Electron. Gov. Res. **8**(3), 78–97 (2012)

Charalabidis, Y., Loukis, E., Androutsopoulou, A., Karkaletsis, V., Triantafillou, A.: Passive crowdsourcing in government using social media. Transforming Gov. People, Process Policy **8**(2), 283–308 (2014)

Charapabidis, Y., Loukis, E., Koulizakis, Y., Mekkaoui, D., Ramfos, A.: Leveraging European union policy community through advanced exploitation of social media. In: Tambouris, E., Macintosh, A., Bannister, F. (eds.) ePart 2014. LNCS, vol. 8654, pp. 13–25. Springer, Heidelberg (2014)

Charalabidis, Y., Loukis, E., Koulizakis, Y.: Social Media in policy making: the EU Community project approach. In: International Conference on e-Democracy and Open Government Asia 2014 (CeDEM Asia 2014), pp. 4–5, Hong Kong, Dec 2014 (2014c)

Conklin, J., Begeman, M.: gIBIS: a tool for all reasons. J. Am. Soc. Inf. Sci. **40**(3), 200–213 (1989)

Conklin, J.: Dialog mapping: reflections on an industrial strength case study. In: Kirschner, P., Buckingham Shum, P., Carr, C. (eds.) Visualizing Argumentation: Software Tools for Collaborative and Educational Sense-Making. Springer, London (2003)

Ferro, E., Loukis, E., Charalabidis, Y., Osella, M.: Policy making 2.0: from theory to practice. Gov. Inf. Q. **30**(4), 359–368 (2013)

Kokkinakos, P., Koussouris, S., Panopoulos, D., Askounis, D., Ramfos, A., Georgousopoulos, C., et al.: Citizens collaboration and co-creation in public service delivery: the COCKPIT project. Int. J. Electron. Gov. Res. **8**(3), 44–62 (2012)

Kunz, W., Rittel, H.: Issues as Elements of Information Systems. Working Paper No. 131, University of California, Berkley (1979)

Loukis, E., Charalabidis, Y.: Active and passive crowdsourcing in government. In: Janssen, M., Wimmer, M., Deljoo, A. (eds.) Policy Practice and Digital Science: Integrating Complex Systems, Social Simulation and Public Administration in Policy Research. Spinger Verlag – Public Administration and Information Technology Series (2014)

Maragoudakis, M., Loukis, E., Charalabidis, Y.: A review of opinion mining methods for analyzing citizens' contributions in public policy debate. In: Tambouris, E., Macintosh, A., de Bruijn, H. (eds.) ePart 2011. LNCS, vol. 6847, pp. 298–313. Springer, Heidelberg (2011)

Maynard, D., Funk, A.: Automatic detection of political opinions in tweets. In: García-Castro, R., Fensel, D., Antoniou, G. (eds.) ESWC 2011. LNCS, vol. 7117, pp. 88–99. Springer, Heidelberg (2012)

Miller, G.A.: WordNet: a lexical database for English. Commun. ACM **38**(11), 3941 (1995)

Pang, B., Lee, L., Vaithyanathan, S.: Thumbs up? Sentiment classification using machine learning techniques. In: Proceedings of EMNLP, pp. 79–86 (2002)

Rhodes, R.A.W.: Policy network analysis. In: Moran, M., Rein, M., Goo-din, R.E. (eds.) The Oxford Handbook of Public Policy, pp. 423–445. Oxford University Press, Oxford (2006)

Rhodes, R.A.W.: Understanding governance: ten years on. Organ. Stud. **28**(8), 1243–1264 (2007)

Riloff, E.: Learning extraction patterns for subjective expressions. In: Proceedings of the 2003 Conference on Empirical Methods in Natural Language Processing (EMNLP 2003), pp. 105–112. Association for Computational Linguistics, Stroudsburg (2004)

Rodrigues, P.P., Gama, J., Pedroso, J.P.: Hierarchical clustering of time series data streams. IEEE Trans. Knowl. Data Eng. **20**(5), 615–627 (2008)

Shirky, C.: The political power of social media. Foreign Aff. **90**, 28–41 (2011)

Skogstad, G.: Policy networks and policy communities: conceptual evolution and governing realities. In: Workshop on "Canada's Contribution to Comparative Theorizing" Annual Meeting of the Canadian Political Science Association, University of Western On-tario, London, Ontario (2005)

Wandhöfer, T., Taylor, S., Alani, H., Joshi, S., Sizov, S., Walland, P., Thamm, M., Bleier, A., Mutschke, P.: Engaging politicians with citizens on social networking sites: the WeGov toolbox. Int. J. Electron. Gov. Res. **8**(3), 22–43 (2012). (GESIS–Leibniz-Institute for the Social Sciences, Germany)

Wandhöfer, T., Allen, B., Taylor, S., Walland, P., Sizov, Z.: Online forums vs. social networks: two case studies to support eGovernment with topic opinion analysis. In: IFIP 12th International Conference on e-Government - eGov 2013, Koblenz, Germany, 16–19 Sept 2013

Wiegand, M., Klenner, M., Klakow, D.: Bootstrapping polarity classifiers with rule-based classification. Language Resources and Evaluation, pp. 1049–1088 (2013)

Author Index